Cultural Exclusion in China

State education, social mobility and cultural difference

Ethnic minorities form a very substantial proportion of the population of China, with over 100 million people in 55 formally designated minority groups inhabiting over 60 per cent of the country's land area. Poverty and economic inequality of minority groups are widely-recognised problems. However, as this book, based on extensive original research, shows, under-lying economic inequality are educational inequality and cultural exclusion, which in turn lead to problems of social mobility and thereby to poverty. The book examines in particular Tibetan, Muslim Hui, Salar and Bonan people. It discusses the policy and practice of education for ethnic minorities, the prevailing chauvinistic Chinese national culture, from which minorities feel excluded, and the attitudes of both majority Han Chinese towards minorities, and of minorities towards their position of cultural exclusion. Besides exploring the forms of cultural exclusion experienced by ethnic minorities, it considers what might be done to promote inclusion, proposing a rethinking of the project of nation building and modernization of state and minority rights in order to achieve the goal of including the minority population of distinctive cultures into wider society.

Lin Yi is Associate Professor of Sociology at Xiamen University. His current research focuses upon culture, inequality and boundaries, with particular reference to class, ethnicity and globalization. Lin's articles have appeared in such journals as *China Quarterly* and *Japanese Journal of Political Science*.

Comparative Development and Policy in Asia Series

Series Editors
Ka Ho Mok *(Faculty of Social Sciences, The University of Hong Kong, China)*
Rachel Murphy *(Oxford University, UK and The Centre for East Asian Studies, University of Bristol, UK)*

Cultural Exclusion in China

State education, social mobility and cultural difference

Lin Yi

Routledge
Taylor & Francis Group

LONDON AND NEW YORK

First published 2008
by Routledge
2 Park Square, Milton Park, Abingdon, Oxon OX14 4RN

Simultaneously published in the USA and Canada
by Routledge
711 Third Ave, New York, NY 10017

*Routledge is an imprint of the Taylor & Francis Group,
an informa business*

First issued in paperback 2012

© 2008 Lin Yi

Typeset in Times New Roman by
RefineCatch Limited, Bungay, Suffolk

British Library Cataloguing in Publication Data
A catalogue record for this book is available from the British Library

Library of Congress Cataloging in Publication Data
Yi, Lin, 1965–
Cultural exclusion in China : state education, social mobility and
cultural difference / Lin Yi.
    p. cm. – (Comparative development and policy in Asia series)
    Includes bibliographical references and index.
    ISBN 978–0–415–45761–3 (hardback : alk. paper) –
ISBN 978–0–203–89527–6 (ebook) 1. Minorities–Education–China.
2. Ethnicity–China. 3. Race discrimination–China. 4. Educational
equalization–China. I. Title.

LC3737.C6Y5 2008
371.82900951–dc22
2007050128

ISBN13: 978–0–415–45761–3 (hbk)
ISBN13: 978–0–415–54115–2 (pbk)
ISBN13: 978–0–203–89527–6 (ebk)

Contents

List of illustrations

Maps

Tables

Chinese Pinyin

Pinyin, used in the People's Republic of China since 1958, is a system which uses the Latin alphabet to represent the sounds of Mandarin Chinese. This alphabetic system is adopted in this book. In what follows I list some consonants roughly compared to English pronunciation.

c is pronounced like **ts** as in 'ha**ts**'.
ch is pronounced like **ch** as in '**ch**alk'.
g is pronounced like **g** as in '**g**o'.
j is pronounced like **j** as in '**j**eep'.
q is pronounced like **ch** as in '**ch**eep'.
sh is pronounced like **sh** as in '**sh**op'.
x is pronounced like **sh** as in '**sh**eep'.
y is pronounced like **y** as in '**y**es'; except that the syllable **yi** is pronounced like **ee** as in 'b**ee**'.
z is pronounced like **ds** as in 'wee**ds**'.
zh is pronounced like **j** as in '**j**am'.

Acknowledgements

Since 2001, when I made a career change (from Chinese literature and language in Chinese to sociology in English), I have received assistance from a wide range of people. First I would like to thank my supervisors Tariq Modood and Leon Tikly, who offered me excellent supervision with their remarkable insight, unbelievable energy and good sense of humour during my stay in Bristol. Without either of these, I do not know where my work would have ended up. A Universities UK Overseas Research Students award (ORS), a University of Bristol bursary and a studentship from the Great Britain–China Centre in London sponsored my study at Bristol, for which I am extremely grateful.

Many other people should be thanked for their help and support during my life over the past decade. I am greatly indebted to Zhen Shangling whose incredible understanding, patience and support, during and after her supervision of my master's thesis, became my main source of inspiration. Hildegard Diemberger, my external supervisor from Cambridge University, oversaw my fieldwork in 2003 and helped to lay a good foundation for my subsequent writing up. The two examiners of my thesis, David Gillborn and Ka-Ho Mok, offered invaluable suggestions, which enhanced the clarity and presentation of my research. Ka-Ho Mok's generosity and encouragement in particular enabled me to convert my PhD thesis into this book. Other people who gave important advice or comments on my PhD drafts at different stages or in different ways include Rachel Murphy, Gerard Postiglione, and Dru C. Gladney. I am also grateful to my colleagues in China, and the Department of Sociology and the Graduate School of Education at the University of Bristol.

I am in particular indebted to Okazaki Masashi, whose very generous financial support significantly facilitated the realization of my dream to study, and to Tim Murphy for his thorough help with my writing and other generous support. The time spent with my fellow PhD students was always a major source of indispensable and wonderful diversion during my stay in Bristol – all one can expect from friendship. Some of them who offered input to my thoughts and writing ought to be mentioned in particular: Angeline Barrett, Annie Bramley, Chamion Caballero, Matthew Cole, Ranji Devadason, Glyn

Everett, Emma Head, Agita Luse, Mutsumi Matsumoto, Karen Morgan, Simon Weaver, Chao-Yu Wu, and finally, Yasu Oiso-Fuller. Yilan Xiao, an undergraduate student of mine at Xiamen University produced the two impressive maps for this book.

I am also grateful to the people I interviewed and the people I received assistance from during the three periods of fieldwork I conducted in 2003, 2006, and 2007 in Qinghai. The Muslim, Tibetan and Han students I interviewed were extremely friendly and open-minded. Other people who offered very important assistance include Xin Jianping, Ma Husai, Ma Caixia, Sylvie Hyvernaud, Kevin Stuart, Deng Qingli, Yang Wenkui, Zhang Fushun, Fernanda Pirie and Nina Fenton. Special thanks belong to the retired schoolteacher Wanma Xiangxiu, who hosted and looked after me so carefully and selflessly throughout the whole course of my fieldwork in 2003, 2006, and 2007 on that chilly, dry and remote plateau.

I also wish to thank my editors at Routledge, Peter Sowden and Tom Bates, for ushering this book through to publication.

Deep thanks inevitably go to my parents, too. Their ever-lasting understanding and support brought me calm and courage that have sustained my reading, writing and thinking in sometimes difficult circumstances.

Finally, I gratefully acknowledge the permission granted by Thomas Publishing Services and Cambridge University Press to reproduce the copyright material in this book, of which I am the author: 'Choosing between ethnic and Chinese citizenship: the educational trajectories of Tibetan minority children in northwestern China', in the edited volume by V. Fong and R. Murphy, *Chinese Citizenship: Views from the Margins*, Routledge, 2006; 'Muslim narratives of schooling, social mobility and cultural difference: a case study in multiethnic northwest China', *Japanese Journal of Political Science*, 6(1), 2005, Cambridge University Press; and 'Ethnicization through schooling: the mainstream discursive repertoires of ethnic minority cultures', *The China Quarterly*, 192, 2007, Cambridge University Press.

1 Introduction

Why do many ethnic minority communities persistently perform poorly in schooling? Why is it that some minority members cannot achieve social mobility as much as they should in accordance with their achievement in education?

The research presented here explores what lies behind the failure of ethnic minorities in the educational system and in social mobility, in a knowledge-economy-driven world in which education is a major route to social mobility. It is concerned primarily with an examination of the relationship between ethnicity and educational performance. This book argues that the failure to achieve inclusion of ethnic minorities of distinctive cultures is largely responsible for poor minority performance in education and social mobility; that is, cultural exclusion perpetuates ethnic minority inequality.

This book examines the forms of cultural exclusion experienced by ethnic minorities in the Chinese education system, and considers what might promote their inclusion. This introductory chapter delineates the ways in which cultural exclusion creates inequalities for (particularly) ethnically disadvantaged groups. It begins with an examination of the factors influencing educational achievement among ethnic minorities. These tendencies are examined by referencing four theoretical frameworks: the social system and community forces, cultural capital, social capital and multiculturalism. Following these discussions, I argue that the theorization of (ethnic) social mobility and equality requires an holistic approach to the socio-cultural context. That is, the extent to which a community with a distinctive culture is recognized by the wider society directly affects their social mobility and position within that society.

Ethnicity and educational achievement

Standardized public education is widely acknowledged as being essential for citizens to gain equal opportunity to access mainstream institutions (Kymlicka 2001: 20), so as to facilitate opportunities for upward social mobility. This idea of equality makes demands in the first place for the equal achievement of students from different backgrounds in education. However, unequal school performance is often closely associated with differences in ethnicity in that some ethnic groups tend to outperform others,[1] as illustrated by data from China as well as the UK and USA.[2]

Kao and Thompson (2003) suggest that three theoretical approaches pervade debates on minority school performanc: namely, cultural orientations of certain ethnic groups that promote or discourage academic achievement; the structural position of ethnic groups that affects the environments of children, parents or schools; and genetic differences. The last approach is largely dismissed in academic discussions today for its racist overtones and the lack of empirical evidence (Kao and Thompson 2003: 419–20). Most academic discussions focus on the interplay of the other two approaches: cultural orientations and the structural position. Notably, some theoretical arguments fall between the two perspectives. Whilst the cultural orientations thesis is directed at the cultural norms of ethnic groups, that of the structural position largely focuses on parental socio-economic status (SES), which is connected with parental participation, quality of instruction, school peers, teachers and other influences.

In his analysis of the persistence of low educational performance of black people in the USA, Ferguson (2005) subtly and convincingly relates socio-economic to cultural factors. He argues there have long existed differences in the ways in which the ethnic majority and minority (for Ferguson, whites and blacks) have coped with and adapted to their positions in the nation's hierarchy of power and privilege, which reflect psychological self-defence mechanisms, social interaction patterns and disparities in access to opportunities. Such patterns help determine 'the economic wherewithal of families to provide for their children, the child-rearing methods that families grow accustomed to using and the ways that they understand and interact with mainstream institutions such as schools' (Ferguson 2005: 316). In a word, the minority socio-economic status is largely associated with race or ethnicity that is socially constructed. This race- or ethnicity-rooted disparity is likely to lead to, for example, the differences in parenting that supposedly prepare minority children for different cognitive or learning styles, on the one hand (Blair 2001; Osborne 2001), and on the other, do not prepare minority children with the necessary knowledge bases before schooling (Ferguson 2005). As a result, minority students appear to have difficulties in understanding what is being taught in schools. In a nutshell, these kinds of pre-school parenting practices result in minority children's under-preparation in skills and knowledge that are needed in formal education (Ferguson 2005).

Ferguson's analysis of the relationship between socio-economic status and cultural factors resonates with John Ogbu's concept of 'community forces'; that is, distinctive minorities foster different cultural models in response to the system or the dominant group's treatment of them (Ogbu 1987; Ogbu and Simons 1998). Such an interactive perspective allows Ogbu to explain why some minority groups have the motivation to perform well (voluntary minorities) while others show resistance or reluctance in school study (involuntary minorities). This classification is justified by Ogbu through providing four distinguishable types of cultural model of ethnic minorities (Ogbu and Simons 1998: 169–76): frames of reference, instrumental responses or folk theories of 'making it', degree of trust in dominant (for Ogbu, white) people and their institutions, and finally, beliefs about the effect of adopting the mainstream (white) ways on minority identity.

Here, Ogbu primarily looks at two dimensions that together lead various minority groups to differing interpretations of and responses to the mainstream group: economic aspirations and the cultural concern. Both of these are significantly informed and shaped by their relationship with the dominant group. This allows for an understanding of minorities' responses both instrumentally and symbolically, and more importantly, of the dilemma and possibility of reconciliation between an expectation for economic success and a desire for cultural well-being. Therefore, the underlying question in Ogbu's approach is: whether or not it is possible to achieve upward social mobility through education and at the same time to maintain a distinctive cultural identity.

However, in explaining minority performance, Ogbu's concept of voluntary and involuntary minorities can be said to be in many cases somewhat misleading, including Ogbu's own cases, as other scholars have criticized (for example, Margaret A. Gibson et al. 1997). More importantly, the association of certain minorities with certain types of response and behaviour can imply that they are responsible for their disadvantaged status and lead to further stereotyping (Gillborn 1997). This is primarily because of Ogbu's failure to recognize the responsibilities the social system has for minority performance in schools. Therefore, his distinction between voluntary and involuntary minorities is not employed in this study. Nonetheless, the system and community forces distinction has heuristic value as a conceptual framework based on power relations between different social forces (in spite of the fact that to neglect the system quite often leads Ogbu to diverging from the underlying concept of his framework, power relations) (also see Navarro 1997 and van Zanten 1997). Correspondingly, methodologically Ogbu's thesis provides a useful conceptual framework, incorporating both macro-level and micro-level analyses, for the empirical study of the relationship between ethnicity and school performance. My empirical studies adopt his framework. This adoption modifies his 'the (social) system' as 'social systems' (plural) to show that the system is not always a coherent whole but diverse.

Educational achievement, cultural capital and social capital

By highlighting community forces, Ogbu shows that cultural and linguistic difference explanations put forward by some educational anthropologists in the USA do not adequately account for the differences in school performance amongst some minorities. Nevertheless, cultural discontinuity between home and school clearly does cause learning problems (Erickson 1987; Ogbu and

Simons 1998: 161). In fact, it is not easy to distinguish between the two cultural themes of community forces and cultural difference. That is to say, when cultural values and norms of minority communities positively or negatively affect their children's educational performance, they are undoubtedly functioning as 'forces'. In this sense, it is more appropriate to see cultural difference as part of community forces, or *cultural orientations*, thereby expanding its theoretical implications.

In this way, cultural sociology – unlike conventional anthropology – suggests an understanding of culture that does not fix the attributes of entire groups and societies. Nor does it merely refer to 'an ideally purer realm of art and morality expressing higher human capabilities and values', an idea that emerged in the course of the Industrial Revolution in England (Spillman 2002: 3). Instead, as Spillman points out, cultural sociology entails analysis of the effects of meaning-making processes in social life. To understand culture in this way is to consider cultural norms and cultural relationships simultaneously. I will return to discuss this at length in dealing with the interrelations between capital, culture and power relations later on in this chapter.

Given these considerations it is difficult to assess what factors, community forces or cultural differences, are more significant in minority school performance. However, Pierre Bourdieu's theory of cultural capital provides support for cultural discontinuity explanations due to its emphasis upon processes of meaning-making in social life. In analysing the educational achievement gap between different classes, Bourdieu explains that distinctive class groups possess differential cultural heritages, some of which are more likely than others to be transformed into cultural capital (Bourdieu and Passeron 1977; Bourdieu 1986).

Cultural capital, according to Bourdieu, takes three forms: embodied, objectified and institutionalized. Its embodied form refers to the domestic transmission of cultural heritage. This is 'the best hidden and socially most determinant educational investment' (Bourdieu 1986: 48).[3] Its objectified state is observable in the form of cultural goods such as pictures, books, instruments, machines, etc. Its institutionalized form is most significantly embodied in academic qualifications or 'credentialization'. That is, the embodiment of a particular culture rather than others is recognized and reproduced through the educational system. This institutionalization has the crucial effect of guaranteeing the monetary value of a given academic qualification. In this way, it ultimately converts culture into economic value.

It is cultural capital that causes divergence between the academic achievements of students from different cultural groups and, further, leads the intergenerational reproduction of this educational pattern. In terms of class disparity, this endowment is associated with ownership by the higher class of 'highbrow' culture and language. The possession of highbrow culture and language confers dominance as this culture and language are institutionalized through the education system. In turn, the possession of cultural capital by higher class children appears as 'merit' in schooling. In such circumstances, while the education system presupposes equal possession of cultural capital for credentialization in school, lower class students are placed in a disadvantaged position due to their lack of cultural capital or 'merit', simply because they are from a relatively 'lowbrow' culture.

This educational or institutional system enables the higher class to maintain its dominant position by legitimating the normative status and reproduction of its cultural heritage. Moreover, the success in schooling of some individuals from the lower class also helps to strengthen the educational system by legitimizing the 'meritocracy' of the dominant culture. This is apparently applicable to ethnicity and education as the anthropologists of cultural discontinuity demonstrate. The theory has been applied to studies of school performance focusing on ethnicity or racial difference (see for instance, Kalmijn and Kraaykamp 1996; Lareau and Horvat 1999; Olneck 2000).

Ogbu's approach to community forces is, in some way, transcended by some other research in which the community can be seen to have been mobilized as an active, intentionally organized social network in helping their (younger) members to achieve upward social mobility through education (Zhou 2005). In Zhou's research, the Chinese ethnic community in the US are not seen as playing a passive or invisible role in relation to social systems, contrary to Bourdieu's class-based theory; nor, as Ogbu suggests, do they merely employ an 'opt-in' or 'opt-out' strategy based on their perceptions of the treatment they have received from the system, aiming either to fit into social systems or to reject it. In fact, the marginalized community, as Zhou illustrates, can play a significant role in the attempt to actively participate in (mainstream) social systems through becoming a 'Do It Yourself' actor in the first instance.

Zhou's approach brings to our attention the concept of social capital. Unlike cultural and economic capital, 'social capital inheres in the structure of relations between actors and among actors' (Coleman 1988: S98). As Robert Putnam states, it encompasses 'social networks and the norms of reciprocity and trustworthiness that arise from them' (2000: 19). Meanwhile, social capital is 'the collectivity-owned capital', which is 'a durable network of more or less institutionalized relationships of mutual acquaintance and recognition' (Bourdieu 1986: 51). Put simply, social capital is a network of connections characterized by mutual knowledge and recognition of its membership. This knowledge and recognition create, maintain and reinforce obligations and expectations between its members. By effectively mobilizing the network of relationships, social capital facilitates conversion from cultural capital to economic capital. By the same token, cultural and economic capitals also act as a basis to form social capital and further, add more value to it (Bourdieu 1986, Coleman 1988, Putnam 2000).[4]

However, an important distinction should be made between three types of social capital: bonding (exclusive), bridging (inclusive or horizontal) and linking (vertical) (Putnam 2000: 22–3, Woolcock 2001: 13).[5] *Bonding social capital* refers to a social connection that tends to stress the identity of a group which is constituted in an inward and homogeneous way, and potentially excludes others who are external to it. In other words, it bolsters narrower selves and in-groups loyalty, and may also create out-group antagonism. *Bridging social capital* refers to a form of social networking that includes people across diverse social cleavages, and 'can generate broader identities and reciprocity' (Putnam 2000: 23). *Linking social capital*, unlike bridging capital that functions horizontally, connects groups or individuals to others in different social positions, for example, more powerful or socially advantaged, and hence refers to a vertical network. It is a linkage to formal institutions from which resources, ideas and information can be leveraged (NESF 2003). Furthermore, different combinations of bonding, bridging and linking social capital are responsible for the variety of outcomes of different cultural groups. In other words, whilst social capital can be mobilized to empower communities, it can also play a negative role. A similar distinction between negative and positive forms is also made by Zhou (2005) as two patterns of (inward) social capital, the ghetto (destructive) and the enclave (constructive), respectively.

Capital, culture and power relations

Whereas every community in theory possesses inward social capital, what makes communities distinctive in socio-economic status is dependent on how communities mobilize that capital. In the cases of dominant groups and dominated communities, the former are rarely in need of mobilization of their *bonding capital* while it is quite often the case with the latter, as Zhou illustrated in her Chinese community case. In other words, the fundamental difference between dominant groups and dominated communities in terms of social capital lies in whether or not a community needs to mobilize its bonding social capital. This need to mobilize *inward* capital is in fact a compensation for the lack of *outward* capital, bridging and/or linking. Therefore, the mobilization of bonding capital is a reflection of imbalanced power relations between the dominant group and dominated communities. Linking capital, as the public institution-related form of outward capital, is more responsible for the different roles distinctive communities play in power relations.

When a community predominantly possesses *linking social capital*, this means that it constitutes the core part of formal institutions, which ensures that it has substantial access to formal institutions. This will enable the community to become *the* legitimate player over other communities. In this condition, its inward social capital substantially overlaps with its linking social capital, and in mobilizing its linking capital in fact the community is also mobilizing its bonding capital. The two forms of capital are interlocked and sustain each other so that the dominant group does not particularly need to separately mobilize its bonding capital. One of the main results in playing this role is to institutionalize its own cultural heritage as capital, as Bourdieu observes. This is quite the reverse with dominated groups, who are deprived of outward social capital and have to rely on mobilizing inward social capital. This is why Bourdieuian theorists, unlike positivists who tend to take inward capital as an analytical basis, are more likely to pay close attention to outward capital in general, and linking or vertical capital in particular. As differential forms of social capital function differently depending on the socio-economic status of various communities, it is necessary to disaggregate the package of social capital, and at the same time to ensure that social capital is not reduced to solely one of its dimensions, inward capital.

The need and significance of unpacking but not reducing the thesis of social capital is fundamentally grounded in mutual knowledge and recognition within a community and between different communities. Whereas mutual knowledge and recognition are relatively easy to achieve within a cultural community, owing to shared cultural norms or values, they are not as easy to achieve between cultural communities. Dominated groups, in order to achieve such mutuality, have in the first instance to acquire the mainstream culture of the dominant group, that is, cultural capital, regardless of whether or not the mutual recognition is eventually achievable. This mutuality-oriented acquisition aims to empower dominated groups themselves through establishing connections with formal institutions, and achieve the goal of putting them on an equal footing with the dominant group. In this light, the ideal pattern for dominated groups is to both keep their own cultural heritage and acquire institutionalized culture or cultural capital, or 'additive learning', from an Ogbuian perspective (Ogbu 1987; Gibson 1988; Ogbu and Simons 1997).

In reality the situation is quite the reverse, however. The acquisition of the mainstream culture is very likely to lead the dominated to subordination to the dominant cultural group. When dominated groups acquire cultural capital, it implies that their own culture is less valuable or inferior and useless, which inevitably further leads to a devaluation of the symbolic image of the possession of their culture. In acquiring cultural capital, subordinated cultural groups are also at risk of being distanced from their own culture and, at worst, of losing contact with it. In other words, the acquisition of the mainstream culture cannot legitimize marginalized cultures and communities; indeed, it can make matters worse, in the sense that they will be put into a more peripheral position.

As a result, those minorities who have succeeded in schooling have paid a higher price to overcome cultural or social gap brought about in their acquisition of the behaviour, values and goals of the mainstream. In other words, they 'could do significantly better and enjoy their education much more were the barriers to their success eliminated or reduced' (Gibson 1988: 167). At the same time, the 'losers' in schooling – either due to a lack of cultural capital because of discontinuities with the mainstream culture, or, on account of a lack of positive inward social capital resulting in their resistance to the dominant group and its (mainstream) culture as a strategy of self-protection – could also be compared by some policy-makers or academic commentators with 'winners' and thereby 'reinforce the idea that race and intelligence are linked, not genetically but culturally' (Noguera 2004: 182).[6]

This is why marginalized group members, in particular those successful individuals from marginalized groups, insist on the importance of their allegedly distinctive cultural heritage and identity even though they are equipped with plenty of cultural capital. What they aim to achieve in their assertion of difference is not the acquisition of cultural capital (if they are willing to 'equip' themselves with the dominant culture), but rather, an appropriate social status in relation to the dominant group. This reflects their desire for more outward, in particular vertical, social capital that is believed to be attainable by making some fundamental changes to power relations in order to provide them with a relationship of mutual knowledge and recognition with the dominant group.

This in the end does not entail acquisition of the dominant culture in the name of mutuality, but rather, a (re)negotiated version of cultural capital between the dominant and other cultures. With this (re)negotiation, cultural capital is expectedly transformed to a 'new landscape', which is justly combined by both dominant and dominated cultures, and is an 'interculturally created and multiculturally constituted' common culture (Parekh 2000: 221). In this light, what is now known as multiculturalism emerged in close association with a movement under the banner of cultural rights. Multiculturalism is a social perspective that emerged in the 1960s and 1970s from the growing awareness of cultural diversity. That is, the importance of diversity for people to have a meaningful life and for a modern society that recognizes and appreciates the richness of humanity expressed through cultural diversity. It is a social paradigm that has been provoked by a social movement on the one hand and advanced by academic discourse and reflection on these movements on the other.

In the meantime, multiculturalism can also be used to orient policy-making. It has been adopted by governments such as Canada and Australia as national policy. In Britain, multiculturalism has not been taken up as a policy whereas in practice the state has promoted a package of multiculturalist measures (Modood 1997). Whilst the distinction between these levels is not always clear-cut, multiculturalism is essentially understood as recognition of cultural diversity in this book. This understanding is directed at a public accommodation of diversity and, more importantly, serves to suggest a new direction in policy-making that considers entitling minorities to social citizenship in the form of their cultural rights or membership in the larger society.[7]

About this book

Social mobility, education and inequality

Departing from these approaches, it is time to re-examine the notion of social mobility. Social mobility is in the first instance measured by economic indicators of income or occupation (profession) (Loury, Modood and Teles 2005). While an income indicator is purely economistic, professional membership is associated with both economic well-being and power and prestige. Nonetheless, both approaches primarily focus upon labour market position. This focus is challenged by a third approach under the concept of social citizenship which sees social mobility in terms of recognition: the degree to which individuals are recognized by others as being equal partners in the community. In addition, the extent to which a group is recognized by others does not necessarily correspond with its position in the labour market but is partially independent (ibid.).

In this light, social mobility can also be understood as 'securing symbolic goods dispensed not by markets, but by private and public institutions' (for example, language policy) (Teles, Mickey and Ahmed 2005: 523). Furthermore, many of the means by which people seek to advance themselves are profoundly shaped by public policies that political institutions have introduced. Therefore, the state plays a central role as a decision-maker and producer of goods in personal advancement. Meanwhile, different social or cultural groups develop different understandings of social mobility, as in individual or group progress, on account of their differential historical experiences and cultures (ibid.). All of this suggests that the socio-cultural dimension of social mobility is equally important when mobility is seen from a perspective of life courses (process) rather than merely measured by economic achievements (outcome).

Like the notion of social mobility, inequality has long been understood in economic terms. This essentially means that inequality is directly associated with the unequal distribution of resources, whilst recognition of cultural difference has little to do with economic equality. Furthermore, this economically orientated view also means that, in order to achieve equality, it may sacrifice cultural well-being to a certain extent when culture is considered to hamper economic development.

This view of inequality is widely accepted across the world, and particularly held in China, where economic development has come to be the top priority of the nation. In this light, ethnic minority cultures are largely regarded as being useless or inferior for modernization of the Chinese nation. As a result, minority cultures are excluded as living cultures from public institutions in general, and from schools in particular. Furthermore, this institutional exclusion is also exercised at the individual level of everyday practice that is demonstrated in my examination of social processes in minority education.

I redress this economistic view by demonstrating how cultural exclusion of ethnic minorities directly or indirectly creates inequality, particularly in the domains of education and social mobility. Education is increasingly seen as the primary route to social mobility. In turn, the impetus for social mobility directly sustains motivations for education. In fact, 'educational aspirations are universally high for all racial and ethnic groups' (Kao and Thompson

2003: 435). This is to say that abstract aspirations are high for all groups despite differences in material realities. Nevertheless, the situation in which minority students on average perform relatively poorly in schools persists, although the degree to which this is the case varies geographically and/or ethnically (also see Chapter 3 for the Chinese case). Furthermore, unequal educational achievement has prevented many minorities from realizing their abstract aspirations. And in fact, even those minorities who outperform their majority peers are still not likely to achieve as well as they should in the labour market (Strategy Unit 2003; Woo 2002).

Echoing this body of scholarship, my findings show that cultural mis-recognition or exclusion of minority communities by mainstream society has blocked or complicated ethnic minorities' access to opportunities for education and related social mobility, and caused many of them to become underachievers in both areas. Cultural exclusion of ethnic minorities principally lies in three dimensions. First of all, cultural discontinuity has caused many minority children to become academic underachievers. Secondly, mis-recognition of cultural difference has set up a glass ceiling for ethnic minorities which inhibits social mobility. Finally, the two factors have in turn diminished minority communities' confidence in and motivation for education, and this has led many of them to becoming perfunctory and ineffective students. In this light, a common ground around the relationship between education and social mobility emerges that brings together both low and high educational achievers of ethnic minorities, who can be regarded as having to overcome specific barriers either in schools or in the wider society of social systems.

This inequality largely caused by social systems is connected to both the cultural and socio-economic dimensions both within and outside schools. This is fundamentally different from the view held by the mainstream[8] that the 'backwardness' of ethnic minorities in education and social mobility, or generally, in community development, lies in their community forces (their cultural norms and actions that promote or discourage achievement in education and social mobility). When largely attributing the minority school performance to community forces, many Chinese academics have left out social systems (the government and the ethnic majority group) that, I argue, are equally responsible for poor minority school performance (see Chapter 3).

In the meantime, the government and the majority group are much more interested in *outcomes* (for example, GDP, annual income, examination results) than the *processes* by which citizens are cultivated. Thus, they measure inequality almost exclusively by outcomes whilst neglecting inequalities which are – to a large degree – perpetuated by processes. This has masked hidden agendas on the part of social systems that disadvantage ethnic minorities as culturally different peoples. I uncover these hidden agendas by scrutinizing the education and social mobility of ethnic minorities to emphasize the responsibilities that social systems should take in the process. Therefore, the two research aims for this book are:

1   To examine the causes and effects of the cultural exclusion of Tibetan and Muslim students in schooling in China.
2   To consider what might improve the inclusion of ethno-cultural minorities in schools.

The first research aim needs to be realized through answering five research questions as follows, whereas the second aim is developed in the concluding chapter.

1   How did Chinese culturalism historically shape ethnic community boundaries and membership, what is its educational legacy and how has this legacy determined the educational experiences of ethnic minorities?
2   What do the existing literature and policy documents tell us about the way in which the mainstream society treats ethno-cultural minorities with regard to schooling?
3   How does the mainstream cultural group in state schools perceive Muslim and Tibetan students and their ethnic communities?
4   What are the attitudes of Tibetan students and parents towards the curriculum, their ethnic communities and their own identity in schooling as well as the larger society?
5   What are the evaluation of schooling, socio-economic status and cultural identity of their ethnic communities among Muslim students and parents?

Research approach and field settings

By focusing on socio-economic and cultural processes rather than merely on outcomes, the 'core' of this book lies in its ethnographic data that substantiates my examination of inequality and processes of cultural exclusion. Furthermore, cultural exclusion is revealed in the context of an historical investigation of Chinese culturalism, and a critical analysis of the government policy and mainstream discourse. Data from these sources are triangulated to give an overall view of the experiences of ethnic minorities in educational terms. Methodologically, this analytical approach is much on the same wavelength with the framework of discursive (or interpretative) repertoires that draws upon a lexicon, or register, of terms and metaphors to characterize and evaluate actions or events (Potter and Wetherell 1987: 138).

The study of discourse aims at the discovery and theorization of pattern and order. To achieve this goal, Wetherell (2001) suggests we need to explore three main domains or *discursive repertoires* in which discourse proceeds: the study of social interaction order, or the nature of social action, meaning the fundamental building block of social life and social science; the study of social actors that is associated with minds, selves and sense-making; and finally, the study of culture and social relations or the historical and institutional features of discourse. In doing so, we can see how contesting or messy discursive repertoires are actually illustrating patterns or orders of power that underlie them. This analytical tool respects the irreducibility of human experience, and acknowledges the messy nature of human life and understandings on the one hand (O'Reilly 2005: 226), and on the other, enables research themes to emerge from substantiation. Thus, it enables me to identify areas of relevance for educators and policy makers to consider, with a view to introducing responsive policies and measures.

My research particularly focuses on an examination of how varied ethno-cultural groups at the periphery of, or excluded from, mainstream institutions, both historically and at present, perceive, react and respond to social systems, with a particular focus on education. Therefore, two aspects of data collection and analysis require close attention: the *interactive* and *comparative* dimensions. Ogbu (1987; 1998) argues, the analysis of interaction based on power relations between different social forces is of fundamental importance. However, my interactive perspective refers to investigating inter-action between social systems and ethnic minority communities at the macro level, and between different ethnic groups at the micro level. This approach allows the research to move beyond traditional ethnography by placing micro fieldwork data within the macro context. Furthermore, it not only deals with ethnic minorities as many similar studies have done, but also probes the perspectives of the ethnic majority in juxtaposition with the former. It thus makes up a multifaceted 'net' of interactions between the state and minority communities, between minorities and the majority, and between different minority (sub)groups (see below).

By doing so, we can see how, for example, the positive or negative inter-action between different ethnic groups, including that between different eth-nic minority groups in the region, is entangled with national ideology that, for instance, relates to social evolution theory (see, particularly, Chapter 3); or whether the dominant Han people homogeneously voice the state's ideology that, for example, regards religion as more negative than positive in terms of social progress (see Chapter 3). I located my study of interaction at a local level where different ethnic groups regularly encounter each other in the course of everyday life, and this interaction shapes their perceptions of each other and of formal institutions (Parekh 2000: 212).

I located my research on the borderlands between Qinghai and Gansu provinces.[9] This is a 'middle ground' (White 1991) that links China proper (*neidi*, lit. 'the interior, inland') to Turkic Muslims in the far northwest Xinjiang, to Tibetans in the Qinghai-Tibet Plateau in the southwest, and to Mongolians in the northeast (see Map 1.1). The region is a nexus where several different ethnic groups have lived and interacted with each other for centuries, respectively identified with Buddhism (the Tibetan, Mongolian, Tu), Islam (the Hui, Salar, Bonan, Dongxiang) and Confucianism or atheism (mainly among the Han). In other words, this is a frontier where the two main minority cultures that centre on Buddhism and Islam encounter each

Map 1.1 Map of China.

other, as well as confront the Chinese Han culture (also see Chapter 4 on the field site).

The region is a hub of agricultural, pastoral and urban populations, revealing different socio-economic patterns. This allows people in this area to have the opportunity to be in contact with different social or economic groups, and to develop open perspectives and aspirations about their socio-economic status and future prospects which may coincide with their cultural traditions. This is very different from the ethnic minorities in remote or difficult-to-access areas, where they are quite isolated from the rest of China and live with few frames of reference beyond the local and few opportunities for social mobility. This is also a buffer zone between the central government and the two politically sensitive regions, TAR and Xinjiang. For the government, it is arguably a testing ground to pilot its minority policies (*minzu zhengce*) and strategies, and to nurture a role model for TAR and Xinjiang along the lines of the state's agenda of integrating ethnic minorities into the Chinese nation in terms of economy, culture and ideology.[10] These features of the field site enable me to consider the various experiences of ethnic minorities in terms of cultural inclusion or exclusion and draw on both socio-economic and cultural factors.

The comparative methodology explores similarities and differences in ethnic minorities' experiences of cultural exclusion that are affected by social systems, and relatedly, by interethnic relations. Comparative studies are carried out between different ethnic groups in a mainstream school, and between different subgroups (rural and urban) respectively from a mainstream school and a minority school. Comparison tackles the issues of achievement, perception and aspiration.

I chose Tibetans and Muslims[11] (Hui, Bonan and Salar, the same hereafter unless indicated otherwise) as my research subjects. This is because they provide good contrasting case studies of the ethnic minority differences in terms of cultural norms, political profile, socio-economic status, and patterns of community forces. Tibetans and Muslims are respectively among the most important representatives of Buddhist and Islamic ethnic groups in China. While Tibetans are the core of Tibetan Buddhism, Muslim Hui are the largest Islamic minority group.[12] The Muslims in this region have a different political image from Tibetans or their Turkic Muslim counterparts in Xinjiang. Both of the latter are internationally politicized, having attracted political attention from the international community, including the USA, the EU and some international organizations; they, correspondingly, receive similar attention in state policy, while this applies much less in the case of my Muslim subjects.

These Muslims are mainly Chinese speakers, which draws a clear-cut line between this bloc and most other minority groups who have their own language and even script, for example: Tibetans and Mongols.[13] Therefore, my Muslim subjects are different from Tibetans and Turkic Muslims in the sense that the latter are among the least sinicized, which is partially attributable to their different linguistic backgrounds. Culturally, as I argue in the remaining chapters – in particular in Chapter 3 – it is relatively easy for the mainstream Han to recognize or even identify themselves with (Tibetan) Buddhism on account of the age-long impact of Buddhism on Chinese culture (which in turn led to the sinicization of Buddhism in Chinese history). By contrast, Chinese Han feel distant from Islam, and vice versa. This is particularly true in the northwest where Muslims are concentrated and largely maintain their tradition.

Furthermore, the Hui, the largest Muslim group in China, are distributed in all walks of life across the country, ranging from politicians to intellectuals, from public servants to self-employed business people, from manual workers to farmers. Most Tibetans, by contrast, are rural and are concentrated in the TAR and the four other provinces neighbouring TAR in West China, Qinghai, Gansu, Sichuan and Yunnan. These similarities and differences between the Tibetans and Muslims are significant for minority education, socialization and identity construction in the wider Chinese Han cultural context. Therefore, the coexistence of Tibetans and Muslims within the same geographic location makes it an apposite site for a comparative study of the various experiences ethnic minorities have of cultural exclusion. These have resulted in differential types of community forces among the minority population as demonstrated in Chapters 4 and 5, and summarized in Chapter 6.

Meanwhile, comparison is achieved through looking at different types of schools, mainstream or ordinary schools and minority schools, in which students from different socio-economic backgrounds are concentrated. This is because in some mainstream schools the majority population may be not from the ethnic majority group, as my investigation reveals.[14] More importantly, the difference in the school choice of ethnic minorities is in accordance with their different socio-economic backgrounds – rural or urban, grassroots or elites – as my case studies show. Taking this kind of information into account can help the process of discovering what has played a critical role in shaping minorities' belief and performance in schooling and their different experiences in schools and the wider society, as described in Chapters 4 and 5, and can prevent the framing of minorities, and their experiences, as homogeneous.

I therefore chose a mainstream secondary school, the only one of its kind in the seat of the regional government, and a Tibetan minority senior secondary school. There are no minority schools for Muslims in the area, which in turn has formed the distinct experiences of Muslims and – implicitly or explicitly – influenced their perception and evaluation of the educational situation in the region, as discussed in Chapter 5.[15]

Outline of the book

Chapter 2 is an historical investigation of Chinese (Han) culturalism and its modern legacy. Central to this culturalism is the belief that China was the only true civilization. Furthermore, Chinese culturalism means that people should be educated according to its universal civilization. Through a thematic sketch of Chinese culturalism, this chapter uncovers how the culture discourse of China takes shape. This belief in the superiority of its culture pervades the education of ethnic minorities in China – both the policy and the educational experiences of the minority population – as is revealed in the proceeding chapters.

Chapter 3 looks into the process through which minority cultures and subjects are interpreted and defined by the cultural mainstream as inferior and less valuable for the modernization of China, and in consequent need of transformation in line with advanced cultures, particularly through education. In dichotomizing advanced cultures vis-à-vis backward ones, this process has ethnicized differences of minorities. However, within the process itself are internal contradictions that render any attempt at actual education self-contradictory and ultimately unproductive. Using three sources of data, government policy, academic discourse, and interviews with Han teachers and students, the chapter provides corroborative evidence relating to the creation of particular images of minority cultures and subjects by the mainstream community. Central to this creation is the idea of Chinese culturalism, in spite of its different vocabularies and strategies from the historically formulated prevailing culture discourse of imperial times.

Based on fieldwork in a Tibetan administrative region, Chapter 4 examines how Tibetan children's efforts to attain social mobility through education were hindered by the Chinese state agenda of integrating them into the Han nation-state. This complication can be understood as a tension between their desire for full social citizenship in the form of rights to employment, education and opportunities, and the requirement that they also adopt Han cultural citizenship, that is, they acquire the knowledge and language for 'belonging' to mainstream society. However, by focusing on integrating and equipping students to become part of the Han-dominated mainstream, educational policies devalued Tibetan culture and language. This situation prevented Tibetan students from acquiring the kinds of cultural capital that would enable them to 'progress' and caused many of them to become academic underachievers.

Drawing upon the interviews with Muslims, Chapter 5 reveals how the Muslim community disengaged from state schools and the wider society as a response to their ethnic identity as a people of 'familiar strangers' in the Chinese Han cultural context. This alien identity received by Muslims from the wider society in general, and in this Tibetan-dominated region in particular, largely blocked their access to opportunities for social mobility and education. As a response, Muslims showed little motivation, enthusiasm for and confidence in state education, which subsequently led to their poor school performance. This was grounded in their pessimistic outlook about their socio-economic status in the future, and the prejudice and hostility they received from individuals as well as institutions. Therefore, education, the major way to achieve upward social mobility, became irrelevant to Muslims to a large extent. In the meantime, Muslims were barely identified by the larger society as Chinese people unless they sinicized themselves, involuntarily or voluntarily, by substantially hiding or removing their ethno-religious markers.

In Chapter 6 I conclude by summarizing social systems that create inequality for ethnic minorities, and the corresponding community forces and their consequences. It manifests the possible reconciliation between economic development, political cohesion and cultural diversity by demonstrating how the three aspects can in fact sustain and reinforce each other in everyday practice as well as in theory. In consequence, the chapter casts new light on the societal environment in which government policies are made. This is directed at achieving the inclusion of ethnic minorities of distinctive cultures into the wider society in general, and in schools in particular.

Finally, drawing upon the second period of fieldwork in 2006 and 2007, a Postscript is annexed to this research of state education to look at and discuss some recent educational programmes sponsored by NGOs. These programmes were designed in particular for Tibetan students. This new development provided alternative paradigms and opportunities for minority education, and cultivated some of the high-achieving students in English and project management. Nevertheless, this trend did not significantly enhance participation of Tibetan minorities in socio-politically important public institutions. In the meantime, it also widened the gap between Muslims and other ethnic groups in terms of their opportunities for education. It therefore created new cleavages between the state and minority communities, and between different ethnic groups. This made it urgent for the Chinese educational system to become (more) inclusive of minority populations.

Terminology

Some important terms have already been explained or discussed in this introduction including: community forces, culture, cultural exclusion, and discursive repertoire. A few more key terms that are used throughout the book need to be clarified. In modern Chinese there is only one word for different ethnic populations within its boundaries, *(min)zu*, which had long been translated into *nationality* in English. However, informed readers may have found that I adopted terms *ethnic, ethnicity* rather than *nationality* in spite of the fact that self-consciousness of ethnic identity was largely absent in the governmental identification of the 56 ethnic groups that was embarked upon some 50 years ago in China.[16] Clearly, official definitions are not merely a result of social engineering, or derived from nowhere; moreover, these definitions have inevitably led to an awareness of ethnic identity among both the Han and non-Han groups. *Nationality*, the English translation of the Chinese concept of *(min)zu*, was gradually replaced by *ethnicity* in its English translation in some government documents and academic research some one to two decades ago. This signals that the concept of ethnicity has been imported into Chinese discourse.[17]

However, my adoption of the term of ethnicity or ethnic is in a more linguistic sense for reasons of convenience even though the term of nationality can also be found on several occasions with regard to historical discourse. On the other hand, my study does not particularly focus on the confusion over the ethnic identity issue. This is also associated with the nature of the ethnic minority groups that this study takes as subjects, Tibetans and Muslims in the northwest. They are more confident about their ethnic identity than many others even though they may not know the official terminology used to describe them until reaching schooling age (R. Ma 2003: 13). However, I identified the ethnicity of some students in the mainstream school in the fieldwork when it appeared to be obscure to me. My records were basically dependent upon their self-consciousness and self-identification. The relevant information can be found in Chapter 4.

I use the pair of terms *minority/majority* in line with the government and public discourse in that (ethnic) *minority* always refers to non-Han groups whether or not they are quantitatively dominant groups, for example, in their autonomous regions. Correspondingly, the term *majority* is directed at the Han community.[18] By the same token, I refer to the majority Han when employing such terms as *dominant, mainstream, ordinary, subordinate* or *common* whereas terms like *dominated, peripheral, subordinated* or *marginal* are used to refer to ethnic minorities, unless indicated otherwise.

2 The trajectories of Chinese culturalism and its educational legacy

Introduction

The culture discourse in China is a shifting discursive repertoire under different historical circumstances, through which the cultural mainstream attempts to maintain control of legitimacy. Central to this culturalism is the belief that China is and has been the only true civilization; this position remained unchallenged even at times of military occupation and threats by aliens due to their alleged backwardness. Furthermore, this cultural outlook means that rulers must and can be educated and govern according to Confucian ways of universal value. This is also applicable to aliens, as asserted Han cultural superiority is believed to rest on education that can potentially civilize and so legitimize non-Chinese (James Harrison 1969, cited in Townsend 1992: 98–9).[1] Firstly, therefore, culturalism has determined ethnic boundaries and cultural membership in history. Secondly, it was institutionalized and reinforced through the running of civil service examinations of imperial China (*keju kaoshi*). This in turn has shaped the Chinese educational tradition that has held up a Confucian-based elitist view at the philosophical level, and operated an examinations-guided institution at the technical level. Finally, it has (re)shaped the Chinese perception of the West in the era of modernization that urges China to conduct a new campaign of *suzhi* education aiming to transform the human quality of the whole nation.

As a legacy, it has largely determined education policy and practice through the modern era of China, and relatedly, the educational experiences of ethnic minorities today, although the exact form that the culturalism takes has changed over time. Changes occurred, in particular in modern history when China and its civilization were seriously challenged and threatened by the West, provoking the New Culture Movement (*xin wenhua yundong*) specifically directed towards democracy and science within its pursuit of European civilization (Dikötter 1992; Mitter 2004). In the meantime, the culturalism has also changed in relation to changing material conditions that is in particular evidenced by the new era of reform and opening-up of China since the late 1970s centring on economic development. Correspondingly, education policy with regard to ethnic minorities has kept changing, whilst being ingrained in the same idea of culturalism.

This chapter falls into two parts. The first part delineates an historical development of Chinese culturalism that results in an education-grounded culture discourse. The second part of the chapter looks into the culture discourse against the backdrop of the Chinese encounter with the West, and how this leads China to seeking cultural legitimacy on a global scale under new circumstances that is hoped to be actualized through *suzhi* education. Nonetheless, a new ethos in education is also seen to emerge under a complex and competing package combining Chinese culturalism, career and self-accomplishment focused educational tradition, increasing competitiveness driven by the knowledge economy, and Chinese ways of governing and engineering society and people.[2]

Historical development of Chinese culturalism

The fluidity of ethnic boundaries

When Fei Xiaotong (1989) likens the process whereby the Han takes shape to snowballing, and Dru C. Gladney (2004) unpacks the category of the Han that is widely assumed to be the equivalent of a homogeneous and monocultural 'Chinese' nation, both are actually revealing the same fact: the Han itself is always undergoing a process of reconstruction from both within and without, historically and at present. So how does the boundary between the Han and non-Han groups come into being and keep changing, and what are the implications for distinguishing between the Han and non-Han groups? What follows is a thematic sketch of Chinese history in relation to the economic, cultural and political dynamics of this age-long boundary drawing exercise. Some names that will be used with regard to the Han and non-Han groups are listed below just before discussion:[3]

- *Han*: Hua, Huaxia, Xia, Zhongguo, Zhonghua;
- *Non-Han*: Dalu, Di, Fan, Man, Miao, Rong, Yao, Yi.

Han was certainly not used as the name of a people until well after the Han dynasty (206 BC–AD 220. See Appendix 1 'History Timeline'). However, a group of people(s) had already been named by itself and/or out-groups, that is either associated to the first dynasty, Xia (2070 BC–1600 BC), or with certain geographically based administrative institutions (for example, *Zhongguo*, lit. the Middle Kingdom, originally refers to 'the capital city'). Both were located somewhere around the middle and lower reaches of the Yellow River (hereafter MLYR) (Chen 1989). The names served as boundaries between this group (and its territory) and other groups around it, and meanwhile were also a reflection of a gradually formulating concept of 'all under heaven' (*tianxia*, or 'the world'). This holistic concept of *tianxia* was actualized by the Qin emperor when he established the first centralized empire in 221 BC. One of the most influential policies the emperor implemented was to standardize the variety of writing systems, which largely facilitated the integration of previous states in economy, politics and culture into the empire, and more importantly, laid a foundation for the empires that followed that lasted for over two thousand years.

The group of people(s) was finally called *Han Ren* (Han people) during the following period of the Wei, Jin, Southern and Northern dynasties (AD 220–581) that was characterized by the influx of nomadic groups from the north and their establishment of many dynasties. Correspondingly, all other groups were placed under a general rubric of *Fan* vis-à-vis *Han* (Chen 1989).[4] Having settled in Zhongguo, a huge number of *Fan* peoples acquired Zhongguo culture, coupled with changes of their surnames to the Han style or their marriage with Han people. This eventually led to their absorption into the Han group. On the other hand, the intrusion of nomadic northerners to Zhongguo also forced a great number of previous Han people to migrate to the south or other marginal areas where they mixed with locals. These previous Han people hence may be labelled or have labelled themselves as other than Han (Fei 1989; Xiao 1995; Ebrey 1996; Lu and Yang 2000; Gladney 2004). Meanwhile, *Han* was used quite freely to include peoples from other origins in some dynastic periods (Jia 1989a; 1989b).

This migratory pattern of people from the north to Zhongguo and from Zhongguo to the south putatively has been an important aspect of the whole history of China, the two most widely known cases being those of the Yuan and Qing dynasties, respectively ruled by Mongols and Manchu.[5] This demonstrates that Han, as the name of a people(s) versus non-Han, is a reflection of the fluidity of the boundary between Han and non-Han. This migratory pattern is also evidenced by linguistic typology – the Chinese language shows a long continuity with the dialects of the north and northwest, being much closer to Altaic compared to dialects in the south, that remain more relics of classical Chinese in a certain sense (Qiaoben 1985).[6]

Culture as the primary criterion in distinguishing ethnic groups

One interesting question with regard to ethnicity in Chinese history is that if the boundary between Han and non-Han kept changing, what was the meaning of this distinction to different groups? A simple answer is that it is primarily associated with cultural differences that are usually addressed through strategically drawn 'symbolic boundaries'. Michele Lamont (2001: 15,341) suggests that symbolic boundaries are expressed through including some groups (likes) and excluding some others (dislikes), and so play an important role in the exercise of power. In the case of China, Wang Mingke (1997) argues that people living in what are now two different types of area, the agricultural areas of the MLRY and the nomadic areas on their northern margins, shared a similar life style of agriculture on account of their similar natural environment, which did not change until about 2000 BC when the global climate gradually became drier. This climate transformation eventually turned the life of the people on the margins into a nomadic style, involving a very different mode of production, and eventually, a different social organization and cultural model compared to those of their agricultural neighbours.

A concern with redistribution of resources became serious, as populations living upon agriculture kept growing. This caused (more) conflicts between different groups, and eventually resulted in a gradual building up of the Great Wall along the marginal areas by the MLRY peoples during the following 2,000 years. Meanwhile, backed up by agriculture, a political system of centralized dynasties of complex bureaucratic institutions also emerged in the MLYR area, which was primarily maintained by corvees and taxes from peasants. This social order was in sharp contrast with what existed outside the Great Wall, which was highlighted by increasing nomadicization, mobility and militarization (M. Wang 1997). More importantly, the process of division of the two types of society gradually forged a consciousness of difference between peoples, which resulted in a difference in the naming distinctive peoples. *Xia, Zhongguo* or *Hua* (see below), therefore became the names of the agricultural populace while the names for (nomadic) out-groups are *Yi, Di, Rong, Man*, etc. This division is epitomized in the juxtaposition of *Hua/Yi* or *Yi/Xia*, with Yi generally referring to non-Xia, non-Hua or non-Han groups until the early period of the Republic.

This mode-of-production-based socio-political division inevitably led to a cultural division that, at the beginning at least on the part of the Huaxia, devalued out-groups in favour of itself. This is understandable given the significance that agricultural life can have in building up a complex and institutionalized society in comparison with the type of society that can be developed in a nomadic life. Furthermore, a nomadic life in that era meant a close tie with animals as well as one inclined to militarization. Both tendencies were thought to represent primitivity or brutality, vis-à-vis advance or humanity of the Huaxia, and thus 'barbarian' in the Huaxia's eyes. This emphasis on literariness over militarization is also reflected in the imperial civil service examinations (see below).

Meanwhile, relatively less concern about a basic standard of living was also more likely to enable development of a splendid lifestyle (for example, 'gorgeous attire and rich ornaments' and sophisticated literature). In fact, the existence of the Great Wall and the militarization process is fundamentally associated with the issue of power as an underlying motive for reinforcing cultural difference or symbolic boundaries between the Han and others. As a result, the cultural dimension eventually came to be the most important criterion in distinguishing between Huaxia and Yi. Rawski (1988: 33) summarizes that Han-ness or Chinese-ness therefore 'became defined by dietary habits (the Chinese did not eat dairy products), by clothing styles, and especially by traditions concerning marriage and death'.

This fluidity left room for Yi people to become Xia and vice versa, dependent upon whether they behaved in Xia ways or Yi ways (Chen 1989, Xiao 1995). The core of Xia ways is what was known as Confucianism, that advocated the rule of rites and traditional morals, which supposedly could and should be acquired through learning the Confucian classics, especially Four Books and Five Classics (*Sishu Wujing*). Therefore, Xia or Confucian ways as a set of institutions became the standard of culture, and were universalized cultural values. Iris Marion Young (1990: 164–6) unmasks the injustice in the process of this universality by drawing attention to three of its oppressive consequences. First, all the rules and standards have already been set by dominant culture before dominated groups participate in the social game. This has resulted in disadvantaging these late-participants. Correspondingly, it is blind to the specificity of the privileged group, and gives them the illusion that their own viewpoint and experience embody a neutral and universal humanity. This universalism in the end leads to internalization of a devaluation of themselves among disadvantaged groups.

Fundamentally, Young sees that while rules and standards are set by the dominant group, these rules and standards are specifically designed to create 'others' and set these groups in a disadvantaged position from the outset. It then doesn't matter as much if the 'others' are latecomers to the game, but, instead, if they are capable of transforming themselves to 'non-others'. This makes up the very concept of hegemony that was most influentially articulated by Antonio Gramsci (1971), and largely explains the alien nomadic peoples' 'voluntariness' in acquisition of Han culture. Ebrey (1996: 23) also similarly infers from the fact of many non-Chinese people claiming descent from Chinese migrants that either they wanted to believe it in looking down upon non-Han themselves or it was in their interest to do so for local politics, social prestige, or whatever.

In this vein, it is also understandable that, when Confucians did not seem to practise the exclusion of various Yi peoples from the Xia group, Confucius himself believed that Yi or *yuanren* (lit. 'people from afar') could be attracted with its 'universal' culture or morals, so as to come under control (*yuanren bu fu, ze xiu wende yi lai zhi*).[7] In other words, those who did not accept the universal values set out by Confucians would be considered to have no willingness to stay in, but to exercise self-exclusion from Chinese society instead. By the same token, when talking about rulers from different backgrounds, Yi or Xia, Mencius argued that they would be similarly accountable so long as their behaviour accorded to Xia ways (*dezhi xinghu Zhongguo, ruo he fujie, xiansheng housheng, qi kui yi ye*).

This method of distinguishing Yi from Xia or Hua (*hua yi zhi bian*) even brought about a protest among English traders in the nineteenth century who were resentful at being seen as Yi people (i.e. barbarian) by the Qing rulers, which led to the creation of a new name *Yang* (lit. 'ocean'), referring to 'foreign' (Chen 1989: 103). This very shift of terminology marks a change in Chinese concern with 'alien' from domestic to Western forces, that has changed the Chinese view of power relations between Chinese and 'aliens', particularly from the New Culture Movement (*xin wenhua yundong*) onward (see below).

This universal culturalism is also reflected in another name of the Han mentioned earlier, *Hua*, that originated from a self-bragging phrase '*yiguan-huazu*' ('splendidly dressed-up group of people'), coined by a group of Han people (Chen 1989: 104). This group emerged after the Eastern Han dynasty (AD 25–225) as scholarship in the classics was gradually controlled by and transmitted privately in certain families, which resulted in men from these families eventually monopolizing the top leadership in the government. This very high status and the related sophisticated lifestyle won respect from Han and non-Han emperors alike, and meanwhile led them to disdain other relatively poor or humble Han families (ibid.).

Eventually, (*Zhong*)*hua* developed into a concept with reference to the culture represented by the classics and/or the people who possess this culture, that is, Han (ibid.). This highlighted a sentiment of the cultural superiority of the Han that was summarized by a scholar in the Tang dynasty as that Zhongguo is called Xia because it possesses great propriety and righteousness (Xia also means 'large, great'), and is named Hua for its splendid clothes and literature (Hua mainly means 'splendid', 'colourful', 'beautiful') (*Zhongguo you liyi zhi da, gu cheng Xia; you fuzhang zhi mei, gu wei zhi Hua*). Correspondingly, phrases naming non-Han people were always associated with negative connotations whatever their original meaning (see, for example, Dikötter 1992: 9).

Undeniably, the history of acculturation never merely moves in a single direction, but both ways (also see below Elman). This is, in the Chinese case, to say that new elements and the content of various Yi cultures were continually brought into Huaxia culture due to constant communication between different communities. A more telling case is of the invention of the Manchu during the Qing dynasty (AD 1644–1912). In order to survive among the wider society of Han – the ruled and also majority – the Qing Empire employed a number of policies and measures through its three centuries' regime to repeatedly define its ethnic identity so as to making Manchus distinctive from Han (and others). These strategies involved making up genealogy and language, emphasizing martial skills and the frugal lifestyle of the 'Old Way' (*jiu dao, jiu feng*) (Crossley 2000, 2006; Elliot 2006). In this process, the Qianlong Emperor (AD 1711–99) and the Eight Banners (*baqi*) system served respectively as the crucial figure and institution in promoting Manchu identity (see esp. Crossley 2000, Chapter 6; Elliot 2006).

Yet, in this making of identity backed up by cultural and institutional initiatives, Manchus were also seen to encounter an identity crisis after long settlement in an environment surrounded by 'the temptations of refined China's culture' (Elliot 2006: 47). In fact, while this settlement contributed to the making of Manchus, it was, as the other side of the same coin, also responsible for the ebbing away of the language and other cultural traits among Manchus as China was moving into its modern era after the demise of the Qing. This is where complexity and complication of acculturation lie. Nonetheless, despite a problematic category of Chinese culture itself,[8] as I argued in the chapters that follow, the culturalism (not culture) of Han as a discourse is still accepted and held by officially identified Han and other ethnic groups as the means of distinguishing between different peoples, some of whom are superior to others.

Institutionalization of Chinese culturalism

The imagined superiority of Huaxia civilization ran through all the dynasties of Han or non-Han rulers. Nevertheless, as both Mitter (2004) and Townsend (1992) similarly point out, culturalism (although only the latter author actually uses this term) is primarily an intellectual provenance. This ideology or movement was not only premised on an abstract concept, but had in fact been institutionalized through, principally, the establishment of the civil service examinations of imperial China, and reinforced in the continuity of the examinations system that lasted for 1,300 years with almost no interruption until the end of the imperial era (Schirokauer 1981: 7).

Education in the imperial period was characterized by two features: public education was largely left to the people, and the civil service examinations system dominated and guided the education domain (Miyazaki 1981: 111–29). The examinations system was formally introduced in the Sui dynasty (AD 581–618) as a means of suppressing the power of the 'splendidly dressed up' aristocrat-literati (*shi*) who had dominated and reproduced top officialdom as a result of their monopolization of scholarship in the classics on a family basis. However, the aristocrat-literati had an advantaged position over other classes when it participated in the examinations, on account of its greater fluency in the classics (or of its cultural capital) (ibid.).[9] And in fact, civil examinations served 'to tie the dynasty to literati culture bureaucratically' (Elman 2000: xxiv).

Meanwhile, Northern Song rulers also employed civil service examinations to limit alternative military power as a strategy against potential military threats that were prevalent in the late Tang and the Five dynasties before the Song (ibid.), which kept military officers subordinated to civilians. Yet, concomitantly, non-Han conquerors in late imperial times (Khitan, Tanguts, Jurchen, Mongols, and Manchus) conferred on their military elites a special status outside the bureaucratic civil system (e.g. the Eight Banners system) that aimed to 'minimize the full implication of the Han civilizing process' (ibid.: 64). Even so, for the victorious outsiders, it was necessary to endure the classical literature and bureaucracy in an effort to ensure their political legitimacy. While this maintenance of Chinese culture resulted in many warriors becoming as civilized as the literati historian in the civil bureaucracy, it also granted Han literati an ideological space (ibid.).

Furthermore, this ideological space was considered to be best filled with

Neo-Confucianism (*daoxue*) that emerged in the Southern Song, became the orthodox classical curriculum for examination candidates after 1300 under the Mongol Yuan, and eventually penetrated Han Chinese society and culture during the early Ming (Elman 2000). Because *daoxue* was believed by the warrior to contain a model set of ideas and facts, which would reproduce classical ideals while cultivating political loyalty (ibid.: 65). In return, the examinations system held up and reinforced the classics of Confucianism as a standard, and eventually became essential for the establishment of imperial autocracy in late imperial China. As a result, it confirmed literati's 'preeminence over the warrior in the precincts of the bureaucracy and on the higher ground of political ideology' (ibid.: 64). This is why Elman illustrates this civilizing process as cutting-both-ways (ibid.: 63), and that civil service examinations became 'a cultural arena within which diverse social and political interests contested each other and were balanced' (ibid.: xxiv).

Undeniably, the civil service examinations system left a profound legacy after its abolition. The system was unusually democratic in that it was open to anyone, regardless of background,[10] and its fairness in the way examinations were conducted with strict discipline. However, the abolition of the examination system itself is evidence of its intrinsic defects. This system embedded a careerist attitude towards scholarship, which to a significant degree has shaped the education focus in today's China that is narrowly centred upon college entrance examinations (*gaokao*).

Relatedly, the examinations system also brought misery to the vast majority of examinees who failed in examinations. This is understandable, given the fact that on the one hand to devote one's energies to the civil service examinations was an extremely costly pursuit, although in fact it was only the middle class who could afford this (so the equality of the system stayed at the level of theory to a large extent). On the other hand very limited demand for more government officials also meant that the number of examinees who could eventually receive a *jinshi* (the highest) degree after going through all levels of examinations was only one out of every three thousand (Miyazaki 1981). Finally, since the literary studies involved narrowly memorizing the Confucian classics and writing poems and essays, one of its main effects was that these intellectuals became inflexible in relation to the new learning, and at the same time too proud to engage in commerce while too weak to do physical labour (ibid.). This disconnection between education and the real world is still a noticeable feature of the modern Chinese educational system, as argued in subsequent chapters.

The examinations system not only served as an examination of the career potential of a person, but also as a means of 'discovering men of high moral character as well as of scholarly and literary attainment' (Schirokauer 1981: 7). As a consequence, those who succeeded in the civil service examinations would then win their honourable status from the emperor, and at the same time their eminence was acknowledged by a public opinion that was formed and controlled by intellectuals (Miyazaki 1981). Therefore, this group of people not only became political elites, but also cultural elites, and this culti-vated the notion of *xiushen* (cultivate oneself), *qijia* (put the family in order), *zhiguo* (rule the country), *ping tianxia* (unify the world in peace). This phil-osophy connected individual cultivation in moral and literary matters to the ruling of the country and the world, and also regarded the management of family life and political life as inseparable. Thus the state was seen as an extended family, or *guojia*, literally meaning 'state-family'. This integration of four levels comprised the ideal package of intellectual accomplishment.

Cultural superiority first and the cultural triumph that followed fostered the very kind of Chinese elites who are always ready to take the world (*tianxia*) as their own responsibility as a result of their confidence in their morality and cultural accomplishment. They believe in the morality and cul-ture they possessed and represented which was the ultimate standard that should be used to manage the world, and the path through which this can be achieved is to educate the masses with this universal culture. In portraying the conviction that was triggered by the New Culture Movement in 1919 as that 'educated classes were the only ones who could save China', Mitter (2004: 269) observes that this conviction 'echoed a mindset that went back even before May Fourth to the Era when Confucianism had dominated'. As a benchmark of career, political, cultural and moral achievement, education has become the ultimate life goal of affordable (or unaffordable!) people in imperial China that has become an essential aspect in Chinese tradition.

This fad for education, or more precisely, for examinations, is condensed in numerous household phrases as principle, practised by the whole nation ever since.[11] To name but a few: 'the worth of other pursuits is small, the study of books excels them all' (*wanban jie xiapin, wei you dushu gao*); 'there are auto-matically gold-made houses in books; and there are automatically jade-like faces [i.e. beautiful women] in books' (*shu zhong ziyou huangjin wu, shuzhong ziyou yan ru yu*); a literary or intellectual family is respectfully called 'a family with book fragrance' (*shuxiang mendi*). Hard work stories in schools were also recorded and passed on in families, schools as well as the larger society since imperial times. The stories are invoked to encourage younger gener-ations to bear hard and bitter study conditions and life, for the very moment when one's name appears on the list of successful candidates in the imperial examinations (*jinbang timing shi*, lit. 'when one's name is inscribed on the golden list'). These kinds of story were not only involved with working hard in straitened circumstances (*hanchuang kudu*, lit. 'study hard by a cold win-dow'), but also, if not more, referred to self-denial, by which to endure, for example, tiredness or sleepiness (*tou xuan liang, zhui ci gu*).

The cultural discourse of China

One of the main reasons why the examinations system could survive for 1300 years was closely connected with the first emperor. As mentioned earlier, one of the most influential policies the Qin emperor introduced was the standardization of the Chinese writing system, Chinese characters (*hanzi*), which became the official writing system of imperial China. This is because only with a uniformed writing system, would it become possible for the state and elites to gain control and exercise power over the masses (Lewis 1999). Needless to say, this standardization could not have been completed without a 'preparation' period that occurred well before the Qin. In unveiling the association of writing with authority in early China (the Warring States period), Lewis (1999: 4) states that writing was employed to create the entire world, a world that 'provided models for the unprecedented enterprise of founding a world empire'. By doing so, the elites 'who composed, sponsored, or interpreted' this world gained authority on the one hand, and on the other, 'secured the longevity of the imperial system and led to the omnipresence of the written graph in Chinese culture'.

This standardized system enabled the literary-based civil service examinations to be conducted across this vast country, where languages in different locations, to a varied extent, were mutually unintelligible. As a result, *hanzi* not only functioned as the conveyor of the classics, but also evolved a highly sophisticated form of art, calligraphy. To acquire Chinese characters is therefore a necessity for people to become literate, and further, to access 'universal' morality and high culture. This is roughly the idea of culture as a separate realm of human expression (Spillman 2002: 3–4) that 'is most valuable about us or others,' and so 'needs to be preserved or express and represent the identity of a group.' As a consequence, Chinese characters became the most basic and important symbol of Chinese (high) culture, and those who fluently master this system were considered highly respectable. This is nonetheless also attributable to difficulties in learning characters which prevent a large number of people from becoming reasonably knowledgeable and fluent in the system. In fact, only those who have been specifically trained, for example, in history or Chinese departments of universities, can possibly fluently master this system and are regarded as having a high cultural level.

Therefore, education in China is technically closely related to the acquisition of Chinese characters, which is symbolically associated to one's 'cultural level' (*wenhua shuiping* or *wenhua chengdu*). This has resulted in 'wenhua', or 'culture', being the preferred vernacular expression in public discourse even after the term 'cultural level' was replaced by 'educational level' in the fifth national census in 2000 (also see discussions below on *suzhi*, i.e. quality). Indeed, this preference for 'culture' complies with the traditional conception: acquisition of Chinese characters, and the whole package of knowledge it conveys (including sciences). So for a long time, learning culture (*xue wenhua*) primarily refers to learning characters. Furthermore, when one is said to 'have culture' (*you wenhua*), it means that s/he has knowledge of Chinese characters and of other subjects wrapped by and/or taught in Chinese characters. In other words, mastery of the kind of cultures wrapped with writing systems other than Chinese characters is probably not regarded as 'having culture' or will be regarded as 'having no culture' (*mei wenhua*). In his illustration of the conception of 'culture' in the Chinese context, Gladney (1999: 59) describes an elderly Hui Hajji who did not think that he had culture despite the fact that this Hajji had spent twelve years living in the Middle East and was fluent in Persian, Arabic, and was a master of the Islamic natural sciences.

This literacy-based education that has apparently fostered a feeling of worship towards scripts is also employed by both the communist government and society to distinguish backwardness from progress. The communist government helped establish writing systems for some 'backward' ethnic minorities who did not have scripts. Meanwhile, when asked about the relationship between ethnicity and education, one of my Muslim Hui informants suggested that the Muslim Salar are even more backward (than Hui) because they do not even have their own writing system corresponding to their language (a kind of Turkish), while Hui, as Chinese speakers, have Chinese characters. This type of education is actually reflected in the two characters of the Chinese word *wenhua* itself. *Wen*, translated as 'literary, literature, script, inscription', is the 'central part of the idea of culture', and *hua*, translated as 'change, transform', is the process of culturing people (ibid.).

Although as a modern Chinese word, *wenhua* is the translation of 'culture' in the European languages that were imported via Japanese in the nineteenth century, it is nevertheless rooted in the classical concept of **wenzhi jiaohua**, for which *wenhua* stands. *Wenzhi* (*zhi*, 'rule, manage, govern') can be understood both as 'government by civilians rather than military men' and 'government promotion of literature and the arts', and is the Chinese mode of governance; *Jiaohua* (*jiao*, educate, train in good manners) is the process of educating people so as to transform them, and hence can be understood as civilized intercourse. Therefore, the notion of *wenhua* covers a wide range of dimensions from elitism, governance to the transformation of people, which is in parallel with the underlying function of the civil service examinations. This is exactly a meaning-making process that echoes the early meaning of 'culture' in English (Williams, cited in Spillman 2002: 13).

However, today *wenhua* can also be used in *shaoshu minzu wenhua* ('ethnic minority cultures'). *Wenhua* in this context does not contain the same meaning as it does in 'having no [Chinese] culture', but rather, refers to the historical heritage of ethnic minorities and so is thought to be static and should be kept in museums (also see Gladney 2004, esp. Chapter 3). Different discourses about the concept of culture are in fact constructed by discursive practices that favour mainstream culture over the others, as Wetherell and Potter (1992) unveil in their portrayal of Pākehā positions in relation to Māori in New Zealand. The former people regard themselves as possessing society, having civilization, and holding a mundane, technical and practical outlook, which are not presented as culture, but as simple common sense. On the contrary, Māori people are thought to possess 'culture' that makes them exotic and abnormal, compared to the normal mode of the Pākehā majority. This culture discourse exactly mirrors that in the Chinese context where an ethnic minority people with their own culture is probably thought not to have culture if they are not educated with the mainstream civilization conveyed by Chinese characters, and/or in mainstream schools, as I document above and in Chapters 3 and 4.

Indeed, minority cultures are deep down understood worldwide in a colonialist view of the primitivity and inferiority of the Other's culture in contrast with the complexity and superiority of their own culture. This is what Harrell (1995: 15–17) portrays as the metaphors of history in conceptualizing civilization projects with respect to relationships between civilizers and civilized. This metaphor is an attempt to find a resolution to the paradox between the idea that minority peoples are primitive and civilizable, and meanwhile innately backward and hence uncivilizable. When minority people are placed on the scale of the development of human history, they are ancient and unchanged, and so the civilizers have some chance of success (ibid.). This idea is a fact of civilizing the uncivilizable that glosses over the nature/nurture dichotomy, and is likewise reflected in the recent discourse of *suzhi*, or roughly, (human) quality (see below), as Kipnis (2006: 297) suggests. In this vein, those who are regarded as being low quality (*suzhi cha*) (usually rural or minority) students are likely to be labelled as being *you zhishi mei wenhua* ('having knowledge but without culture') even though they possess a university degree. Subtly enough, *Wenhua* in this context is largely interchangeable with *suzhi*, whereas it is more associated with Chinese characters in the context of *mei shenme/duoshao wenhua* ('having little culture'), which reflects a gradual development of the connotation of *wenhua* itself.

The culture discourse in the modern era

Culturalism under nationalistic sentiment in modern China

Dikötter (1992) suggests that no serious challenge was posed to universal culturalism until the nineteenth century when China encountered both internal disorder and the external intrusions of foreign countries. These crises were highlighted by a reluctant reflection upon the Confucian ideology in the first place, followed by an acute attack on the imperial orthodoxy, which eventually led to an entire rejection of the Confucian legacy and the upsurge of the New Culture Movement. The New Culture Movement specifically directed at 'science' and 'democracy' within China's pursuit of European civilization, which were hoped to displace or transform Chinese traditional culture. And indeed, the significant ruptures in pre-modern culture that arrived with the modern era were seen in many aspects of (urban) social life of the time. These include new concepts of the role of individuals in society, freethinking possibilities, increasing numbers of factory workers and jobs for women, experiments with ideas of 'free love', language reform from the old classical to vernacular form – which particularly made Confucian ideas now an alien form for most Chinese (see, for example, Mitter 2004). Above all, this movement signalled a shift of Chinese concern with 'alien' from traditional nomadic forces to ocean forces, and initiated a 100 years' attempt to define China's modern identity. It has underpinned a new Chinese view of power relations between China and 'aliens' in the modern epoch.

Nonetheless, in the Maoist era (1949–76), China isolated itself from the West, which suspended the tradition of the New Culture Movement. This isolation was exacerbated during the Cultural Revolution when both the Western civilization and Confucianism tradition were overthrown. Needless to say, however, this 'deviating' episode was, in part, driven by a similar pursuit of a modern identity. It was not until after the late 1970s when a new cultural reflexivity among cultural intellectuals occurred as a movement competing with the official communist ideology. This is what has been called 'culture fever' (*wenhua re*).[12] In this culture fever, a very wide range of cultural intellectuals, after survived from Mao's Cultural Revolution, were seriously considering what would be a new Chinese culture that would become the motor for Chinese modernization. This reflection largely and eagerly drew upon Western culture in examining Chinese traditional culture, in particular its weakness, and relatedly, the elements that supposedly undesirably prolonged Chinese history. In this resonance with the call that their predecessors made for science and democracy some seventy years before, a television documentary series entitled *Heshang* ('River Elegy') in particular stirred up the nation in the late 1980s (also see Mitter 2004). The authors of *Heshang* argued that China should abandon its too somnolent and peaceful inward-looking culture that had made its civilization wane. Instead, it should embrace the 'deep blue' (*wei lan se*) of the ocean, that is, the outward-looking, creatively destructive culture of the West that represents new ways of thought and living (ibid.: 265).

Nevertheless, the loss of confidence in Chinese Han culture does not necessarily alter the Han view of the superior status of their culture in relation to its minority cultures. In spite of various relationships between the Han and different minority communities, a culturalist attitude among the 'Han' towards all other groups that were seen or defined as an ethnic minority or nationality has changed little over time.[13] *Zhonghua*, with its superior connotation to peripheral groups, was not applied to all ethnic groups in the Chinese territory until the twentieth century, when Sun Yat-sen, the leader of the Nationalist Party and the Republic of China, incorporated the other four ethnic groups (Manchurian, Mongolian, Hui and Tibetan) in the *Zhongghua Minzu* (Chinese nation) after realizing the limitation of merely equating *Zhonghua* with *Han* when confronting foreign intrusions (by the West and Japan). This was progress, compared with his earlier slogan, 'drive away *Dalu* [Manchurians, the rulers of the Qing dynasty], restore *Zhonghua* [Han China]' (*Quzhu Dalu, huifu Zhonghua*). Sun also gradually engaged with the notions of minority self-determination (*minzu zijue*) and minority autonomy (*minzu zizhi*). All of this apparently mirrored a new era of restructuring China with regard to both domestic and international affairs, as a response to the emergence of the modern nation-state that posed a threat or challenge to China in every significant way.

However, this 'progressive' idea still could not move beyond an essential concern or an ultimate goal of 'Chinese' nationhood. This is in the first place associated with Sun's perception of what placed China under threat from foreign forces. He thought that the differences of the other four ethnic groups from the Han in language, territory and custom precluded their frontiers and those of China proper from integration and unification, and further, could not protect the whole country from foreign intrusion as an effect of vulnerable frontiers inhabited by these alien groups. In this light, the task of the rulers was to assimilate the four minority groups into Chinese Han culture (Songben 2003: 73–155). To bind the five ethnic groups together (*wuzu gonghe*) as the Chinese nation was thus a political strategy, a top goal on the Republic agenda, although it was substantially shaped by the cultural dimension, as the case below shows that people in China were divided into three groups. This was the demand from the serious international situation China was facing, and also was underlined by and an echo of the historical concept of 'all under heaven'.

Yet, to merely refer to the five ethnic groups reflects Sun's limitation with regard to ethnic composition in China. Sun simply took over the legacy from the Qing dynasty to whom these minority groups were vassals whereas other minority populations, for example, those living in the southwest, were delineated as 'assimilated' and 'lowly civilized' (ibid.). This type of thinking about the ethnic composition of China was embedded in the way that Han scholars viewed ethnic minority groups in general in the early twentieth century as a result of their limited knowledge about non-Han peoples.

These scholars categorized ethnic groups into three types, A, B and C, by the criteria of the geo-political importance of the territory in which ethnic groups were located, their cultural level and disposition of intelligence. As a result, the ethnic group at Level A (the highest) was the Han. The four ethnic groups mentioned earlier constituted category B. Those who were scattered in the southwest, such as *Miao, Yao* and *Yi*, comprised Level C for the presumed absence of civilization and their geo-political insignificance (ibid.). The extreme version of the ignorance of minority groups is found in the kind of state ideologies that arbitrarily alleged that ethnic minority groups are merely large or small branches of the same blood lineage of the Han (Jiang Jieshi 1944, cited in Xie 2004: 51). This can be seen as shades of biological racism, under the impact of racial discourse from Europe since the nineteenth century.

Following on from the Nationalist approach but also in relation to its own experiences and ideology, the CPC (Communist Party of China) developed a more sensitive and sensible standpoint towards ethnic minorities. It was aware of the existence of more groups beyond the five ethnic communities, and also once guaranteed ethnic minorities rights of self-determination (Songben 2003: 184–201). The Ethnic Identification Project (*minzu shibie gongzuo*) that was carried out after it came to power in 1949 is another proof of its divergence from the historically formulated assimilationist pattern, that had aimed to sinicize minority groups with presumably superior Han culture, or simply overlooked minority groups. Nevertheless, like the Nationalists, the CPC's concept of minority determination eventually gave way to the ideology of Chinese nationhood that resulted in the introduction of the concept of minority (regional) autonomy (ibid.: 201–32). Concomitantly, the recognition of the minority population and the endowment of it with the regional autonomy system did not lead the CPC to full respect for minority customs or religions. Rather, the idea of respect largely stays at the level of legal formalities, which conceals the real inequality between the Han and the minority population (Xie 2004).[14] This was particularly striking during the Mao period, when minority customs and religions were accused of being backward and feudal and this was coupled by the destruction of numerous religious buildings such as monasteries or mosques, or when the minority population was forced to melt (*ronghe*) into the Han under the CPC's civilizing projects, an arguably different version of the assimilationist model from that of the Nationalists.

New developments in the culture discourse

The recent practice of a civilizing mission is highlighted by the *suzhi* campaign that was largely introduced into public discourse in the 1980s. Literally 'essential character', and generally translated as (human) 'quality' or 'character' in English, '*suzhi* is an amorphous concept that refers to the innate and nurtured physical, intellectual and ideological characteristics of a person' (Murphy 2004: 2. Also see Kipnis 2006). Therefore in academic discussions of *suzhi*, the concept is divided into *shenti suzhi* (physical quality) and *wenhua suzhi* (cultural quality), and the latter is principally connected to educational level. The former largely refers to the idea of eugenics that was imported with the discourse of race from Europe at the turn of the twentieth century (also see Dikötter 1992, Chapter 6), and more recently was embodied in the state one-child-per-couple policy. This policy is interpreted as *shaosheng yousheng* ('bear fewer and superior children') or *yousheng youyu* ('bear and rear superior children'). The *suzhi* agenda, as a new official ideological concept, aims to transform the low quality Chinese populace at the periphery that are characterized by tradition, poverty and agrarianism to modernity, prosperity and industrialism (Murphy 2004: 3). This transformation is particularly hoped to be realized through *suzhi jiaoyu* (lit. 'quality/character education'), in which educational objectives should shift from traditional examination-driven rote learning to emphasizing 'self-expression, manual dexterity, life skills appropriate to the local environment and extra-curricula activities such as music, sport and art' (ibid. and Chapter 3).

In spite of the primary orientation of the *suzhi* project towards peripheral populations, it is nevertheless an agenda aiming to make fundamental changes in the Chinese national character as a whole, as similarly observed by Mitter (2004: 269). That is, *suzhi* is a set of all-round standards for 'the Chinese nation' as a whole to foster the capacities needed for competition on the international stage in the long run. Kipnis (2006: 305) further attributes this *suzhi* idea to China's imagination of its struggling for survival and supremacy with other nations. This is an inevitable result of the ambivalence that Chinese have towards its culture after encountering Western values in the nineteenth century, and of a long period of self-enclosure under the CPC regime later on. Both experiences led to agonizing about the legacy of Confucianism (regardless of what it actually connotes) that provoked the New Culture Movement and culture fever, and meanwhile fostered the catalyst of the Chinese nationalism of elites and the masses alike (also see Townsend 1992).[15] This ambivalence or ambiguity can be seen from China's moving back and forth between aversion to and promotion of foreign ideas, between repudiation to celebration of national traditions, and between the Cultural Revolution to post-Mao modernization through modern Chinese history (ibid.: 101). It is not an exaggeration to say that a hundred years' pursuit of modernization (e.g. and esp. 'enrichment of the country and strengthening the military' (*fuguo qiangbing*)) is also a pursuit of a new confidence in Chinese cultural identity.

In the light of the economic success of East Asia that arguably benefited from the legacy of Confucianism, and of the disorder of the world system that is believed to be primarily caused by the Western new imperialism, the sentiment of superiority of Chinese culture has found room to voice itself, both within its territory and on the international stage.[16] Chinese culture is taken as the ideal model to conduct *suzhi* education as well as to foster a new confidence in Chinese culture so as to reconstruct a strong Chinese nation.[17] A very important part of this reconstruction is to unify ethnic groups under the same polity, and under the Han-based 'China culture'. The reconstruction is backed up by a belief that the Chinese nation has been historically formulated as a result of interaction between and integration of different ethnic groups. In this version of history, Han culture supposedly became a nucleus of the civilization of the Chinese nation that consists of many different ethnic cultures. This is allegedly because nomadic groups submissively and actively melted into the Han after entering plains, where the type of agricultural society with intensive and meticulous farming was located (Fei 1989: 31).[18] This thought fundamentally reflects the hegemony of the victors rather than an historical knowledge of struggles, and so is a version of subjugated knowledges or of regimes of truth (Foucault 1980: 81–2). This victors' version of history is called *zhengshi* ('official history') in Chinese history-writing, regardless of the ethnicity of the succeeding rulers.

When China first drew global attention for its assumed role of threatening or driving international economic growth, one of the *Heshang*'s authors started to publish his latest major work that he claims draws on his observations in mainland China and beyond, and his reflections on human civilization over the last years (Xie 2004/2005). Entitled 'Chinese Civilization Integrates the Globe' (*Zhongguo Wenming Zhenghe Quanqiu*), this work turns its back on *Heshang*, and argues that European or Western colonial civilization is in fact a secular one of anti-Christianity, and the disintegration of the Eastern European bloc is the beginning of the end of the European colonial system. Hence Europe or the existing post-colonial civilization system has lost power over itself and cannot resolve the most serious problems facing human beings today, such as environmental pollution, species extinction, immorality and war. On the other hand, the challenge from Islamic fundamentalism to the world order is not worrying because it is anyway within the existing system of civilization and thus controllable.

It concludes that Chinese civilization that centred on *lizh* (lit. 'rite system'), that is, a system pursuing inter-balance between a central (capital) city and local vassal autonomy, is a suitable one to resolve increasingly salient extremist tendencies and so integrate human beings as a whole. Correspondingly, East Asians, the creators of this culture, are claimed to have the highest intelligence that is alleged to have been evidenced in historical studies, cultural philosophy and political development, as well as by the latest anthropological reports. The asserted superiority of the East Asian race(!) is therefore justified by history, culture and science (ibid.). In other words, even though Chinese culture lost its confidence at times in particular in modern history when confronting Western culture, culturalism is always waiting there for the moment when it can take the opportunity to stand out again over other cultures.

In summary, Confucianism-oriented Chinese culture has admittedly been challenged and changed throughout history in general, and in the modern era in particular. Whilst the changes and challenges have disturbed so many important aspects of Chinese life, they have also awakened, cultivated and reinforced the consciousness of Chinese cultural identity on the one hand, and on the other, driven the cultural mainstream to continue its civilizing projects towards its peripheral peoples more urgently in attempts, and in the name, of the modernization of China. All of this demonstrates that culture is always changing as the cultural group copes with and adapts to its position in regional, national or global hierarchies of power and privilege. Regardless of the different forms Chinese culturalism has taken, due to changing historical circumstances, its underlying ideology is constant in that Chinese culture is believed to possess the kind of power to educate the masses and to transform so as to integrate other groups inside and outside of its territory. In other words, despite the shifting discursive repertoire, the normative discourse that Chinese culturalism complies with always looks forward to Chinese culture being taken as the tool (or remedy) for an all-round development of human beings as opposed to more physically (technically or militarily) orientated cultures. The implication of this view is intimately associated with the interest in Chinese culture being (re)located at the centre of power (or of 'soft power', in Joseph S. Nye's words (2005)). And this interest is encouraged and strengthened by some commentators based in the West, who, unlike Max Weber, are seen to interpret Confucianism alongside Protestantism and Judaism in opposition to Catholicism, Orthodox Christianity, and Islam, mainly on account of the recent economic growth of China (Harrison and Huntington 2000).[19]

The current ethos in education

As argued above, education, or examination-driven education, had long been the most important official way of achieving upward social mobility in imperial China. The educational system in modern China that is seemingly driven by examinations is, to a significant extent, the legacy of the imperial system. Learning from the lesson of Mao's devastation of scholars and the knowledge and education they represented, and also under rapid development of the global knowledge economy, the Chinese government in the late 1970s proposed the slogan of 'respect knowledge, respect talent' (*zunzhong zhishi, zunzhong rencai*).[20] This indicated the beginning of a new era in China since then, an era of reform and opening-up (*gaige kaifang*). The pursuit of knowledge came into fashion again, marked by reintroducing nationally uniform college entrance examinations in 1977. Thus, to successfully enter higher education means that someone from a low socio-economic urban family will achieve significant social mobility, whilst one from a rural family will become entitled to permanent urban household registration (*chengzhen hukou*).[21] This is associated with the government that will allocate university graduates a job in a state work unit, which secures a regular salary as well as all other kinds of state welfare benefits. This policy inevitably recalls the way in which the imperial system worked in selecting government officials. Nevertheless, unlike in imperial times, examinees or pupils did not pay for the education run by the Party-state until well after the economic reform. That is, state-run schools before 1990s were primarily open to everyone that largely focused on cultivation of an elite class (through allocating jobs in state sectors to graduates). Hence, the democracy of the imperial examinations seems to have been achieved more thoroughly under the rule of the CPC. In addition to this career benefit, successful examinees have also won respect for their assumed cultural and moral merits as part of the educational achievement, which is partially a continuity of the role of education in imperial times.

Since the mid-1980s, to be engaged in commercial business increasingly became more and more profitable owing to an increasingly free economy, and this is said to have stirred up a new tide of 'study is useless' thinking (*dushu wuyong lun*), that was once popular in the Cultural Revolution when Confucius and his doctrine and all Chinese intellectuals he supposedly represented were under acute attack. This was particularly salient between the mid-1980s and mid-1990s, which was characterized by a severe brain drain – public servants, teachers or even students turned away from state work units or schools to the 'commercial sea' (*xiahai*). The cessation of assigning jobs by the government to school or college graduates in 1996 exacerbated the situation. On the other hand, the continuity of the reform also means that the state gradually introduced policies (for example, raising the salary of employees working in the state system, or providing other kinds of welfare benefits) to attract more knowledgeable, cultured and young talent into state employment, while stopping a further brain drain from state sectors. At the same time the new policy of privatization and devolution of the state-run enterprises was also introduced. This policy led millions of mainly unskilled or semi-skilled workers in these enterprises to be laid-off from their formerly secure positions, to became 'go-off-post workers' (*xiagang gongren*).

The reform of the public servants system and of state-run enterprises has shed new light on the benefits that education can bring. Education has again come to be the essential concern of individual families as well as of the government at all levels, although it may be different as to what subjects to offer by the government, and what subjects to study on the part of the masses as the socio-economic situation keeps changing. The bottom-up strategy based in families aims to successfully enrol children in (good) colleges or universities, and in popular subjects; the top-down policy made by the central government aims to expand education to reach a wider population by increasing enrolment rates at all educational levels under the impact of a knowledge-economy-based global competitiveness.[22] This educational carnival has been marching forward rapidly at the expense of appropriate and sufficient human and material resources for a quality education. This carnival has also rendered parents, schools and society in a position, in which they are increasingly putting pressure on students to achieve highly, in particular in examinations. This has resulted in a highly competitive culture in education that has led to negative effects on the socialization of children (H. Jiang 2004). Therefore, a new 'examination hell' has been created (also see Chapter 4). In a word, education has come to be the top priority again under the impact of global development and the revival of the educational tradition of China.

This (particularly college entrance) examinations-driven and competitive schooling has made demands for a highly standardized educational system, which has inevitably resulted in a degree of blindness to difference in gender, class, ethnicity and locality. Although the educational system in the past, imperial times or otherwise, was also largely blind to difference in various cultures (broadly understood), an educational system blind to cultural diversity today is difficult to account for, given the growing consciousness of cultural difference and the importance of recognition of it for a meaningful life among the government, academic commentators and the masses. In fact, in this blindness, Chinese (Han) culture has been under threat itself at the global level, and correspondingly, other cultures than the dominant one in China have been pushed to a more peripheral position. Nonetheless, at the national level, Chinese Han culture still firmly holds hegemony, and is also hoped to play an important role on a global scale as suggested earlier. Nevertheless, the requirement for 'blindness' in education has brought in a wider gap between students owing to their differential backgrounds in socio-economic status, gender, ethnicity or locality. Meanwhile, education has also been reduced to a merely careerist instrument that no longer emphasizes individual cultural or moral accomplishment as the imperial system did. The idea of *suzhi* education was hence proposed under this societal climate.

However, this blindness in education is not entirely something that social entities deliberately exercise – either governments or various social or cultural communities. In fact, as argued in more detail in the next chapter, both governments and social or cultural communities have made efforts to narrow the educational gap caused by a wide range of factors. All of that is grounded in a broad consensus among governments, academics and the public that one primary aim of education ought to ensure a form of equality that is mainly indicated by equal achievement by students from different backgrounds. Where such achievement is unequal, it is crucial to explore what underlies these differences in achievement. Nonetheless, equality in education seems to be a long-term goal to achieve for two major reasons. First, a marketized or fee-charging education system is likely to exclude people from worse-off backgrounds, and this will be exacerbated if (sufficient) policies of aiding disadvantaged families are not in place accordingly and in time (see Chapter 4).[23]

Second, an education that is driven by a knowledge-economy based global competitiveness is actually leading to a more standardized knowledge package for teaching in schools that is supposedly going to benefit an economically oriented society. This is inevitably leaving even less room for consideration of the kind of cultures that are derived from difference in gender, class, ethnicity or locality. As a consequence, this education has and will put students from different cultural backgrounds on an unequal footing in that they supposedly possess standardized aptitude, or the cultural capital in Bourdieu's terms (Bourdieu 1977, 1986), for schooling.

As a consequence, both historical and global impetuses have made up an educational context that is combined with age-long Chinese culturalism, career and self-accomplishment focused educational tradition, increasing competitiveness driven by the knowledge economy, and Chinese ways of governing and engineering society and people that is depicted as pastoralism (Murphy 2006; Fong and Murphy 2006). This is a complex and competing package in which contestation not only exists between different cultures, but also between economy and culture, as well as between the government and various social or cultural communities. In the meantime, these dimensions are also achieving a 'new' set of compromises, a new alliance, and new power bloc led by neo-liberal governmentality, as similarly observed by Michael Apple (2006). This new and much more complicated educational architecture, in which the culture discourse of China has been deeply ingrained, has been shaping governmental policies of education and impacting (not only) ethnic minority educational experiences. Taking from the current ethos in education, I examine in the subsequent chapters how this educational system works. This examination focuses on current policies, practices and the mainstream discourses concerning the education of ethnic minorities (Chapter 3), and on how ethnic minorities evaluate their situation in relation to education, culture and social mobility in society (Chapters 4 and 5).

3 Ethnicization through schooling

The mainstream discursive repertoires of ethnic minority cultures

Introduction

This chapter looks into the process through which minority cultures and subjects are interpreted and defined by the cultural mainstream as inferior and less valuable for the modernization of China, and in consequent need of transformation in line with advanced cultures, particularly through education. In dichotomizing advanced cultures vis-à-vis backward ones, this process has ethnicized differences of minorities. However, within the process itself are internal contradictions that render any attempt at actual education self-contradictory and ultimately unproductive. Using three sources of data, government policy, academic discourse, and ethnographic fieldwork, the chapter provides corroborative evidence relating to the creation of particular images of minority cultures and subjects by the mainstream Han. Central to this creation is the idea of Chinese culturalism, in spite of its different vocabularies and strategies from the historically formulated culture discourse of imperial times.

The chapter consists of four parts: the education of ethnic minorities in China, government policies for minority education, academic evaluations of minority education, and mainstream individual perceptions of the minority population in relation to education. The main analytical tool used in the chapter is the framework of discursive repertoires. This approach allows us to uncover the implementation of discourses that work together *and* against one another in actual settings (Potter and Wetherell 1987: 138; Wetherell and Potter 1992: 90. Also see Chapter 1).

Education of ethnic minorities in China

Ethnic minorities of China

China has 55 officially identified ethnic minority groups. The minority population in total increased from 6.06 per cent (35,032,085) of the total population as recorded in the first national census of 1953 to 8.47 per cent (105,226,114) of the total population as recorded in the latest (fifth) national census of 2000 (RhSKTS and JF 2003: 2–3). In 2000, minority groups with populations of more than 5,000,000 included the Zhuang, Manchu, Hui, Miao, Uygur, Tujia, Yi, Mongolian and Tibetan.[1] Despite the relatively small ethnic minority population, the CPC's particular concern about minority groups is evident in its official recognition that the Chinese nation is constituted by different ethnic groups. The CPC's view developed into the concept of minority regional autonomy (also see the previous chapter), and was formally put into practice in 1947 when the first minority autonomous region (at the provincial level), the Inner Mongolian Autonomous Region, was established.[2] By 1965, the other four autonomous regions of its kind were all established: Xinjiang, Guangxi, Ningxia and Tibet. In the meantime, a considerable number of minority autonomous prefectures and counties (*minzu zizhi zhou, minzu zizhi xian/qi*) were also set up.

Among 55 minority groups, 44 groups, amounting to 75 per cent of the minority population in the country, have their own autonomous territory. Minority autonomous regions account for 64 per cent of China's territory (Wang and Chen 2001: 4). Most of the minority population inhabit the Chinese border areas of the northwest, southwest and northeast (RSKTand JF 2003: 2–3) (see Map 1.1). There are political tensions between these regions and China proper, based on territorial disputes as well as on cultural differences; there are significant populations of the same ethnic groups on both sides of the border, from the Far East of Russia to Central Asia, and then down to South and Southeast Asia (see Map 1.1). Furthermore, over 50 per cent of the minority population (53,492,763) is concentrated in western regions, which are traditionally referred to as the three minority autonomous regions (Ningxia Hui, Tibet, and Xinjiang Uygur), six provinces (Gansu, Guizhou, Qinghai, Shaanxi, Sichuan, and Yunnan) and one municipality (Chongqing). In the government's 'Open Up the West' campaign (*Xibu Da Kaifa*), the other two minority autonomous regions, Inner Mongolia and Guangxi Zhuang, are also incorporated in this category; the minority population in the 'new' West thus amounts to nearly 80 per cent of the total (RPB and RhSKTS 2002; RhSKTS and JF 2003).[3]

One of the major distinctive features of minority cultures is the diversity of their languages (61 identified, with others awaiting identification), belonging to five of the world's language families: Sino-Tibetan, Altaic, Austro-Asiatic, Austronesian, and Indo-European. As far as the minority writing system is concerned, except for Manchu and Hui, who use Chinese characters (and language), there are 39 different minority writing systems used by other minority groups, with 24 being created by Chinese linguists (Teng and Wang 2001: 326–8). There are also around 20 minority groups who generally use the Chinese writing system in the absence of their own writing system (Teng and Wang: 432–8).

Another cultural dimension is their commitment to religious beliefs, which is in sharp contrast with largely, though arguably, secular Han culture.[4] About half of the minority population believe in a certain faith, which is also half of the religious believers across China. In comparison, believers among the majority Han who constitute the other half of religious believers make up only 5 per cent of its whole population (Guojia Minzu Shiwu Weiyuanhui 2002: 4). Buddhism and Islam, 'at least in terms of scale' (Mackerras 1999: 23), are the most important faiths among other religions. While (particularly Tibetan) Buddhism is the faith of Tibetans, Mongolians, Tu, Yugur and Monba in western and northern China, Islam is adhered to by ten minority groups, who are largely concentrated in northwest China, from far west Xinjiang (Uygurs, Kazakhs, Kirgiz, Uzbeks, Tatars and Tajiks) to the Gansu-Qinghai-Ningxia regions (Hui, Dongxiang, Bonan and Salar). This last region is where I carried out my fieldwork in both 2003 and 2006, and to a lesser degree, in 2007.

The educational level of ethnic minorities

The normative criterion to assess the educational level in China (as it appears in the official statistics) is called the cultural level (*wenhua chengdu*) or level of received education (*shou jiaoyu chengdu*).[5] This is measured by looking at the number of years of education received or completed in the state educational system.[6] Another categorization method is to divide the 15-year-old-plus population into literate and illiterate groups.[7] I take the latter as the main measuring tool to look at the educational development of different ethnic groups. This is primarily because illiteracy in the minority population is a more serious problem in terms of its persistence and much larger scale compared to that in the majority population (RhSKTS and JF 2003). For this reason, to eliminate illiteracy in the minority population is always the top agenda of the government (Jiaoyu Bu 2004b, 2005).

Meanwhile, it is also difficult to compare the minority and majority populations at the primary, secondary and tertiary levels, because the education of ethnic minorities is primarily carried out in minority schools, colleges and universities. This means that minority education is largely separated out from the mainstream education that usually leads to segregation between minority and majority groups in the labour market, as I discuss in Chapters 4, 5, 6 and Postscript. As a result, even if a minority community has a higher, for example, graduate rate than the Han, it does not necessarily means that the group is also more competitive in the labour market than the Han as I demonstrate in the empirical chapters.[8]

The kind of data relating to educational achievement by ethnic group that is available is at the national level. Meanwhile there is far from sufficient and valid data at the provincial, prefectural and county levels that are available to me. Given the wide range that different minority groups, as well as different members within a minority group, are distributed geographically, and their varied economic conditions, occupational patterns and educational traditions, it is necessary to combine at least two criteria, ethnic and regional differences in the attempt to find out the relationship between ethnicity and educational achievement (also see Lamontagne 1999). Therefore, my analysis as a whole mainly focuses on the educational level according to the national census. I also highlight the educational gap through a comparative analysis of educational development by ethnic group and by regions (at the provincial level).

Table 3.1 produces two types of information with regard to the ethnic educational level: the illiterate population of each ethnic group and the distribution in different provinces of each ethnic group. The illiteracy rate across ethnic groups varies from 62.88 per cent of Muslim Dongxiang to 1.98 per cent of Muslim Tatar, with the national average 7.75 per cent and that of the Han 8.60 per cent. There are six ethnic groups with some of the highest illiteracy rates (around or above 50 per cent), Tibetan (47.55 per cent), Muslim Salar (49.11 per cent), Lhoba (50.79 per cent), Muslim Bonan (55.94 per cent), Monba (56.21 per cent) and Muslim Dongxiang (62.88 per cent).[9] At the other end of the spectrum, the most literate groups (an illiteracy level of less than 4 per cent) are another ten minority populations (from 1.98 per cent for Muslim Tatar to 3.81 per cent for Ewenki). However, the number of ethnic groups with an illiteracy rate higher than that of the national average is 40 (who amount to 70.78 per cent of the national minority population), and the average rate is 23.01 per cent, which is about three times higher than the national level of 7.75 per cent. In the meantime, the average illiteracy for the minority population as a whole is 17.86 per cent, more than twice as high as that for the Han.

Table 3.1 Ethnic groups by illiterate population and distribution in different provinces

EG (population)	IL (%)	DDP
NA	7.75	
Dongxiang (513,805)	62.88	Gansu, Xinjiang, Qinghai, Ningxia
Monba (8,923)	56.21	Tibet
Bonan (16,505)	55.94	Gansu
Lhoba (2,965)	50.79	Tibet
Salar (104,503)	49.11	Qinghai, Gansu
Tibetan (5,416,021)	47.55	Tibet, Qinghai, Sichuan
Lisu (634,912)	32.54	Yunnan, Sichuan
Nu (28,759)	32.02	Yunnan
Pumi (33,600)	30.06	Yunnan
Hani (1,439,673)	29.76	Yunnan
Unidentified (734,438)	29.14	Guizhou
Dulong (7,426)	26.80	Yunnan
Bouyei (2,971,460)	23.77	Guizhou
Lahu (453,705)	23.72	Yunnan
Va (396,610)	23.51	Yunnan
Blang (91,882)	23.43	Yunnan
Yi (7,762,272)	23.20	Yunnan, Sichuan
Tu (241,198)	23.20	Qinghai, Gansu
Shui (406,902)	22.06	Guizhou
De'ang (17,935)	21.25	Yunnan

(*Continued overleaf*)

Table 3.1 continued.

EG (population)	IL (%)	DDP
Miao (8,940,116)	19.83	Guizhou, Hunan, Yunnan
CCFD (941)	19.71	
Gelao (579,357)	18.23	Guizhou
Hui (9,816,805)	17.77	Ningxia, Gansu, Henan, Xinjiang, Qinghai, Yunnan, Hebei, Shandong, Anhui, Liaoning, Beijing, Inner Mongolia
Jinuo (20,899)	17.13	Yunnan
Jingpo (132,143)	15.71	Yunnan
Dai (1,158,989)	15.71	Yunnan
Naxi (308,839)	15.21	Yunnan
Yugur (13,719)	14.62	Gansu
Achang (33,936)	13.56	Yunnan
Tajik (41,028)	13.32	Xinjiang
Li (1,247,814)	12.09	Hainan
She (709,590)	11.81	Fujian, Zhejiang
Tujia (8,028,133)	11.71	Hunan, Hubei, Guizhou, Chongqing
Bai (1,858,063)	10.99	Yunnan
Dong (2,960,293)	10.87	Guizhou, Hunan, Guangxi
Qiang (306,072)	9.42	Sichuan
Yao (2.637,421)	9.32	Guangxi, Hunan, Guangdong, Yunnan
Uygur (8,399,393)	9.22	Xinjiang
Kirghiz (160,823)	9.05	Xinjiang
Han (1,137,386,112)	8.60	
Mongolian (5,813,947)	8.40	Inner Mongolia, Liaoning, Jilin, Hebei, Heilongjiang
Jing (22,517)	7.92	Guangxi
Maonan (107,166)	7.52	Guangxi, Guizhou
Zhuang (16,178,811)	6.83	Guangxi
Mulao (207,352)	5.96	Guangxi, Guizhou
Gaoshan (4,461)	5.58	
Manchu (10,682,262)	5.54	Liaoning, Hebei, Heilongjiang
Ewenki (30,505)	3.81	Inner Mongolia, Heilongjiang
Russian (15,609)	3.64	Xinjiang, Inner Mongolia
Oroqen (8,196)	3.48	Heilongjiang, Inner Mongolia
Daur (132,394)	3.46	Inner Mongolia, Jilin
Hezhe (4,640)	3.06	Heilongjiang
Korean (1,923,842)	2.86	Jilin
Xibe (188,824)	2.71	Liaoning, Heilongjiang, Xinjiang
Kazakh (1,250,458)	2.68	Xinjiang
Uzbek (12,370)	2.50	Xinjiang
Tatar (4,890)	1.98	Xinjiang

Key
CCFD = Chinese citizens of foreign descent
DDP = Distribution in different provinces
EG = Ethnic groups
IL = Illiteracy
NA = National average

Sources: RhSKTS & JF 2003; RPB and RhSKTS 2002

The most literate ethnic groups are largely concentrated in Xinjiang in far northwest China or in Heilongjiang, Jilin or Liaoning in northeast China (the former Manchukuo), or in the Inner Mongolian Region. Possible reasons cited in the literature for the relatively high achievement of these groups include a tradition of modern education and at the same time high socio-economic status, for instance, among the Tatar, Uzbek, Russian, Daur and Korean; some have rapidly enhanced educational performance to a high level with the special aid of the state due to the relatively easy manageability of ethnic communities that have a small population, such as Oroqen and Hezhe (Ma and Wang 2002; Dongfang Minzu Wang); some are much sinicized, for example Zhuang.[10] Minority groups with a higher illiteracy rate than the national average are substantially settled in western regions, amongst whom the six most illiterate ethnic minority groups are primarily distributed in Qinghai, Gansu and Tibet. The three Muslim groups are settled in the borderland areas between Qinghai and Gansu while the other two small groups, Monba and Lhoba, live along the border regions between Tibet and India. The largest group among the six, the Tibetans, are widely spread in the Tibet Autonomous Region and the vicinities in its neighbouring provinces, Qinghai, Gansu, Sichuan and Yunnan.

Lamontagne (1999) conducted a survey in which he divides ethnic groups into four phases with regard to illiteracy by examining the 1982 level of illiteracy and the degree of progress made between 1982 (the third national census) and 1990 (the fourth national census): (1) the low-slow phase; (2) the low-fast phase; (3) the high-fast phase; and (4) the high-slow phase. Here the 'low-high' division refers to the 1982 level of illiteracy, and the 'slow-fast' distinction indicates the degree of progress made between the two censuses. The ethnic groups at the low-fast and high-fast phases are 'the moderately advanced nationalities' (i.e. ethnic groups) who 'have made significant progress during the 1980s towards catching up with the most advanced nationalities' (Lamontagne 1999: 147). The high-slow phase indicates that educational development approaches a ceiling or saturation point. The low-slow phase points to the situation in which 'although the least advanced nationalities have made some progress, the gap separating them from the moderately advanced nationalities has widened' (ibid.). As a result of a comparison, the four communities at the low-slow phase in Lamontagne's survey (ibid.: 146), Salar, Tibetan, Bonan and Dongxiang, are still among the most illiterate populations in the 2000 census as can be seen from above.[11] This is to say, from a developmental perspective, the four groups still perform poorly.

In 2000, the illiteracy rate across province-level territories varied from 4.93 per cent in Beijing to 47.25 per cent in Tibet, with a national average percentage of 9.08 per cent (see Table 3.2). Among the ten territories with the least illiterate populations (including Beijing, Guangdong and Shanghai), none of them are situated in western regions. On the other hand, the highest illiteracy rate (an illiteracy level of 15 per cent or more) is found in western

Table 3.2 Illiteracy and minority population in province-level territories

Province	IL (%)	MP (%)
National average	9.08	8.47
Tibet	47.25	93.94
Qinghai	25.44	45.97
Guizhou	19.83	37.84
Gansu	19.68	8.75
Ningxia	15.72	34.56
Yunnan	15.44	33.42
Anhui	13.43	0.67
Inner Mongolia	11.59	20.83
Shandong	10.75	0.70
Sichuan	9.87	5.00
Shaanxi	9.82	0.50
Hainan	9.72	17.38
Fujian	9.68	1.71
Hubei	9.31	4.34
Chongqing	8.90	6.47
Hebei	8.59	4.35
Zhejiang	8.55	0.86
Henan	7.91	1.25
Jiangsu	7.88	0.36
Xinjiang	7.72	59.43
Jiangxi	6.98	0.31
Tianjin	6.47	2.71
Heilongjiang	6.33	4.89
Shanghai	6.21	0.63
Hunan	5.99	11.13
Liaoning	5.79	16.06
Jilin	5.74	9.15
Shanxi	5.68	0.32
Guangdong	5.17	1.49
Beijing	4.93	4.31

Key
IL = Illiteracy
MP = Minority population

Sources: RhSKTS & JF 2003, RPB and RhSKTS 2002

regions, Tibet, Qinghai (25.44 per cent), Guizhou (19.83 per cent), Gansu (19.68 per cent), Ningxia (15.72 per cent) and Yunnan (15.44 per cent). As a whole, these western regions have an average illiteracy rate of 18.87 per cent, more than twice as high as the national level.

By and large, the minority populations have a higher illiteracy rate than the majority Han across the country, and the minority groups with a higher literacy account for a very small proportion of the minority populations. The highest illiterate population are concentrated in western regions, particularly in the Qing-Zang (Qinghai-Tibet) Plateau areas that spread from the border areas between Tibet and India to the borderlands between Qinghai and

Gansu provinces. The areas are home to the six minority groups that top the illiteracy league table.

Government concerns shaping minority education policies and practices

The modern education of ethnic minorities has long been recognized as different from ordinary education in Han-dominated regions. The establishment of several schools for ethnic minorities (mainly for Manchurians, Mongolians and Tibetans) around 1910 is regarded as the commencement of education of ethnic minorities in China (Cui, Zhang and Du 1999: 803–4; Teng and Wang 2001: 265–6). This tradition was taken over and enormously developed by the CPC after it came to power in 1949. With more than 50 years' development, the education of ethnic minorities in China has been to a large extent systematized, with various levels as well as forms of schooling for ethnic minority people (Teng and Wang 2001: 267–91).

In the Party-state's attempt to realize its goal for minority education, preferential policies (*youhui zhengce*) are at the centre of the official agenda. These policies range from material support to cultivation of minority personnel that include: financial investment; establishment of minority schools, colleges and universities; compilation of textbooks in the minority writing systems; cultivation of minority teachers for bilingual education; establishment of governmental departments at national, provincial and local levels overseeing minority education; requirement that more developed provinces give aid to minority concentrated regions through material or personnel support, or through running minority schools or classes in their own territories; the preferential policy for minority students to have priority in getting admitted if the results of their college entrance examinations are the same as or relatively lower than, mainstream Han students (Guojia Jiaowei and Guojia Minwei 1992; Guojia Minwei and Guojia Tongjiju 2000; Guowuyuan 2002; Jiaoyubu 1986, 1995, 1998; Minzu Jiaoyu Si 1992; Minzu Weiyuanhui 2001; Quanguo Renmin Daibiao Dahui 2004; Teng and Wang 2001; Xinwen Bangongshi 2005).[12]

This emphasis on preferential policies reflects the government's deep concerns in recognition of the difference of minority education, which shape minority education policies and practices. The particularities of minority education are deemed by the CPC to be embodied in some 'special difficulties and problems' that are recently illustrated in an official government document (Guowuyuan 2002):

> Due to a variety of historical, social, physical, and particularly economic reasons, minority education in our country is still facing some special difficulties and problems. The ideas about education relatively lag behind, educational reform proceeds very slowly, and education lacks strong bases. Popularization of compulsory education and development

of all other types of education are relatively sluggish. Teachers are insufficient in quantity and poor in quality. Inadequate financial investment makes it difficult to improve the conditions for managing schools, therefore the problem for the schooling of students is rather salient, and the pay for teachers is in need of further improvement ... In recent years, hostile forces from overseas and religious extremist forces from neighbouring countries collude with domestic nationalistic separatists to create incidents in some minority areas in our country, and to conduct ethnic separatist activities. They try vainly to infiltrate our educational field, to foster ethnic separatist forces, and to contend with us for the next generation.

In the concerns of the government, perhaps the most salient feature of minority education policy is that it is shaped by a fear that ethnic and religious allegiances may undermine the capacity of minority people to be loyal political and cultural citizens of the Chinese nation-state. For the government official, the difficulty in education in China is in rural areas, and in particular in minority areas (Jiaoyu Bu 2002). This is embedded in the reality that the ethnic issue (*minzu wenti*) highly intertwines with the religious issue (*zongjiao wenti*) in education in most minority areas.[13] This applies particularly to West China, where Muslim and Tibetan areas are thought to harbour 'violent and terrorist forces, religiously extreme forces and ethnic divisive forces' that are regarded as a particular threat to the unity of the nation, and the safety, stability, peace and order of the state (Renmin Ribao Shelun 2001).[14] Therefore, religion is often under suspicion for being responsible for political or ideological wars between religious communities and the Marxist-Leninist orientated CPC.

A concern for diluting those kinds of knowledge bases that threaten to produce alternative forms of cultural citizenship has caused educational planners to separate out religion from popular education. One way in which this occurs is that Party functionaries educate the masses in general, and school students in particular, about atheism, materialism and scientism, and encourage citizens to establish a scientistic view towards the world and religion so as to consciously resist feudal superstition, cult (*xiejiao*, lit. 'evil or pernicious doctrine') and ethnic secession (Jiaoyu Bu 2002; Jiaoyu Bu Bangong Ting and Guojia Minwei Bangong Ting 1999; Guowuyuan 2002; D. Li 2002; Renmin Ribao Shelun 2001). In this light, religious elements have not been permitted in state education since the Religious Reform (*zongjiao gaige*) of the late 1950s, unless they are inextricably linked to aspects of a bilingual education, or are deployed as a target of criticism in textbooks, in which religion is claimed ultimately to wither away (*Lishi* 2001: 116).[15] Nevertheless, the Constitution guarantees citizens freedom of religious belief, which in education appears in some religion-related practices such as diet, dress, funding of religious schools or even inviting a few religious clergy to act as language teachers (Gladney 1999: 84; Mackerras 1999: 38, 43–4; Postiglione

1999: 6; Teng 2002: 269–70). Even so, this freedom is circumscribed by several 'must-nots', including proscriptions against propagation, instruction or practice of religion in the school, for religion is assumed to be presented by some religious or social groups as a force to contend with the Party-state for younger generations (Jiaoyu Bu 1983).[16] The direct result of this policy that excludes religion from schools or other formal institutions is a marginalization of religion in both the classroom and the wider society.

Caution on the part of Han pedagogies towards alternative bases of knowledge for cultural citizenship also means that minority education is characterized by chauvinistic approaches towards the language, history and other cultural aspects of the curriculum. In spite of periodically encouraging bilingual education over the past fifty years, government policy concerning bilingual education epitomize the civilizing missions of the Party-state, and is also the result of a concern with the political threat possibly posed to the wider national form of cultural citizenship. So when officials have permitted, for example, Tibetan language and literature to be introduced into the curriculum of Tibetan minority schools, it was within the wider context of Mandarin instruction in the core subjects with the wider emphasis on encouraging Tibetan students to master Chinese to facilitate their integration into the mainstream in the long run (see, for example, R. Ma 2001: 231–49, Teng and Wang 2001: 311–12). Meanwhile, the demand for a course on Arabic by some Muslim minority schools is rejected by the government under the suspicion that the aim of this demand is to offer the subject of religion in the name of a language lesson (Jiaoyu Bu 1983).

With regard to the history component of the curriculum, minority history barely exists except when being represented in the contexts of social evolution and national unity. With regard to social evolution, all ethnic groups are ordered from a primitive to an advanced stage, with Han on the top and bearing an obvious responsibility for 'civilizing' the less civilized minorities (Harrell 1995; *Zhongguo Jindai Xiandaishi* 2000: 148–9; *Zhongguo Lishi* 1995: 187–9).[17] The history curriculum also devotes much space to mapping out the historical process by which different ethnic groups have closely interacted with one another, and as a result contributed to the emergence of a Chinese nation that has a unified national culture and identity. The Han are said to be the nucleus of this unity (*ningju hexin*). This is the core of the influential concept of *duoyuan yiti* (plurality and unity) (Fei 1989).

Instruction in other aspects of minority cultures in the curriculum is even more limited. On the whole, publicity and education in minority cultures, wherever there is any, is not a systematic instruction or introduction; instead, minority cultures are frequently equated with colourful dress, beautiful dance and song, special dwellings, exotic food, or language and script against the Han culture (Teng et al. 1997).[18] This representation of minority cultures is fragmented and tokenized.

A final issue affecting minority education policy has been that the 'troublesome' or 'disloyal' minorities are concentrated in the economically least developed regions of West China (Hu and Wen 2002; Tang 2003). These regions have rural populations and rural-urban inequalities that are above the national average[19] and harsh and inhospitable physical environment (Shen 1995; Zhou 1957). These disadvantages that face ethnic minorities have been described by Han officials as the 'three backwardnesses' (*sange luohou*) of economic productivity, cultural and educational level and living standards (D. Li 2002). The Party-state has increasingly designated a role for education in 'developing' the West and integrating it with the rest of China. Much of this policy has invoked the familiar developmental discourse of 'catch up'; it has been widely assumed by both the government and the mainstream Han and minorities themselves that, if they did not want to be 'phased out' (*taotai*), they have to catch up educationally in schools, which in turn, it is believed, will contribute to them catching up economically, ideologically and culturally in the long term.[20]

The academic discourse of minority education

Government policy discourses reveal an unoptimistic view of minority education (particularly in many western regions), and researchers of minority education and my mainstream respondents share a similar standpoint. The following two sections examine how Chinese academics assess and diagnose poor minority educational performance in their research articles, and further, how my Han interviewees (teachers and students) perceive the minority population in educational terms. Academic assessments and diagnoses are a reflection on, analysis and conceptualization of government policy discourses. In the meantime, government policy discourses have explicitly or implicitly informed the mainstream perceptions of the minority population. The focal question for the government, academics and mainstream individuals is: which is (more) responsible for (poor) minority performance, community forces or social systems?

Concern with community forces

Among a wide range of factors, many academics highlight a backwardness in the thinking modes of minority people as the fundamental element that is responsible for the poor educational achievement and the persistent poverty of ethnic minorities. It is claimed that minorities' low view of education (apparent in their lack of enthusiasm and motivation for education) lies at the centre of these modes of thinking. This inadequate evaluation of education is believed to be embedded in minorities' isolated environment, both physical and cultural, which are causatively intertwined.

Commentators said that ethnic minorities usually live in isolated (nomadic or agricultural) areas and thus are unfamiliar with modernization, in which education plays an important part (Li, Cai, Li and Wang, 1995; Lin, Jin and Chen 1990; Liu 1994; Ma et al., 1996; Wang and Liu 2002; Yuan, Yang and

Li 2003). Meanwhile, the sluggish local economy has forced them to prioritize their needs for (more) labour, which inevitably leads to a high birth-rate and so aggravates their poverty. All these elements, according to commentators, form a vicious circle centring around poverty, limited education and large families. In light of the conceptual framework of social evolution, such disadvantaged status is largely traced back by academics to the backward socio-economic patterns of the minority population (ranging from primitive to feudal society) before the CPC brought them into allegedly advanced socialist society (Li, Cai, Li and Wang, 1995; Lin, Jin and Chen 1990; Liu 1994; Ma et al., 1996; Wang and Liu 2002; Yuan, Yang and Li 2003).

The isolation of minorities is also thought to be a result of their cultural and, in particular, religious tradition, which is argued to discourage their engagement in education and reinforce their insularity. Minority communities have been investing considerable amounts of money and time into religion whilst school-aged children have been sent to religious institutions. At a more fundamental level, religion is seen as encouraging believers to obey and preserve tradition, leading them to resist other cultures or cultural innovations (Li, Cai, Li and Wang 1995; Lin, Jin and Chen 1990; Liu 1994; Ma et al. 1996; Wang and Liu 2002; Yuan, Yang and Li 2003).

Minorities' intelligence in schooling is also called into question, despite the contrasting claim that their intelligence can be improved through appropriate training (Meng 2002). Minority students are presumed to encounter obstacles in the development of their mental ability in comparison with their Han peers (Ding 1997). These obstacles could be caused by adverse physical environments which usually result in malnutrition. The obstacles could also be caused by their human or cultural environments, ranging from lifestyle (their closed, isolated life coupled with interbreeding) to their ways of parenting, child-rearing and pre-school preparation (which are usually unlikely to nurture an aptitude for schooling) (Chen 1998; Ding 1997; Zhang and Huang 1996; Zhang 1994).[21] As a result, minority children tend to be sluggish in developing academic ability (Deng 1997; Ding 1997; Meng 2002). Furthermore, their background is also said to affect their personality, resulting in their being more likely to suffer from low self-esteem or passivity in modes of thinking (Deng 1997; Ding 1997; Meng 2002). The implication is that the lack of intelligence caused by both physical and cultural environments is significantly responsible for poor minority school performance.

Concern with social systems

In spite of the supposed evidence, these arguments have made limited connection between community forces and the wider society, in which minority communities have coped with and adapted to their positions in the nation's hierarchy of power and privilege. This reflects disparities in access to opportunities and helps determine their economic status, as Ferguson (2005) observes. It is thus unsurprising that these arguments are not agreed with by some other commentators. These academics suggest that minorities' disengagement from education or ineffective academic outcomes are largely due to their lack of access to education, or of the irrelevance of education to their local socio-economic situation or cultural values.

For these academics, the national curriculum has an immediate effect on the failure of minority education due to its lack of responsiveness to locality and ethnicity in minority areas, in basically two ways. Firstly, it is not designed so as to accord with the present physical or socio-economic conditions of minority areas, and therefore confidence in school education among minority communities has significantly declined (Guo 2003; Li, Li, Zheng and Yang 1994; Palden 1998). The irrelevance of the curriculum also relates to it being divorced from historically-shaped socio-economic patterns of minorities in terms of social evolution. That is, minority communities are thought not to be fully in concert with the presumably advanced socialist system, in either social or economic terms, though it is supposedly the case in political terms (Palden 1998).

The failure in response to minority needs stems primarily from the Chinese Han tradition of an elitist approach to education that focuses narrowly upon college entrance examinations; this is largely the legacy of the civil service examinations of imperial China as discussed in the previous chapter. Indeed, where education is managed to meet the requirements of the masses rather than those of the elite, ordinary people are reportedly far more enthusiastic for schooling (Cairangcuo, Chen and Liu 1997; Meng, Qi and Kan 1998; Meng 2002). Taking children's life experiences, and other related factors which may have affected their patterns of cognitive development into consideration, would also significantly facilitate their learning in schools. In this fashion, what is more important is that the view that minority children are intellectually inferior would also largely be corrected in both majority and minority communities (Cui 1995; Palden 1998).

To pay close attention to local situations also requires considering various minority cultures in the curriculum, which is interrelated and overlaps with local socio-economic needs.[22] The curriculum not only serves as an instrument to help create human capital, but also as a tool that guarantees and enhances the cultural well-being of minority groups. For commentators, this is associated with whether or not, or to what extent, minority languages (not necessarily religions!) are provided in the curriculum. Despite substantial bilingual education initiatives across the country, this is regarded as a far from perfect system, and needs to resolve several crucial tensions. Amongst others, the fundamental tension is that between the efficiency and effectiveness in learning brought about by employing a bilingual education for minority students, and decreasing opportunities of using minority languages in the wider world (Teng et al. 1997; Teng and Wang 2001; Teng 2002). However, bilingual education is considered to be essentially important in providing minorities with more confidence in valuing their own cultures and their intellectual quality (Ma and Xiao 2002; Teng et al. 1997).[23]

Ignorance of locality and ethnicity of minority areas also means that minority education often has little to do with minority communities. Schools are not keen to get minority communities involved in education, and if they do, their attempts are very narrowly, i.e. instrumentally, directed, for example, to certain religious leaders. These leaders are encouraged to help with minority education in raising funds, persuading parents to send their children to school, or becoming teachers themselves of the minority language in some understaffed schools (Liu 1994; Ningxia Jiaowei 1998; Teng 2002). It is arguably an implementation of the government policy of religious freedom in practice. This is why, when mentioning the limited textbooks that pay regard to ethnic minorities, commentators criticize the textbooks as merely providing skin-deep knowledge about minority cultures, and tending to confuse students by their inappropriate representations of the latter (Jin 1998).

Furthermore, state preferential policies for minority education are criticized by many commentators for fostering an inclination among minorities towards relying upon government special policies and treatment (Minzu Jiaoyu Si 2002; Tang 2002). The preferential policy in the enrolment of ethnic minority students is said to form a vicious circle of lower entry requirements, laxity in learning and the limited academic outcomes of minority students, which eventually leads them to a situation of having a certificate but no quality (*you wenping mei shuiping*) (Li, Li, Zheng and Yang 1994; Tang 2002).[24] As a result, many educators argue that the system of separating minority schools from ordinary schools should be abolished.[25] This not only would create an environment of healthy competition, make education resources be used more effectively or teachers more professional, but would also enhance mutual understanding between, and self-reflexivity of, students of different ethnic groups so as to promote ethnic unity (Bai Jierui 1994: 35).[26]

Evaluation

In so far as community forces and social systems are concerned, however, commentators from both sides are similarly shocked by some reports with regard to minority education. Some minorities are reported to be unwilling to send their children to schools even when the government or school rewards them in material form if they do so. Some other minority parents would even 'employ' some people to go to school instead of their own children by paying these people money (Yuan et al. 2003). In sharp contrast to this, it is widely reported (usually as a subject of criticism) that some minority families would rather make a donation to their religious institutions from their limited budget. The conclusion drawn by academics is that minorities are reluctance or even resistance to engage in education. Therefore, whilst a number of mainstream academics acknowledge that the physical or socio-economic situation and the school curriculum are all in need of change, essentially it is minority subjects' backward modes of thinking that are seen as being in urgent need of transformation.

This concern about the backwardness of minority modes of thinking is typically reflected in the mainstream discourse of *suzhi*, or quality.[27] Low quality is not only the cause of poverty, but 'also affects the potential for capital to grow' (Yan 2003: 494).[28] And at the very centre of this *suzhi* improvement is located consciousness, or the subject's 'intendedness' towards the object (for example, development), which is supposedly the key for the (cultural) poverty relief of ethnic minorities (Spivak 1985: 73; Yan 2003: 500.). It is fashionable for both critics and supporters of the minority population to label minorities as a people or labour force of low quality. This is even reflected in their comments on the failure of the government policy of separating minority schools from mainstream ones. When suggesting abolition of this policy, Chinese academics are in fact attributing the failure to the embedded low quality of minorities. This fashion is derived from the ways in which the mainstream has viewed minorities, and is fundamentally rooted in their conceptual framework, shaped in line with the social evolution ideology of the Party-state. Academics from both sides take the evolutionary framework so comfortably for granted as seen above, that no research bothers to question its validity or applicability to widely varying contexts.

The resulting convenience for discursive construction is that the backwardness of the minority peoples can be easily located in terms of their history, so as to primordialize this backwardness. Therefore the minority population is essentially in need of being enlightened, not only in the field of knowledge or skills transmission, that aims to cultivate human capital, but also, more fundamentally, in the field of the cultural transmission of advanced modes of thinking and moral standards. And enlightenment in these two fields should be conducted in Chinese, in which advanced culture is presumably grounded, and by which science and technological knowledge are conveyed (See, for example, Halike and Muhabaiti 1997: 90–2). In a nutshell, this enlightenment is believed to serve as a tool to transform the minority population, and so their intellectual quality and socio-economic situation, in the long term. This echoes the discourse of 'cultivation' used by my informants (see below).

Stevan Harrell shows how the mainstream discourse regards the peripheral as childlike and historically static in its metaphors of education and history (Harrell 1995, also see the previous chapter). In this discourse, minority peoples are assumed to be primitive and so civilizable on the one hand, and historically innately backward and hence uncivilizable on the other hand. It is this very paradox that provides civilizers with the eternal reason for carrying out their civilizing missions and also with some chance of success. This discourse construction is particularly useful when the abovementioned two fields are difficult to reconcile with each other. So whilst Tibetans are criticized as being so deeply poisoned by religion that they are very passive in participating in the market economy, Muslims are rebuked for favouring material benefits by prioritizing commerce at the expense of their children's education. In this context, Tibetans are thought to be unaware of the importance of

education for modernization or development that is particularly characterized by the commercial economy. However, despite their active economic
performance, Muslims are denounced as short-sighted profiteers and so
are in need of education for enhancing moral standards in order to redress
the imbalance between economy and morality among them. A similar view
regarding Tibetans and Muslims was expressed in more detail by my mainstream interviewees, as illustrated below.

In this discursive construction, what is also true is that scholars would
rather avoid a direct clash with the political mainstream by keeping silent if
they consider that their discussions would not comply with the conventions
set out by the Party-state. One salient example is the mainstream attitude
towards religion in education. Academics are most likely either to parrot
the Party-state's policy (for example, insisting on the negative character of
religion, that is believed to be distracting minorities from the importance of
schooling), or to evade the issue (in contrast to substantial and detailed
arguments on bilingual education). Correspondingly, only limited research
has implicitly posed questions about why schools have failed to win students
in this 'culture war' with ethno-religious communities (Ding 1991). In the
end, in examining responsibility for poor minority performance, the mainstream discourse, at best, has largely reduced social systems to the curriculum
by merely seeking 'school-based solutions to school-based problems' and
ignoring 'structural and historic relations of domination' (Gillborn 2005:
487).[29] Therefore, this ignorance or reductionism has significantly singled out
social systems that have primarily shaped education policies and practices.

The mainstream narratives of ethnic minorities

As with governmental officials and academic commentators, the mainstream
teachers and students that I interviewed, who had immediate and intimate
contact with minorities, also considered their minority (fellow) students
largely as poor school performers. While attributing poor minority performance to a variety of elements, the dominant view among these interviewees
was that the minority performance depends decisively on community forces –
the educational level, the attitude, and more generally, the quality of their
families or communities. This section looks at how this view takes shape
through everyday discursive formation.

Concern with social systems

A range of factors determines the 'low quality' and low achievement of
minority students. In the case of the mainstream school, a few teachers
alleged that the school policy driven by the pursuit of high scores of students
might be unfair on minority students. The school designates different ratios
of students who meet certain score levels in key examinations, and teachers
face salary deductions if they fail to meet these targets. As a result, students

will be punished or ultimately abandoned if they do not satisfy teachers with expected scores. Due to the low academic achievement of minority students in general, they are most likely to be abandoned by their teachers (also see Chapter 4). This is true, in relation to classroom study primarily, and in disciplining with the consequence that many drop out without the teacher making any effort to keep them in the school, as I was told by two teachers.

A few teachers also partially attributed poor minority school performance to social networks minorities have. This is particularly connected to the Muslim students. Due to the abolition of allocating jobs to college graduates, it is said that it becomes quite pointless for Muslim parents to send children to colleges or universities. 'Because many Hui are ordinary families (that is, no people work in the state system), from a social relations perspective, they do not have a strong background. They are hence relatively realistic', a teacher commented. The 'realistic' point means that Muslim parents believe that their children anyway are very unlikely to find a job even with a degree, unless they have got the kind of social connections with public sectors as many Han or Tibetans do.[30]

As with some academic commentators, many of my interviewees did not regard the idea of separate minority schools and corresponding preferential policies as very effective (also see Chapter 4). They thought that the practice of concentrating minority students in separate schools (in this case, Tibetan minority schools) had actually isolated Tibetan students from mainstream schools and interaction with high quality (Han) students. In minority schools, students were seen as being of low quality, and yet being educated in separate low quality environments. More government funding has also supposedly undermined the dynamic of the quality of education.[31] These elements had together formed a 'vicious circle' among minority school students. This view of minority schools is in parallel with that of academics, and developed in more detail below in their discussions of low quality students in minority schools in comparison with high quality students of the mainstream school.

Another factor is related to teachers. My respondents said that the government assigns teachers of higher educational levels (automatically coupled with 'higher quality' in their minds) to mainstream schools and those of lower levels to minority schools. One extreme example I was told about by a teacher is that a college graduate who studied fine arts was assigned to a Tibetan village school to teach English. 'How can he improve himself? And how can he enhance the quality of his students?'

(In)dispensable minority cultures

For both teachers and students, religion-centred minority cultures are not as negative as school policy, a reflection of government policy, implies. Most respondents believed that religion, the core of a meaningful life for both Tibetans and Muslims, cannot be seen simply as an entirely useless or even negative component within education. This view firstly emphasizes the bene-fit gained from learning about different cultures for mutual understanding and respect. Secondly, it considers that inclusion of religion in public institu-tions is positive because minority students can thereby foster and promote self-esteem in their ethnic identity. A large number of mainstream members also treated minority cultures as a means of entertainment, equating minority cultures with beautiful dancing, colourful dress, or mysterious legends, a tendency that some academics have also noticed as seen earlier. In this fash-ion, one student (S) illustrated his interest in minority cultures to me (M) as follows (emphasis added):

S: I like history, so I like to learn histories of other *races* (*zhongzu*). [As for] other things, I am not interested.
M: So [you mean you] are interested in this subject (history) rather than ethnic minorities [of the history]?
S: Yes. . . . The Han, does not seem to have its own history; the Hui, *if* they are minorities, they have their own ethnic history . . .
M: What did you mean that the Han does not have its history?
S: I meant, from my point of view, the Han, seems, it is not like ethnic minorities who have something like legends, such as an ethnic [minority] group, when did it come to being, what was its source?

This entertainment idea about minority cultures inevitably recalls Pākehā positions in relation to Māori in New Zealand, in which the image of the former is seen to be mundane and so invisible whereas that of the latter is visibly exotic (Wetherell and Potter 1992). The mainstream civilizing projects illustrated by Harrell (1995) and the alleged 'in-museum' characteristic of minority cultures depicted by Gladney (2004) also reflect this ethnicization of minority differences. Thus it is not surprising that the appeal of minority cultures for the mainstream group does not really lead to a substantive know-ledge of them. This is due to the lack of opportunity to learn offered in institutions, specifically in schools, and also reflects their deep-down attitude that minority cultures are largely a kind of decoration in mainstream daily life. Meanwhile, the awareness of the importance of learning about minority cultures for a better mutual understanding largely stopped at the level of theory alone (partially connected with the idea of political correctness which many mainstream members would like to show). This is mainly because for my interviewees, religion-centred minority cultures cannot bring any tan-gible benefit. Three students in their respective interviews suggested that 'these things [in religion] are a little bit too illusory, no realistic meaning', 'no scientific grounds', 'superstitions'. A teacher explained this view as follows:

If a student is too pious with regard to religion, it will certainly invite a clash with our moral education . . . especially in such an era and environ-ment [in which society is becoming more secular and science-driven] . . .

for instance Islam . . . ultimately aims to . . . enable [its disciples] to enter Heaven. We now advocate atheism . . . there is no such things as ghosts or gods. Our ultimate goal is to realize communism.

Holding such a view of minority cultures, it is no surprise that the majority of the mainstream is far from enthusiastic to learn about minority cultures. They do not consider it to be a serious problem that there is limited space for minority cultures in public institutions, or even believe it is right to exclude them from the public sphere. So what about minorities' self-esteem and cultural identity, that are supposedly fostered and promoted by an inclusive curriculum? As I present it here and in Chapters 4 and 5, minority cultures in the school are largely politicized in the way in which they are treated in the curriculum and cultural practice, in line with state policies. In everyday life practice, minority cultures are simply tokenized in the way in which the mainstream members 'appreciate' them. It is thus that minority cultures remain on the periphery of the public and private life of the cultural mainstream.

Discursive repertoires about Muslims

There is an apparent contradiction in the mainstream narratives of minority cultures. This contradiction can be further illustrated in two cases respectively concerning Muslims and Tibetans, in which the mainstream ethnicizes differences of minorities. While in theory affirming the positive role of religion as a whole, some of the mainstream respondents showed scepticism about religion as discussed above. Even so, when asked which religion they would tend to believe in, if they had to choose, all the interviewees pointed to Buddhism rather than Islam.[32] They reasoned that Islam is not the religion of the Han, but of 'those Hui', so they know little about it and have no interest in it; Islamic doctrines were also considered to be too stern. Hence they concluded that Muslim students, regardless of their academic achievement, are all very pious, and so Muslims are 'inborn disciples'. While they believed that to be pious is a good thing for self-discipline, they also associated this 'Muslim character' with conservatism or self-enclosure. This closure is supposedly strengthened by the Muslim tendency toward living together in a compact community, 'which is simply a Muslim village', as one schoolteacher commented.[33] For the mainstream, this isolated nature of the Muslim community is deep-rooted and functions as the fundamental determinant that sustains and even reinforces their 'feudal customs' like patriarchy.

Meanwhile, Muslims were without exception labelled as 'innate merchants'. This 'innate' character determines that Muslims are not willing to invest in education that cannot create immediate profit (so they are short-sighted). One teacher told me about a consensus among teachers with regard to Muslim parents:

They [teachers] say that at home [Muslim] parents tell [children], 'you just go to school like this, no need to work hard. It would be fine so long as you will have a certificate in hand when you graduate from Junior Three [*chusan*, the final year of compulsory education]. Just learn some [Chinese] characters, then go to do business.' Parents speak to children in this way very directly, and then they [children] do not work hard.

Many of my interviewees held a similar view that, for Muslim parents, to send children to schools is either to enable them to acquire basic literacy and numeracy knowledge for business, or to get a certificate for a diploma-dominated society (*wenpin de shehui*). Guided by this goal, my respondents concluded that no more education is necessary in the eyes of Muslim parents, for it just involves spending money. In this view, Muslim parents were said to tend not to send children to kindergarten, a place that is regarded by main-stream parents as a significant starting point of the socialization of their children. All of that is claimed to be ingrained in the low quality of the Muslim community, in particular in their low educational level. In justifying her argument, a teacher gave me an example that happened in a parent-teacher meeting:

> There was one parent who struck me most. She ran to me, with the grade report form [of the class] and said: 'teacher, could you have a look for me at where my child [his name] is [on the report form]?' Can you guess how she held the form? She simply held it upside down. Then I said: 'parent, your kid is here.' I reversed the form to show her.

This inadequate educational level among Muslim parents, their little enthusiasm for but pragmatic attitude to education, are all believed to be a seed-bed for the lack of motivation of their offspring for education, and also to lead to Muslim children's inferiority complex in schooling. When this view of Muslims is mixed with the Chinese traditional view of trade that believes there is no single merchant who is not unscrupulous, and that one cannot be a merchant if one is not unscrupulous, Muslims are profiteers, and so untrustworthy in their eyes.[34] In this sense, Han actually perceived that Muslims are smart people, and so could have achieved highly in schooling. Unfortunately, I was told, Muslims are not keen to utilize their intelligence for schooling or enhancing their cultural quality, but for commercial business or disruptive behaviours instead. This is why their smartness was believed to have reduced to cunning and calculation.[35] To convince me, many of them quoted a popular saying describing a common view of Muslims among the local Han (and other ethnic groups as well): Muslim [Hui] food is edible, Muslim words are unlistenable (that is, untrustworthy) (*Huihui di fan chicheng li, Huihui di hua tingbucheng*). Having spoken about Muslims in this way, my informants were trying to prove that Muslims are culturally foreign and morally evil, by the criterion of Chinese cultural tradition. Since these characteristics of Muslims are inherent, as perceived by the Han, Muslims are hence uneducable and untransformable, as well as being unapproachable and untrustworthy.

Discursive repertoires about Tibetans

Having so criticized Islam and Muslims, more than 90 per cent of interviewees claimed that Buddhism and its believers are relatively 'approachable' and thus 'trustworthy'. Beyond the fact that Buddhism is one of the sources of Chinese culture, the very important implication here is that Buddhism is far from conservatively strict or feudal in comparison with Islam. This can also be translated into the idea that Tibetans are not cultivated as strictly as Muslims, because the former do not appear to be as self-contained as Muslims. Nonetheless, this is not the whole story; in fact, this view laid the ground for my respondents to comment negatively on Tibetans. They explained that Tibetans are usually much less restrained by their families or community, and so they are quite uncultivated as an ethnic group. Tibetans therefore tend to be much less self-disciplined, and rather to be disruptive or violent instead. A lack of cultivation and discipline also presumably results in their limited intellectual merit.

In the attempt to prove this 'Tibetan character', many respondents provided some examples by comparing the differences between Tibetan students who are being educated in mainstream schools and those in minority schools – the latter were seen as 'more' or 'typically' Tibetan. They considered that the former were less hard to communicate with because they had a good command of Chinese and were generally somehow of a higher 'quality' (that is, obedient, self-disciplined and understanding).[36] Contrary to this, it was seen as being impossible to reason with disruptive and violent Tibetans in minority schools, as two girls told me. In terms of academic achievement, several teachers also suggested that top Tibetan students in minority schools were only capable of reaching the average level when they were studying in the mainstream school.[37] In this sense, when they asserted that Tibetan students in minority schools tend to work harder, the comment (and tone!) in fact highlighted their perception of Tibetan intellectual inferiority. This is because, as I was told, Tibetan children who attend minority schools usually come from rural areas and so have limited 'merit'. In short, morally poorly disciplined and intellectually inferior, 'typical' Tibetans were considered unable to easily fit in with an increasingly modernized society. Furthermore, preferential policies for minority schools were thought to deprive Tibetan children of being enhanced in quality, language and dynamics.

On the contrary, several teachers judged that parents who sent their children to mainstream schools have foresight, which they owe to their experience in Chinese Han education and/or in public sectors as a cadre (*ganbu*).[38] This is because, according to a teacher, they 'clearly know that they are not good', 'know that they lack quality [for study]'. Teachers explained that the educational experience in the mainstream school helps Tibetan parents become aware of the importance of education in mainstream schools for having a high cultural quality and social status, which is exemplified by the ideal end-result of becoming a cadre. This in turn shapes a 'virtuous circle'. This cultivation of Tibetan students in the mainstream school was argued to be capable of eventually enabling the Tibetan community as a whole to transform the quality of its population (*renkou suzhi*).

To justify their viewpoint of the cultural and educational superiority of the mainstream school, both teachers and students unexceptionally agreed that it is mainstream schooling that functions as an institution for cultivating useful people of a higher academic standard. Apart from the convenience for both daily life and a future career, a good command of Chinese would gain them mainstream cultural citizenship; it was a signal of high cultural quality, and 'would win the respect of society, and further, could boost one's cultural confidence', two students commented in this way. Moreover, several students also claimed that Chinese is more profound than other languages, because it offers a broader cultural horizon than, for example, Han culture, which they did not believe to be offered in similar depth in minority schools.[39]

In this vein, whilst Tibetans, under the encouragement of state preferential policy and as the dominant group in the region, reckon themselves to be no longer inferior to the Han, or do not share the value of sending children to Han schools, a large number of mainstream members showed their scepticism or criticism towards this policy. They said that this has made Tibetans (who are of low quality!) feel proud of themselves, and even come to be arrogant. Some examples they gave are that Tibetans will ask them to shut up if they are trying to discuss Buddhism with the latter, because Tibetans do not believe that the Han understand Buddhism as well as they do. Tibetans consider that they are dominant in this region and everyone should be required to learn the Tibetan language. In some teachers' eyes, this was definitely 'retrogressive' (*daotui*). 'How does it come to be possible for everyone to learn Tibetan? It is more reasonable (for everyone) to learn English (if not Chinese)!' Two government officials also commented with disapproval on the Tibetan head-teacher of a local minority school, who insisted on the Tibetan language as the medium of instruction throughout the school while some minority schools adopted Chinese for teaching. They thought this was evident of a (backward) ethnic consciousness.

These mainstream discursive repertoires about Muslims and Tibetans are exactly in parallel with the academic idea of enlightenment, as discussed earlier. They were typically reflected in the discourse of 'cultivation', when my interviewees evaluated and judged minorities by the degree to which different groups sought to adapt themselves to Han Chinese culture in general, and mainstream education in particular. Cultivation is a good thing when it works along the lines of Chinese culture. In this light, my respondents praised the Tibetan community, that in general has been making an effort to approach this benchmark (for example, by voluntarily sending their children to mainstream schools) (also see Chapter 4). One teacher declared that because some Tibetans have improved themselves significantly in this direction, they could hardly be distinguished, even physically, from the Han. This is evidence of the educability of Tibetans.

Meanwhile, cultivation can also play a retrogressive role when it is adopted as a tool to reinforce ethno-religious tradition, as has occurred in the Muslim case. Unlike Tibetans, Muslims in the Han's eyes still appear to be very nationalistic, as a student put it: 'if you say something about Muslims, they resist very acutely'. This led the mainstream to the view that the way in which Muslims are cultivated within their ethno-religious tradition has in fact resulted in their resistance to Han culture within, as well as without, the school. Thus they are uneducable within the framework of supposedly advanced Chinese culture, which is coupled with the fact that they still look distinctive in their features from the Han, as a teacher put it. Therefore, 'uneducable' Muslims are seen as being more in need of education. Having ethnicized Tibetans and Muslims in this way, Chinese Han practise a 'racial nationalism', in Sautman's words (1997), toward minorities. This practice was seen in particular in their refusal of making contact with minority students in schools on account of the claimed low quality of minorities. This is because, according to a teacher, 'everyone likes excellent people'. Evidence of this Han chauvinism is further confirmed by my minority respondents in the following two chapters.

Conclusion

Through this investigation into the mainstream discourse at the macro (governmental), mezzo (academic) and micro (individual) levels of the minority population in particularly educational terms, some general conclusions can be drawn.

This discourse construction reveals a shifting discursive repertoire. On one level, in the mainstream diagnosis and evaluation of minorities, one principal feature lies in many on-the-surface competing arguments regarding such issues as separate school, bilingual education, religion and education, and community forces. One major consequence is that it is hard to establish convincing causal relationships between numerous symptoms – physical environment, cultural differences, mental ability, and socio-political concern – that are diagnosed by the mainstream as affecting minority education. Put differently, in explanations of poor minority performance, arbitrariness makes up a striking feature of the mainstream discourse. On another level, in doing so, the symptoms are also very likely to be used to arbitrarily form more 'vicious circles' for the minority population in the mainstream discursive formation. This in fact leads to the implication that the poverty or 'stupidity' of the minority population is their 'habitus', i.e. 'a system of durable and transposable dispositions' that is shared by its members (Bourdieu 1977: 72).

Indeed, as seen throughout the chapter, even contradictory or divergent accounts from different parties or individuals echo each other ideologically, proving and reinforcing one another and so underlying the view of minority's presumed retardation for the modernization of China. Therefore, the main-stream discourse has proceeded mainly in the manner of 'blaming victims', through which symbolic boundaries (Lamont 1992) between the advanced and backward were drawn. This in turn has fulfilled its ethnicization of minority cultures and subjects. This has firstly justified and legitimized the way in which cultural-political mainstream continues to carry out its mission of civilizing these culturally alien minorities through its on-going integrative agenda. Secondly, it has also justified the necessity to (fashionably) put a neo-liberal governmentality in place in order to devolve responsibility to the largely rural-based minorities. That is, minorities are encouraged to raise their *suzhi* themselves and so to prosper at little cost to the state, as both Murphy (2004) and Yan (2003) similarly observe in their studies of rural migrants. The neo-liberal way is seen to push minority cultures to the peripheries of the market economy to a significant extent, whereas the civilizing mission has been excluding minority cultures from public institutions. Both ways together have intensified the marginalization of minority cultures in the wider society.[40]

Concomitantly, this mainstream approach also allows for uncovering the ambivalence and ambiguity of the state agenda of modernization. This agenda strives to integrate the hard-to-compromise ideas of political loyalty, economic development and cultural diversity into a coherent whole. This has particularly resulted in the gap between the formal level of laws and the informal level of public discourse and attitudes, as Kymlicka (2001) similarly presents in his case studies. In other words, even though the Constitution guarantees citizens' freedom of religion, the societal culture that the Party-state has offered to Chinese citizens tends to exert control over a wider range of aspects, such as language, religion or recreation. This is largely on account of 'the same old pastoral relationship' between the Party-state and the masses that 'formed an intrinsic part of the governing *for* rather than *by* the people' (Murphy 2006: 17, 19. Emphasis in original). This has resulted in ambiva-lence or ambiguity, not only in government policies, but also among the majority and minorities alike, toward minority cultures, as I argue in this chapter and Chapters 4 and 5.

Yet, when these aspects appear to be in conflict, to justify and legitimize its regime by focusing upon and fostering political loyalty in the masses, and centring on economic development, usually comes to be the priority of the Party-state at the expense of second-rate minority cultures. This is effectively delineated by Heberer (1990) as the 'borderline integration' (in comparison with assimilation) of the minority policy in China. In this justification and legitimization, the discourse of culture often serves as a toolkit to draw sym-bolic boundaries for the cultural-political mainstream to retain its privileges and power – and correspondingly for minorities to avoid further marginaliza-tion in the larger society, where education, the cultural battlefield, is grounded. Following on from this point, the subsequent two chapters move to minorities' evaluations of their educational situation within the wider socio-economic and cultural environment, with which social systems have provided them.

4   Choosing between 'ordinary' and minorities

The Tibetan case

Introduction

This chapter examines how Tibetan students' efforts to attain social mobility through education were complicated by the Chinese state agenda of integrating them into the Han nation-state. This complication can be understood as a tension between their desire for full social citizenship, in the form of rights to employment, education and opportunities, and the requirement that they also adopt Han cultural citizenship – that they acquire the knowledge and language for 'belonging' to mainstream society. However, by focusing on integrating and equipping students to become part of the Han-dominated mainstream, educational policies devalued Tibetan culture and language. This situation prevented Tibetan students from acquiring the kinds of cultural capital that would enable them to 'progress', and caused many to become academic underachievers. Meanwhile, those who have managed to stay in 'mainstream' are caught in the predicament in which they vainly make an effort to re-establish linkage with their ethnic culture.

The following sections draw on fieldwork in Tongren County in Huangnan Tibetan Autonomous Prefecture in Qinghai Province to examine the predicament that Tibetan parents and students face in school choice. Section one provides a geographical and historical background to ethnicity and education in the field site of Huangnan Tibetan Autonomous Prefecture, Qinghai Province. The next three sections examine how governments have created opportunities for the social mobility of Tibetans, and the positive attitude of Tibetans towards schooling and their hopes for social mobility, at the same time describing educational policy and practice in two different schools: a mainstream or 'ordinary' school and a minority school.

The chapter goes on to consider how parents justify their decisions to send their children to either ordinary or minority schools, and students' evaluations of their own schooling type versus the alternative form of schooling. Following on from this, it discusses the predicament that Tibetan parents and students face in school choice, which is rooted in their ambivalence towards the value of their culture – an effect of its subordination to the dominant discourse of advanced culture (*xianjin wenhua*). The conclusion reflects on whether or not inclusive education for Tibetans is possible and whether or not fully inclusive social citizenship – social and economic rights, and equal opportunities – can be achieved whilst at the same time preserving Tibetan cultural integrity. These empirical sections flesh out tensions between the desire of Tibetans for personal advancement in an era of economic change, counterbalanced against their competing desires to sustain the integrity of their culture and identity – tensions which exemplify their marginal position in the Chinese nation-state.

Huangnan Tibetan Autonomous Prefecture: an overview

Huangnan Prefecture is located in the southeast of Qinghai Province. It adjoins two Muslim autonomous counties in northeast Qinghai, and is surrounded by the three Tibetan autonomous prefectures in Qinghai and Gansu provinces in the northwest, southeast and southwest (see Map 4.1). Huangnan consists of four counties; two of these are largely agricultural (Jianzha and Tongren), while the other two are pastoral (Zeku and Henan). In 2002 the minority population accounted for 92.19 per cent of the total. The breakdown of the ethnic minority population is as follows: 65.94 per cent Tibetan, 13.65 per cent Mongolian, 8.01 per cent Muslim, 4.55 per cent Tu and 0.04 per cent others (HZT 2003a, 2003b). The Tibetan people were distributed mainly in Tongren and Zeku counties (39.80 per cent and 37.09

Map 4.1 Map of the Qinghai-Gansu Borderlands.

per cent respectively), and to a lesser extent, Jianzha (22.76 per cent).[1] The ethnic population in Tongren, the seat of the prefectural government, was 72.06 per cent Tibetan, 5.55 per cent Muslim, 10 per cent Han and 12.16 per cent Tu (HZT 2003b) (see Table 4.1).[2]

According to the Census, in 2000 the rural populace accounted for 72.16 per cent of the population in Tongren County and 78.29 per cent of the whole of Huangnan Prefecture. The Han and Muslims of Tongren County mostly resided in Longwu *Zhen* (Longwu Township), so they were urban dwellers. By contrast, most of the Tibetans were rural, engaged in agriculture and some animal husbandry.

Also according to the 2000 Census, Huangnan Prefecture was one of the three worst performers for education in Qinghai province, having an illiteracy rate of 30.30 per cent – the other two poor performing prefectures are Guoluo (34.81 per cent) and Yushu (43.77 per cent). Together these three prefectures form the *Qingnan Diqu* (South Qinghai Area), the least developed area in Qinghai as measured by economic and educational indicators. At the other end of the educational spectrum, Huangnan had a lower proportion of the college and university graduates (2.39 per cent), as well as secondary school and vocational secondary school graduates (6.84 per cent) than the provincial level (3.3 per cent and 10.43 per cent) (see Table 4.2).[3]

Since 1990 there were 13 secondary schools in Huangnan Prefecture. Four of these were located in Longwu Township, the seat of the prefectural and Tongren county governments. Two were ordinary schools; the *Huangnan Zhou Zhongxue* (Huangnan Prefecture Secondary School), the oldest school

Table 4.1 2002 ethnic minority population in Huangnan TAP

Area	TP	EMP(%)	TbP(%)	MP(%)	MuP(%)	TuP(%)	OP(%)
Prefecture	212,504	195,897 (92.19)	140,126 (65.94)	29,013 (13.65)	17,011 (8.01)	9,672 (4.55)	75 (0.04)
Tongren	77,165	69,442 (90)	55,602 (72.06)	129	4,285 (5.55)	9,385 (12.16)	41
Jianzha	49,672	44,151 (88.89)	31,873	46	12,075	131	26
Zeku	54,761	52,545 (95.95)	52,161	15	303	58	8
Henan	30,906	29,759 (96.29)	490	28,823	348	98	–

Key
EMP = Ethnic minority population
MP = Mongolian population
MuP = Muslim population
OP = Other population
TP = Total population
TbP = Tibetan population
TuP = Tu population

Source: HZT 2003b

Table 4.2 2000 illiteracy rate, college and university graduate rate, and secondary school and vocational secondary school graduate rate in Qinghai and Huangnan

Area	TP	IR2000 (%)	CUGR (%)	SSGR (%)
Province	5,181,560	18.03	3.3	10.43
Huangnan	225,462	30.30	2.39	6.84
Tongren	80,856	23.04	3.33	9.58
Jianzha	48,971	27.72	2.44	6.14
Zeku	57,334	39.97	0.73	3.08
Henan	33,707	38.31	1.23	3.88
Yushu	268,825	43.77	0.76	3.85
Guoluo	140,397	34.81	1.33	5.76

Key
TP = Total population
IR = Illiteracy rate
CUGR = College and university graduates rate
SSGR = Secondary school and vocational secondary school graduates rate

Source: HZT 2002

in the prefecture with a history of more than 40 years, and the *Tongren Xian Zhongxue* (Tongren County Secondary School). The other two were minority schools: the *Huangnan Zhou Minzu Gaozhong* (Huangnan Prefecture Minority Senior Secondary School), established in 1990, and the *Tongren Xian Minzu Zhongxue* (Tongren County Minority Secondary School). Since minority education in Huangnan Prefecture refers primarily to the education of Tibetans or Tibetan speakers (Mongolians or Tu), it is not surprising that Tibetan students comprised the majority of the student body in the two minority schools. Han students traditionally dominated Huangnan Prefecture Secondary School, the prestigious school of the prefecture. Muslim students made up the largest part of the student body in Tongren County Secondary School (half of the students). This ethnic composition of the student body in the two schools reflected residential patterns in Longwu Township as well as the government policy of 'attending the neighbourhood school' (*jiujin ruxue*) (also see Chapter 5).

Historically, Longwu Township was called Longwu *Jie Qu* (Longwu Street District). The town emerged to meet the daily needs of the monks of Longwu Monastery (Longwu *Si*) and its dependants. It formally became a market town at the end of the nineteenth century when the reincarnation of Buddha in Longwu Monastery permitted the business people from Gansu, Xunhua[4] and the vicinities to engage in trade in the Longwu area. After the Longwu market area came into being, the Tibetans, the locally dominant ethnic group, called it 'jiakeri', which means 'the Han city'. Half of these business people were Muslims and they eventually became the main residents of the Longwu market area. From 1954 onwards, a new town was built up to the west of the Longwu market town. This new settlement became the seat of both the prefectural and county governmental administrations (HZZBW 1999; TXBW 2001; HZT 1999, 2002, 2003a, 2003b).

On account of this history, Longwu Township was divided into two parts: *xianshang* (the county part), previously the Longwu market area, and *zhoushang* (the prefecture part), which was the new town centre. The new town centre was home to both prefectural and county administrative sectors in Longwu and commercial and entertainment blocks. In accordance with the 'attending the neighbourhood school' policy, Huangnan Secondary School, which was located in the prefecture part, mainly recruited students from the new prefecture part of the town. As is also noted by Wang (2006) regarding migrant children in her study, this schooling policy meant that residential and socio-economic forms of inequality became reinforced within the school setting. In the case of Huangnan Secondary School, most students were the children of government officials, public servants, teachers, factory workers and/or from Han background. By contrast, Tongren County Secondary School, which was situated in the county part, mainly recruited students from the old part of the town. The students included Muslim children as well as those from some other ethnic backgrounds whose families were usually engaged in business.

The two minority schools recruited predominantly Tibetan students, with most from the agricultural or pastoral areas in the prefecture and Tongren. In the mid-1990s, a donation from Shao Yifu, a Hong Kong businessman enabled another minority junior secondary school to be set up next to Huangnan Secondary School, named the *Yifu Minzu Zhongxue* (Yifu Minority (Junior) Secondary School) which recruited Tibetan or Tibetan-speaking students. In September 2002, Tongren County Secondary School merged with Huangnan Prefecture Secondary School because of the decline in student numbers owing to demographic transition.[5] Hence Longwu Township retained four secondary schools, but the ethnic make-up of the student body in secondary education changed considerably over the course of twelve years.

Opportunities for social mobility

State policy gave Tibetan graduates in Huangnan Prefecture priority access to top leadership positions in government.[6] The Tibetans were specifically selected, cultivated and employed as cadres at all levels of administration and in all kinds of scientific and technological positions within the autonomous government organs (*zizhi zhengfu jiguan*). They were similarly favoured by the recruitment practices of state work units, and also received preferential treatment for enrolment in local schools, minority colleges or universities (*minzu yuanxiao*), within the province as well as nationwide.[7]

As early as 1955, just two years after Huangnan Prefecture was established, Tibetans became the majority ethnic group among cadres in Huangnan Autonomous Prefecture (HZZBW 1999). Although the Han represented a higher proportion of cadres, Tibetans nevertheless formed the dominant group in terms of absolute numbers. The proportion of Tibetan cadres was especially high when compared to the proportion of cadres from other ethnic minority groups (see Table 4.3).

In addition to privileging Tibetan people within the government, the local government also established a number of Tibetan-oriented key pre-fectural organizations and institutions for ethnic minority studies covering subjects such as Tibetology (*Zangxue*), ethnic folk art, and ethnic medicine (HZZBW 1999). The Longwu Township area was host to establishments such as the Rebgong Art Gallery (*Rebgong Yishu Guan*),[8] the Prefectural Ethnic Song and Dance Ensemble (*Zhou Minzu Gewu Tuan*), and the Prefectural Tibetan Medical Hospital (*Zhou Zang Yiyuan*). Longwu Township was also home to four (Tibetan) minority schools and a (Tibetan) minority teachers college (the latter was also turned into a minority school to meet the need to re-adjust the local educational structure in 2007). In fact, Tongren was recently honoured as a National Historic-Cultural Renowned City (Town) (*Quanguo Lishi Wenhua Mingcheng*) for its Tibetan culture, the only town of its kind in the province.

These positive policies and measures towards Tibetan people and culture, coupled with a resurgence and popularization of Tibetan Buddhism among both Tibetans and Han,[9] fostered pride in Tibetan ethnic culture and a cele-bration of Tibetan ethnic identity among Tibetans. For example, among my informants, some Tibetan elites are particularly keen to adopt the word *bodajingshen* (extensive knowledge and profound scholarship) to describe their culture. A number of 'Tibetan discos' (Langma Ting) were also opened on the main street, where most of the time young Tibetans performed or watched their ethnic songs and dances. The first Tibetan non-governmental organization named Rebgong Cultural Centre was also launched in 2004 (see also Postscript).

Education as the means to upward mobility

This largely top-down creation of opportunities for occupational mobility gave Tibetans, both rural and urban, a strong incentive for better social

Table 4.3 2002 ethnic population and government officials in Huangnan

	Han	Muslim	Tibetan	Mongolian	Tu	Others
EP %	7.81	8.01	65.94	13.65	4.55	0.04
OPC %	38.28	4.62	44.88	6.93	4.95	0.33
OP %	32.86	2.86	45.71	10	7.14	1.43

Key
EP = Ethnic population
OP = Government officials at prefectural level
OPC = Government officials at both prefectural and county levels

Source: Fieldwork 2003

status and quality of life. This section considers the different ways in which these opportunities created incentives for parents from rural and urban backgrounds to value education for their children.

Rural Tibetans observed the life opportunities enjoyed by their compatriots in state work units, and became aware that their lives could improve if they too could become cadres. They saw education as the most direct route to upward mobility. This perception was not confined to the younger generation. Members of the older generation also prioritized education for their children, partly because they missed out on these opportunities for themselves. As some of my interviewees said, they would definitely secure the opportunity for their children to study in schools even if they had to ask for loans or postpone new house building plans.

Individuals from rural backgrounds who managed to escape farm and pastoral life through employment in a state work unit had a particularly strong sense of the importance of education. Some of these people were recruited into state work units because of their talents in aspects of Tibetan culture, for example *Zangxi* (Tibetan drama), while others received work unit employment as compensation after land was requisitioned from their village. These people personally experienced the contrast between the hard and bitter life of labouring in the countryside and the easy and relaxed life and regular wage that comes with being in a state work unit. Daily experiences in their new urban working lives further revealed to them the importance of the Chinese language education. One informant told me: 'this is what I can never forget – I cannot even write a *qingjia tiao* (a note asking for leave) (in Chinese). If I could have gone to school in those days, I would have probably been a county magistrate (*xianzhang*)'.

Long-time urban Tibetans also valued education, though for different reasons to those who came recently from the countryside.[10] Whereas people from rural families had land for their children to fall back on, should they fail in college entrance examinations, the only outlet for established urbanites was to find temporary jobs such as being a waiter or shop assistant in the township area.[11] These jobs could not guarantee a financially stable life, particularly given the low levels of economic development in the area. The enthusiasm for and investment in education by these families therefore became a priority. This can be seen in their undiminished enthusiasm for education even after the government abolished the job allocation system for university and college graduates in 1996. Under the new policy, when students graduate, they are not guaranteed a job by the state but need to find one by themselves. This meant that they were at risk of unemployment after graduation (*biye ji shiye*). But this did not stop them from investing more energy and money in education, and many parents encouraged if not forced their children to study harder in order to enter secondary schools and ultimately a university.[12] Some parents went further by encouraging their children to try their best to enter a key or famous university (*zhongdian daxue, mingpai daxue*), whose graduates were better able to find a good job.

Among all Tibetans, but especially those with better access to information, there was a growing tendency towards pursuing education abroad, a development that mirrors nationwide trends. This is not surprising, given that many Tibetans felt a closer affinity with foreign countries than with China, on account of the politicization and internationalization of the 'Tibetan question' (*Xizang wenti*). Some of my interviewees told me that they had relatives working abroad, and that they expected their overseas kin and relatives to sponsor their education, and perhaps even help them to go abroad if they could demonstrate good school performance. These kinds of expectations were usually fostered by their awareness of others who had enjoyed such support.

To sum up, rural people identified education as the main way of freeing themselves from poverty and hardship, while urban dwellers saw it as a means for moving up the social ladder, and eventually joining the elite group wherever this was possible. Tibetan people's evaluations of education were therefore positively equated with material well-being and upward social mobility.

Two schools: an 'ordinary' school and a 'minority' school

As is common in many minority areas, Tibetan students in my fieldwork site could choose to be educated in either an ordinary or a minority school. School choice is fundamental to the citizenship formation of individuals, because as is also discussed by Wang (2006), the category of school influences the type of labels that are placed on students, the kind of knowledge they obtain, and the set of resources and opportunities to which they ultimately receive entitlement. Among four secondary schools in Longwu, Huangnan Secondary School and Huangnan Minority Senior Secondary School were under the administration of the Education Bureau of the Prefecture; the other two schools, Tongren County Minority Secondary School and Yifu Minority Junior Secondary School fell under the jurisdiction of the Education Bureau of Tongren County. In this section, I compare the two prefectural schools – Huangnan Secondary School and Huangnan Minority Senior Secondary School.

Huangnan Secondary School

Huangnan Secondary School is a prestigious local school. After it merged with Tongren County Secondary School in 2002, it has become the sole ordinary school in the Longwu area. Consequently it experienced a noticeable increase in the number of the minority students in general, and Muslim students in particular. According to figures provided by the school official, in the academic year 2002–3, there were over 800 junior and senior school students in six grades, of whom nearly half were female. Among these, minority students made up 65.21 per cent. The ethnic breakdown of the minority students was Muslim 31.63 per cent[13] and Tibetan 24.09 per cent.[14] With a slightly lower percentage than the Han (34.79 per cent), the Muslim students comprised the second largest group in the school. In other words, the only ordinary school in Longwu Township was significantly 'minoritized'. All the Tibetan students were from urban areas and were residents of Longwu Township; many had parents working in state work units at county or prefectural level, while a few had a parent working as a self-employed business person. The students usually paid 400 or 500 yuan per term, for tuition, facilities[15] (computing), textbooks and exercise books, and some miscellaneous fees.

Of the 76 teachers at Huangnan Secondary School, 9.21 per cent were Muslims and 25 per cent Tibetans, while the remainder were Han.[16] There were no teachers of music and fine art, and there was a shortage of teachers of physical education and English. Qualifications-wise, 100 per cent of the teachers for the junior grades met the requirement for an associate college degree (*dazhuan xueli*) or higher, while 46 per cent of those who taught senior classes held a university graduate degree (*benke xueli*) or higher.

Like other secondary schools in China, Huangnan Secondary School very much 'danced to the baton of college entrance examinations' (*genzhe gaokao zhihuibang zhuan*). This was clear in both discipline and course arrangement. The students in year three at the junior level (*chusan*) and above were required to spend in excess of nine hours per day in school during weekdays, and nearly eight hours devoted to classroom study. In addition, they had to attend school for five hours on Saturdays. When key examinations such as national college entrance examinations were pending, they even attended school on Sundays.

The school had rules and regulations that rewarded students for high achievement and punished them for truancy or other disruptive behaviour. Once a student had been punished officially (*chufen*), he or she would not be able to get credentials issued by the school if the punishment had not been discharged by the time of graduation. On the whole, both the school and the teachers were satisfied with the attendance rate of the students, and few students dropped out.

Teachers at Huangnan Secondary School were subject to strict punitive regulations for teaching performance. For instance, if a teacher did not meet the required number of teaching hours, he or she will had to pay a fine. This was despite the fact that the insufficient time usually resulted from the school official not allocating the requisite number of teaching hours to the teacher. One of the regulations that the teachers complained about most bitterly was that they were fined when the percentage of students who had passed the end-of-year examinations fell short of the required number designated by the school official. Almost every teacher had been punished for this 'transgression', the amount they had to pay varying depending on the percentage of failing students. Fines generally ranged from 40 yuan to some 6,000 yuan (for reference, the teachers' monthly salary was usually between 700 and 2,500 yuan). The key point of criticism of this policy was not that the school had introduced such a regulation, but rather, that the criteria were not justifiable: the school had not set the percentage according to local conditions and abilities, but according to standards in Xining, the capital city of Qinghai Province, where the quality of education was the highest in the province.[17]

Like schools in other parts of China, the students were divided into two different classes when they entered *gao'er* (year two at senior level): *wenke ban* (class for liberal arts) and *like ban* (class for science). This eventually led to their study of specific subjects in universities. The school complied with the national curricula, and so used standard issued textbooks (*quanguo tongbian jiaocai*). Because of a shortage of teaching staff, music and fine art were not offered; once-offered courses in manual dexterity (*laodong jishu*) and demography (*renkou*) were cancelled. Additionally, there were some textbooks on local history and geography that were distributed to the students mainly for self-study, such as *Qinghai Lishi* (Qinghai History), *Qinghai Dili* (Qinghai Geography) and *Minzu Zhengce Changshi* (General Knowledge of the Policy of Ethnic Minorities). The medium of instruction was exclusively Chinese Mandarin (*putonghua*, lit. 'common language').

Huangnan Minority Senior Secondary School

Huangnan Minority Senior Secondary School had a much shorter history than Huangnan Secondary School, but it enjoyed a high profile nevertheless. In 2002–3 it attracted nearly 500 senior school students in its three grades. The student body comprised Tibetans (60 per cent), Mongolians and Tu, and equal numbers of males and females. All the students were Tibetan speakers. They studied in minority primary schools and junior secondary schools before attending Huangnan Minority Senior Secondary School. Most of the students came from agricultural or pastoral areas, and boarded at the school. The frequency of home visits varied greatly, according to the distance between home and school – once a week at one end of the spectrum, once a term at the other, though most returned once every one to two months. The students paid 200–300 yuan per term for their study and boarding, and received a grant-in-aid (*zhuxuejin*) of 40 yuan from the government per term.

Students were expected to spend more than eight hours a day in school, with more than seven hours of classroom study. There were no classes on either Saturdays or Sundays. The students also had to go out for physical exercise (*chucao*) at seven o'clock in the morning, five days a week.

The school had rules and regulations that rewarded and punished students, but compared with Huangnan Secondary School, discipline was quite lax. Unlike Huangnan Secondary School, there was no school uniform for the flag-raising ceremony or any other special occasions. But like the ordinary school, the attendance rate of the students satisfied both the school and the teachers, and there were rarely any drop-outs.

There were 35 full-time teachers at the school, half of whom were Tibetan, nearly half Han, and a few from other ethnic backgrounds. The teachers were well qualified, with 85.70 per cent of them having an undergraduate degree. Even so, there was a strong need for physics and chemistry teachers. Unlike Huangnan Secondary School, there was no serious punishment system directed at the teachers' work.

Apart from the courses that were commonly offered in both the ordinary and minority schools, Huangnan Minority Senior Secondary School offered a course that had been tailored in accordance with government policy, that is, *Zang yuwen* (Tibetan language and literature). This was the only course delivered in the Tibetan language at the minority school; all the others were taught in Chinese. *Han yuwen* (Chinese language and literature) and *Zang yuwen* were the only two courses that used *Wushengqu Tongbian Jiaocai* (uniformly compiled textbooks by five provinces and regions in West China where there are Tibetan residents, namely TAR, Qinghai, Sichuan, Yunnan and Gansu provinces). Fine art was also a Tibetan-related course, in which the students could learn Tibetan Buddhist painting (*Tangka*), and for which Tongren was renowned both within and beyond the Tibetan area.

As in Huangnan Secondary School, the students in the minority school were divided into the arts and sciences streams from year two (at senior level) onwards. They were entitled to sit college entrance exams in Tibetan.[18] The majority of the students would enter local minority colleges or universities and major in Tibetan literature or science. In the past few years, the number of the students who chose science subjects increased and was now slightly higher than those who chose Tibetan literature, the most popular subject in the past. This was possibly in part influenced by the abolition of the job allocation system. In the past, university graduates were guaranteed jobs regardless of whether or not there was a social or economic demand for their subject. Since students had to find their own jobs, subjects had to be chosen with more attention to the job market. So even though the scientific subjects were among the most difficult for the students in Huangnan Minority Senior Secondary School (also see below),[19] they still tended to devote themselves to these subjects. There were nevertheless a high proportion of students who chose Tibetan – this choice usually enabled them to enrol in a minority university or college more easily.

The parental dilemma: where to send children?

Justification for opting for minority schools

There were the differences among Tibetan parents with regard to school choice. Generally speaking, rural parents (farmers or village government officers), and working class parents in state sectors sent their children to (Tibetan) minority (primary) schools in their villages of origin. The parents chose this type of school because of low fees, convenient travel to and from school, Tibetan language instruction and Tibetan students and teachers. Students with this kind of early schooling usually continued their education in minority junior secondary and then senior secondary schools, which tended to be located in urban areas.

Parents preferred to keep their children within a Tibetan minority school environment because they feared that their children would not perform as well as their Han peers if they attended an ordinary school. Conversely, they thought that it would be easier for their children to study in their mother tongue and in a Tibetan cultural environment: language and thought are inseparable and Tibetan students often experience difficulty in grasping concepts and communicating within a Han language and cultural environment. For example, in ordinary schools, Tibetan students could hardly understand common sense aspects of the school routine that were taken for granted by the Han. So, even a brilliant Tibetan child who was able to perform excellently in a minority school remained, at best, an average student in an ordinary school.[20]

Parents who decided to send their children to minority schools were aware that many people in the larger society saw the Tibetan language as useless. But these parents felt that the language would nevertheless be useful if the student had a good command of it. This meant that when their children came back to Huangnan Tibetan Autonomous Prefecture as university graduates, they could still work in the government, for instance, in a law court or village governmental sectors, where cadres need to know the Tibetan language to deal with local people. The view that Tibetan is useful stemmed from a belief that their children would normally return to Huangnan Tibetan Autonomous Prefecture after graduation. This was because Tibetan parents thought that their children lacked the knowledge, social contacts and cultural background to be able to compete with Han people in finding employment outside the Tibetan areas.

Parents also preferred minority schools because they believed that their children – and themselves as well – should be able to speak Tibetan before studying other languages, cultures or subjects. To justify their choice, they also addressed the negative effect of studying in ordinary schools. They said that their children would be affected by the Han way after studying in the Chinese language and cultural environment and would adopt a Han way of thinking. As a result, the children would become disobedient and lazy and demand too many material comforts like those children from better-off families.

Many parents told me that nowadays a Tibetan child could learn everything in a minority school that they could in an ordinary school. They pointed out that due to the adoption of the national curriculum in all state schools, their children could learn advanced knowledge like Chinese, English, and computing even in a minority school. At the same time, they could also learn some Tibetan subjects like painting, literature and language, and some dance and song in regular or extra-curricula classes and so acquire their own ethnic culture in a Tibetan environment.

Justification for opting for ordinary schools

The parents who sent their children to an ordinary school usually worked in state work units at either the county or prefectural level (but not as manual workers) and had been educated in Chinese in ordinary schools, or else they had been educated in minority schools followed by recruitment into a state work unit where the working language was Chinese. Their primary concern in school choice was the limited opportunity to use the Tibetan language: 'even in this Tibetan Autonomous Prefecture' Chinese was the working language in state work units, including Tibetan-related institutions such as the Prefectural Ethnic Song and Dance Ensemble, the Rebgong Art Gallery, and minority schools.[21] Some examples they gave were that all documents from the authorities had to be drafted in Chinese, although they are also usually coupled with a translation into Tibetan, and the formal language in meetings and conferences was Chinese, even when the majority of the participants were Tibetan.[22] The conclusion was thus that one must learn Chinese regardless of whether one stays in Huangnan or moves elsewhere. In their understanding, the dominance of the Chinese language was determined by its status as the national language, and by the fact that it is the first language of the Han majority. Competence in Chinese would enable a Tibetan student to study in Chinese at a regular rather than a minority college or university, and this would definitely be an advantage when looking for a job in competition with the Tibetan graduates from minority colleges or universities (also see below).

In short, a good command of Tibetan without Chinese caused inconvenience in daily life, and became a ceiling to personal occupational advancement. My respondent of a government official also proved this by telling me that in 1996 all the people appointed to work in the Prefectural Government and Committee of the CPC were those who majored in Chinese, or Han from other areas, or those from other ethnic backgrounds who were largely sinicized. And this was also the case in 2006. Importantly though, among my Tibetan informants, no one who held this view explicitly endorsed the idea of giving up Tibetan. They still expressed willingness or claimed to require that their children master oral Tibetan, and to a lesser extent, written Tibetan. Another consideration in discouraging children from learning or using Tibetan was that, as Huangnan Tibetan Autonomous Prefecture is a multi-ethnic area (*minzu zaju qu*), it would be inappropriate to adopt Tibetan as a major means of communication. Moreover, many parents also argued or implied that the quality of education in ordinary schools was higher than that in minority schools.

Some other reasons that informed the choice of parents who sent their children to ordinary schools were beyond an instrumental concern with language or quality of education, but were more ideological. One opinion was that Tibetan culture was closely connected with Buddhism, particularly when it went up to certain levels. As a religion, Buddhism was a good choice in cultivating one's moral character and nourishing one's nature (*xiushen yangxing*). But this was not very useful for the progress and development of society, and could even play a hindering role in this respect. This was a popular view among some middle-aged Tibetans who were educated during the Cultural Revolution, when religion was uniformly criticized as feudal superstition (*fengjian mixin*), and as backward and opposed to advanced materialism (*weiwu zhuyi*). Another disadvantage in studying Tibetan culture was the view of some parents that such study could cultivate an antagonistic sentiment among Tibetans towards the Government and the CPC, and further, foster a consciousness of secession.

Where do students want to study?

Evaluations of the students in Huangnan Secondary School

In Huangnan Secondary School, more than 90 per cent of the Tibetan students (10 in 11) in my investigation expressed a preference for studying in Huangnan Minority Senior Secondary School. On the whole, the students saw life in Huangnan Secondary School as unattractive and boring. This was because major courses (*zhuke*) were usually too demanding on account of focusing on college entrance examinations; the students would have preferred to study minor courses (*fuke*) and extra-curricular activities such as music, art and sports. In addition, they would have welcomed the opportunity to study courses such as Tibetan language and literature. But these options were either not offered or were reduced to a bare minimum. For example, even though there was ethnic minority content in the textbooks, many teachers did not bother to cover this material in class, and instead instructed the students to read it by themselves. The content of some teaching materials on ethnic minority issues was often perceived by Tibetan students to be antagonistic, and this sense of antagonism was exacerbated by the negative ways in which some teachers spoke about Tibetan customs in line with the notion of social evolution.

They said that, in contrast, Huangnan Minority Senior Secondary School students could not only study all subjects that were offered in Huangnan Secondary School, including Chinese, English and computing, but also a range of minor courses in ethnic culture. In discussing why it was not possible for them to study the kinds of ethnic culture courses offered in Huangnan Minority Senior Secondary School, the students at the ordinary school explained that their school could not offer such courses because they were not part of the core content of college entrance examinations. Moreover, educational planners assumed that the Tibetan students obtained culturally relevant knowledge from their families anyway. When asked why they were keen to study their own language and culture, more than 90 per cent of them described their embarrassment about their insufficient Tibetan, and explicitly expressed their need to improve their Tibetan. They thought that one should master one's own mother tongue – 'the Tibetan language is a symbol of [our] ethnic group'. They felt that it would be disgraceful if their descendents were not able to speak Tibetan and that poor Tibetan made it difficult for them to communicate with their Tibetan compatriots, with whom they spent most of their time. As for their interest in and enthusiasm for studying their own culture and religion, they explained that it was always good to acquire more knowledge; (their) religion advises people to be virtuous; they would have enough motivation to study excellently if the school offered courses in their culture and religion, and this would enhance their confidence in learning other subjects.

In addition to curriculum issues, the overly stern discipline and the cultural chauvinism of the teachers exacerbated their boredom with school life. Generally the school and teachers kept requiring the students to study hard in order to be able to enter a (good) university. Meanwhile, as mentioned earlier, in order to keep up academic competitiveness, the school official also set up strict punitive regulations for teacher evaluation. The teachers therefore faced punishment if exam targets were not met, so they transferred this pressure onto the students through harsh discipline, for example, giving an official punishment, or beating or scolding the students. In contrast, the students perceived that their counterparts in Huangnan Minority Senior Secondary School were not disciplined so harshly. They believed that the teachers in the minority school respected and understood the students, treating them as their own children, because 'they are also Tibetan'.

When it came to the practice of ethno-religious customs in Huangnan Secondary School, the students told me that the practitioners of religion were teased by the fellow students and even by the fellow Tibetan students. They explained that some teachers did not even allow them to share or explain their customs: they told the Tibetan students not to bring 'minority things' (*minzu de dongxi*) into the school, because they might be eccentric (*xiqigu-guai*) and unhealthy (*buliang*). Some more informed students pointed out that this was because that the school culture was based on Han culture. The students of Huangnan Secondary School also had the impression that Minority Secondary School did not discipline its students too strictly because they were able to wear their ethnic clothes and other ethnic- or religion-related accessories, such as Buddhist prayer beads.

A final reason that the Tibetan students at Huangnan Secondary School thought that they would have preferred to attend Minority Secondary School was because their classmates would be fellow Tibetans who they felt to be more straightforward, authentic, broad-minded and cheerful. By contrast, they saw their fellow Han students in Huangnan Secondary School to be tricky, hypocritical or insular. Moreover, some of their fellow Han students were not interested in making contact with the minority students. This tendency was presumably embedded in the Han self-perception of their higher intellectual quality; this led the Han students to believe that they could have a higher academic achievement in the school, and consequentially a higher socio-economic status in society. Tibetans therefore faced the prejudicial view that they were intellectually poor, and could not perform as well as the Han students. Although a couple of Tibetan students said that they did not make friends along the lines of ethnicity but personal character, they expressed a preference for the personality that was usually perceived to be possessed by the Tibetan students as mentioned above.

Evaluations of the students in Huangnan Minority Senior Secondary School

In Huangnan Minority Senior Secondary School, 60 per cent of the students (25 in 41) in my investigation said that they would have preferred to study in Huangnan Secondary School. Language was the first concern: they believed their Chinese would have improved if they had studied in the ordinary secondary school. They also held a positive view towards the teaching quality and educational standards of Huangnan Secondary School. And they felt that they would have benefited from studying alongside the Han students who they saw as knowledgeable and academically talented. Relatedly, they thought that studying at Huangnan Secondary School would have the added advantage of enabling them to make friends with Han.

Among Huangnan Minority Secondary School students who expressed a preference for staying in their own school, language was the main consideration; with poor Mandarin they felt that they would not be able to keep up with their Han classmates if they studied in the ordinary secondary school. This is understandable if we consider that ever since primary school they had received instruction in their mother tongue of Tibetan. The perceived academic superiority of the Han students in Huangnan Secondary School was another factor that precluded some of them from feeling confident enough to choose Secondary School over Minority Secondary School. While recognizing the social function of the Chinese language, they were not particularly interested in Han culture; even among those who would like to study in Huangnan Secondary School, only one out of 25 students expressed an interest in Han culture. By contrast, the minority school students showed high enthusiasm for their own culture, religion and language. This was another key attraction of Huangnan Minority Secondary School – that they could study their own culture, language, religion and history. Lastly, to study in an environment of Tibetan compatriots made them willing to stay in Huangnan Minority Secondary School.

To be 'ordinary' or minority: the cultural dilemma

Tibetan students and parents both valued education as a way of producing useful people who could benefit their own ethnic group, their family and themselves. In other words, they were not content with their status quo. Conversely, they strived so much for socio-economic mobility that sometimes this resulted in a desperate pattern of study without break and serious frustration with the ineffectiveness of their study, particularly in Huangnan Minority Secondary School. There are two examples that are worth mentioning. A teacher in a minority school told me that some of his students had to spend 40 minutes just trying to memorize a physics theorem in Chinese (so they were regarded as intellectual inferiority). Secondly, many students I investigated in the minority school eagerly requested in their questionnaires that I instruct them how to study effectively.

Tibetan internalization of the dominant critique of Tibetan culture and people

Apart from the instrumental function of upward mobility, education was symbolically important for Tibetans because it was seen as a way to transform the traditional image of themselves as a backward people (*luohou minzu*) into an advanced people (*xianjin minzu*). One of the most often used words in interviews was *xianjin* (advanced). They sensitively avoided employing *luohou* ('backward') to describe their ethnic group by simply emphasizing that Tibetans needed to absorb or study the advanced culture in order to 'get the traditional culture reformed and nurtured' (*buyu*). Without this reform and nurture, they feared being 'phased out'. In their mind, the advanced culture was *Zhong*yuan *wenhua* (Central Plains culture, that is, Chinese Han culture), and *waiguo wenhua* (foreign culture). In this vein, some of them even argued that when sending children to study in school, it was also necessary to teach the children how to distinguish between *zongjiao* (religion) and *mixin* (superstition). Others emphatically explained to me that nowadays many Tibetan practices were not *religious practices*, but *customs* – custom was at the top while superstition was at the bottom in their ideological ranking system, with religion in between.

What is more, some Tibetans who migrated from other sinicized areas or with a sinicized education even acutely criticized Tibetan culture, by claiming that the Tibetan modes of thought (*guannian*) were outdated and backward in the Huangnan Tibetan Autonomous Prefecture, because Tibetan tradition was so deeply rooted in this area. What I found most striking was the comments of a Tibetan school administrator, who was also a teacher of Tibetan language and literature and a would-be reincarnation of Buddha. When discussing the achievement of the Tibetan students in his minority school, he kept repeating:

> Here it is a place the Tibetan people are concentrated, the modes of thinking (*sixiang guannian*) of the people are backward, and the economy is not developed, the desire for pursuing knowledge (*qiuzhiyu*) is low.

As a school official, he anticipatedly ethnicized economic and educational achievement by making a cause-effect link between cultural backwardness, economic underdevelopment and lack of motivation for education.[23]

This kind of view was echoed by the Tibetan students from both Huangnan Secondary School and Huangnan Minority Senior Secondary School when they compared Han and Tibetans. They thought that the Han students had more aptitude for analysis and inference (*fenxi tuili nengli*), and were more knowledgeable, open-minded (*siwei kaifang*) and rational (*lizhi*). For instance, unlike Tibetans, a Han student commonly conceded to avoid trouble, while the former tended to fight to the finish. In their eyes, Han students had a higher study level (*xuexi shuiping*) and cultural level (*wenhua shuiping*), and so were of high quality (*suzhi gao*). The Han teachers in Huangnan Secondary School also possessed more up-to-date knowledge. These factors allowed for a better study ethos (*xuexi fengqi*) in Huangnan Secondary School. By contrast, they considered that the Tibetan students had lower academic achievement, were more conventional (*chuantong*) or conservative (*baoshou*), and less sociable (*shejiaoshang buxing*). Essentially, Tibetans thought themselves to be of poor quality (*suzhi cha*) and morally degenerate (*daode baihuai*). As evidence of this, they cited an inclination to drink or fight, which even scared some of their teachers. It was not surprising that the negative comments on the Tibetan students were said in relation to those students at Huangnan Minority Secondary School, and by the Tibetan students in the ordinary school.

The comments of Tibetan parents and students about the advancement of the Han and the poor quality and backwardness of the Tibetans suggested that they had internalized the critique of the dominant culture regarding their people, customs and cultural values. Furthermore, the criticism of their Han fellow students by the Tibetans in the ordinary school as being tricky, hypocritical and insular, as depicted earlier, in fact reflects an unconscious or subconscious rejection of this internalization of their inferiority when facing distance and even disdain from Han students and teachers. Their resulting ambivalence about their own cultural identity could be seen at even a very young age. When jokingly asked by some adults 'which ethnic group do you belong to', some young children who lived in a state work unit environment were very likely to identify themselves (and the people they had intimate relations with, for example, their mother) with Han, but regarded others (even their father or siblings, for instance) as Tibetan, as I was told by some informants.

Discrimination against Tibetans

Although few parents or students explicitly stated during the interviews that they (or their children) had experienced discrimination, this did not seem convincing, given the exaggerated tone of their denials. In fact, information about discrimination was evident in some of the stories they told. For instance, when a parent explained why he was not interested in attending parent-teacher meetings, he gave the example of a parent-teacher meeting that he had once attended when his daughter was in the primary school:

> I asked the teacher 'how is my kid performing?' 'Your Tibetan kids are all like that' was the reply. There is more to it than meets the ear. At that moment I wondered to myself why he said that, 'Tibetan students are all like that!' Like what? I did not fully understand but did not ask for his further elaboration. However he was the teacher of my kid . . . I have not attended a parent-teacher meeting since then.

Another parent told me that when his son was in the primary school, fellow students bullied him because he was a minority (*shaoshu*). The continued bullying slowly but surely reduced his enthusiasm for study and school life. This contributed to his mediocre academic achievement and disruptive behaviour. The parent concluded by saying that if the teachers had intervened with these bullies, his son's situation would not have been so bad:

> The form master should have cared about and paid more attention to this kind of [minority] kid, rather than seeing them as the same [as the majority] and then leave them there carelessly.

He finally sent his second child to a minority school.

Some of the Tibetan students mentioned a word that was usually used by the other ethnic students to describe them: *fan*. This word basically refers to the nature of a type of person who is slow in response (*chidun*) and has mental problem (*naozi you wenti*). Sometimes even some of their teachers would make a connection between a student and rural Tibetan people when criticizing his or her stupidity by saying 'you are just as stupid as those pastoral Tibetans' (*muqu lai de Zangmin*). Here, pastoral Tibetans were located in the lowest position, in comparison to urban and farming Tibetans.[24]

The dilemma facing the Tibetans emulating the Han model

This devaluation of Tibetan culture and people by the Han schools and society led to cultural ambivalence and alienation among Tibetans who had been sent to ordinary schools for their education. As some of my interviewees commented, in a cultural sense these Tibetans could barely harmonize with their own ethnic group, particularly with the older generation, nor could they integrate with the mainstream Han – though perhaps in the future their own children would(!). Knowledge-wise, they could not specialize in Tibetan language and culture, or Han. They then come to be 'nothing' (*shenme ye bushi*), and only pain or tragedy remained.[25] They explained this to be the very reason why these Tibetans, after becoming parents, tended to send their own children to minority schools instead of following the example of their own parents and making sacrifices to send their children to 'advanced' Han schools. Some other parents also expressed their regret about their choice to send their children to ordinary schools because it resulted in introducing and widening a cultural and linguistic gap between generations. They therefore wanted to stay in their village of origin after retirement so as to nurture their grandchildren with Tibetan culture. Some parents also tried to arrange some family tutorials for their ordinary school children in Tibetan culture and language. But most such 'experiments' were ineffective, due to the difficulty of finding time outside their children's school study, which focused on college entrance examinations. In addition, Tibetan culture and language lessons could also stir up conflict between parents and their children. A common response on the part of the children was: 'now you are forcing me to study these, why did not you send me to a minority school in the first place?'

The dilemma facing the Tibetans opting for minority schools

Compared to the ordinary school, the average academic outcome for the students in Huangnan Minority Secondary School was limited, since it focused on preparing the students for exams in many 'useful' or 'advanced' subjects like Chinese, English or science, to which the students had little exposure in their previous rural and/or minority environments. At the same time, they were usually required or encouraged to study these subjects in Chinese, a language that was unfamiliar to them since the medium of instruction in their primary and junior secondary schools was Tibetan. In other words, their background and previous education did not equip them for dealing with Chinese language instruction in unfamiliar subjects. Following the *minkaomin* preferential policy of the state,[26] graduates from minority secondary schools usually entered local, mostly minority colleges or universities. The admission requirements for these institutions were usually lower than for regular universities. As a result, employers understandably preferred non-minority university or college graduates.

Ineffective study and the above-mentioned perception of the better quality of education in ordinary schools became the immediate dynamics which drove some of the minority students to dream of studying in ordinary schools, while simultaneously pushing others further away from the ordinary school education. This desire to study in ordinary schools was informed not just by a concern with education alone, but also by an eagerness to become more 'sociable' and 'advanced'. Because most of the students in Huangnan Minority Secondary School were from rural areas, had few social relations with the outside world, boarded at school and were viewed negatively by both local urban dwellers and their counterparts in Huangnan Secondary School, it was more difficult for them to socialize with off-campus society. All these reasons plus their language difficulty isolated them from both their far-away home community and the host community of their school.[27]

Attending minority schools reduced considerably both the competitiveness of Tibetan graduates in the job market and their opportunity to acquire a modern self-image. Under such circumstances, Tibetan students in the Minority School became increasingly devoted to the 'useful' subjects associated with advancement and socio-economic mobility, which were taught in Chinese. At the same time, that they needed to master Chinese and the unfamiliar subjects taught in Chinese meant that they must de-prioritize their own ethnic cultural studies. Furthermore, in minority schools the opportunity to study minority cultures was very limited – the only tailored course for ethnic minorities was minority language and literature, which according to the teachers of Tibetan language and literature was no more than a training in language and writing skills. Another difficulty was that the impracticalities of distance limited students' opportunities for home visits. These factors contributed to a fall in the standard of the Tibetan language among the students. Some Tibetan language teachers feared that this diminishing exposure of minority school students to Tibetan would lead to their alienation from their community, people and culture, which would eventually undermine the ethno-religious community as a whole.

This picture was quite different from that perceived by the parents who sent their children to minority schools. They claimed that their children had access to all the necessary knowledge and their own culture in minority schools. But the study of necessary 'useful' knowledge nevertheless resulted in ineffectiveness and the ethnic cultural content of the curriculum was reduced to the minimum. The only appeal of Huangnan Minority Secondary School, apart from practical reasons (lower fees, grant-in-aid, boarding, etc.), was that the majority of the school people were Tibetan. The reason 40 per cent of students in this school said they preferred the idea of staying in their own school and did not want to attend the ordinary school centred on the idea that they wanted to feel safe rather than be exposed to a competitive, uncertain and even humiliating environment. In my investigation, the only Tibetan student who had studied in minority schools, and then opted to attend the ordinary school for a better education, transferred back to the Minority School after the first semester. She listed the reasons as follows: I could not get used to the teaching methods they used there, and also wanted to strengthen my Tibetan and learn more about our ethnic culture. I can better settle down to study (*geng anxin de xuexi*) in an environment of my own ethnic compatriots.

At a superficial level, staying at Huangnan Minority Secondary School seems to be a voluntary decision on the part of the parents and students. Most Tibetan students at that school, however, felt they had no other choice. Likewise, few students from Huangnan Secondary School had actually transferred to Huangnan Minority Secondary School despite the large proportion of them who expressed their desire to do so. Both the students and the parents were very aware of how much they may lose for their future if they pursued education in a minority school. The Tibetans that I met in this ordinary school recognized the need to be absorbed into the mainstream in order to progress. They prided themselves on being more advanced than their counterparts in minority schools when speaking about the 'low quality' of the latter as seen earlier. In the meantime, they were also frustrated by their *de facto* exclusion from the Han circles that aroused their criticism of their

Han peer students. Concomitantly, this frustration partially contributes to the fact that I was told on some informal occasions that there was a much higher proportion of Tibetan children in the most prestigious primary ordinary school compared to two or three decades ago.[28] One parent explained that this was because Tibetans were 'no longer biased against learning the Han Chinese language' while another suggested that this happened under the pressure of the state policy.

Conclusion

In the process of making decisions about schooling, Tibetans in both ordinary and minority schools found themselves in a predicament. While they struggled against the perceived threat of being 'phased out' economically or culturally by working hard in school and emulating the Han model of 'advanced culture' and 'high quality', this seemed to devalue their own culture and to put them at risk of losing contact with it. They were therefore placed in a situation where they voluntarily pursued education but then found themselves involuntarily alienated from their own culture, and further, degraded as the owner of their culture.[29]

Tibetan parents, students and intellectuals responded by starting to think about what kind of education they needed. Some argued that transmitting Tibetan culture and language was not only a private responsibility, but also the obligation of public institutions like schools. For instance, some individuals started to appeal for Tibetan to be the medium of instruction at all levels in minority schools. Others advocated combining the advantage of monastery culture and rural culture with the school curriculum in order to preserve and develop the local culture. These efforts were even seen to develop in the direction in which different forms of non-government-organizations (NGOs) were introduced recently when I returned to my field site in 2006 and 2007 (see also Postscript). From all of this we can see how Tibetan elites were mobilizing their ethnic community capital to move the whole community to achieving social mobility in the wider society, which is classified by Zhou (2005) as the 'enclave' pattern of a positive and active form of social capital.

Yet, within the state system, it seemed unlikely that both the preservation of Tibetan culture and the education of Tibetan people for socio-economic mobility could ever be achieved. Factors from two sides contributed to this pessimism. First, on the side of schools and society, schools discouraged the desire for a Tibetan relevant curriculum in favour of the mainstream national culture. One of the typical remarks on this issue came from a top administrator who was also a history teacher in a mainstream school:

> [A student] is a secondary school student first, and then a minority student . . . Minority students should be equal with Han and other students, and cannot surpass the other students. The school treats all students from different ethnic backgrounds the same (*dui ge minzu xuesheng dou*

yishitongren) . . . [When the students are] in the school, they should hold back (*baoliu*) some of their ethnic or religious customs; otherwise it will bring about a negative effect (*buliang yingxiang*) in teaching and among their fellow students. As for the curriculum, we offer courses of ideology and history in order to educate students with the correct view towards ethnicity and religion. For example, in history lessons [we] teach [students] the tradition of upholding unification of the country . . . We are an ordinary school rather than a minority school, even though we also have minority students. But if we practised distinguishing features (*gao tedian*) for this reason, it would become purposeless for the state to run schools (*shiqu guojia banxue de zongzhi*).

Even if a school, particularly a minority school, was willing to equally incorporate Tibetan language, religion and history into the curriculum, this would not be enough to counter the potency of a national mainstream ideology that devalues Tibetan culture. Indeed, as one interviewee noted, 'the school is run by the state'.[30]

The other source of pessimism was the self-depreciation of the Tibetans themselves. The national agenda centred firmly on 'fitting' Tibetans into the mainstream and this had the effect of cultivating among Tibetans a 'self-loathing' or 'an internalized devaluation' of their culture and group (Young 1990: 165). The deep internalization of this mindset was exemplified by the ways in which Tibetans criticized their own group and culture. For instance, when one girl's parents invited some Tibetan monks to perform rituals to supplement the hospital treatment of an unwell family member, she asked uncomfortably: 'Isn't it enough that we just see a doctor?' One Tibetan teacher, who was very comfortable about his own incompetence in Tibetan, claimed that he could not accept the idea that people considered him to be a local Tibetan, because the Tibetans in this region 'lag behind other ethnic groups in both cultural quality and personal sociability'.

Through the dual process of being-made and self-making (Ong 1996), Tibetan culture and groups in Huangnan were clearly pushed to the periphery in opposition to the mainstream centre. Yet from this marginal position, Tibetans still had to face the question of where, what and how to study. In other words, they had to choose, or had no choice about what they needed to sacrifice in an attempt to 'catch up' – catch up intellectually, economically or culturally? This suggests the need for policies that could endow Tibetans and other minorities with full cultural membership in the larger society on their own terms.

5 The social disengagement of 'familiar strangers'

The Muslim case

Introduction

This chapter reveals the Muslim community's disengagement from state schools and the larger society, as a response to their ethnic identity as a people of 'familiar strangers' (Lipman 1997) in the wider Chinese Han cultural context. This alien identity received by Muslims from their wider society in general, and in this Tibetan-dominated region in particular, largely blocked their access to opportunities for social mobility and education. As a response, Muslims showed limited motivation, enthusiasm for and confidence in state education, which led to their poor school performance. This was grounded in their pessimistic outlook about their socio-economic status, and the prejudice and hostility they received from individuals as well as institutions. Therefore, education, the major way to achieve upward social mobility, became irrelevant to Muslims to a large extent.

This chapter first depicts briefly who are Muslims and who are Hui, and their educational setting and educational level. It then reveals how Muslim parents and students perceived their socio-economic status, evaluated the school curriculum from their ethnic point of view, and how this perception and evaluation resulted in Muslim students' resistance to or disengagement from the mainstream school. The conclusion to the chapter argues that the social disengagement of Muslims from mainstream society has reduced their desire and capability to participate in social and political life of the wider society. This disengagement is difficult to overcome if Muslims cannot see social systems delivering significant improvement with regard to the socio-cultural membership of their community.

Who are Muslims, who are Hui?

In Chapter 1 I highlighted the rationale of choosing Muslims on the borderlands between Qinghai and Gansu provinces as my research subject. It is necessary to say a few more words about Muslims and Hui in China. There are ten officially recognized ethnic minority groups committed to Islam in China, who can be basically divided into two blocs, those mainly residing in

Xinjiang (Kazak, Kirgiz, Tajik, Tatar, Uygur and Uzbek) and those across all China but especially in the Gansu-Qinghai-Ningxia (GQN) borderland areas (Bonan, Dongxiang, Hui and Salar). Unlike the former, who are indigenous to Xinjiang, the latter are mainly the descendants of local people and of Muslims who migrated to China from the Middle East or Central Asia between the seventh and fourteenth centuries largely for business reasons or in the wake of war. This difference helps foster different ethnic identifications among, for instance, Uygur and Hui, respectively the largest groups in the two blocs. Academically, Muslims in Xinjiang are labelled 'Turkic and Indo-European Muslim', while the Hui are labelled 'Chinese Muslim'. In this chapter, 'Muslim' refers to the GQN bloc. Binding these four different Muslim groups together is not only due to the fact that many of them speak Chinese, but also that they identify with one another. This is observable from their predominant pattern of marriage and social connections with each other, and their indifferent attitude towards some non-Muslims, who see all of them as Hui. And in fact, the four groups were under the same rubric of Hui, without clear awareness of their different ethnic identity from one another, before the CPC embarked upon the Ethnic Identification Project some 50 years ago, when the three small groups were officially distinguished from the Hui.[1]

From the history of relationships between Muslim Hui and Chinese and other regimes and society, we can in particular see why Lipman (1997) relates Muslims to 'familiar strangers' in China. One of the major features of the GQN Muslim communities lies in their diverse sects (*jiaopai*) within their Islamic system. It was partially the cause of some major conflicts between these GQN Muslim groups or between their subdivisions. In the meantime, these conflicts also complicated the relationships between these Muslim communities and the Qing rulers. This often meant serious conflicts between the rulers and the communities that ended up with the brutal repression of Muslims by the Qing as a response to their rebellions that shook the Qing regime.[2] This resulted in the Hui coming to be seen and treated as rebels, and hence the Qing regime lost its interest in guaranteeing their lives and faith (Songben 2003).

Under these circumstances, Hui survivors of elites from the Qing dynasty in the Republican era started to explore how to clear up Han biases (the Qing were not, of course, Han) and so safeguard their lives and freedom of religion. Furthermore, they reconciled their attempts to revive their religion and to make a contribution to the Chinese revolution. This reconciliation was promoted by and also strengthened their awareness that they were not able to overwhelm the Chinese, and so it did not make much sense to establish their own regime. As a consequence, they became co-operators with the Chinese Han, although the Nationalist Party, based on the view of making a single Chinese nation, supported the idea that this Muslim group were Han who believed in Islam (ibid.).

The Muslim community in the region[3]

My field site was Longwu Township, the seat of Huangnan Tibetan Autonomous Prefecture. As depicted in the previous chapter, Longwu consisted of two parts, the old town and the new town. In 2002–3, there were three primary and four secondary schools in the town. Among them, the First and Third Primary, and Prefecture Secondary were mainstream schools with Chinese as the medium of instruction; another boarding primary and the other three secondary schools adopted Tibetan as the medium of instruction.[4] Hence the three mainstreams were the schools for Muslims,[5] who were mainly Chinese speakers.

I disclosed in the previous chapter that the Muslims in Longwu Township arrived in the area in response to a call from the reincarnation of Buddha in Longwu Monastery. The call was made for business people from Muslim areas nearby at the end of the nineteenth century. This led to an emergence of the local market town, with Muslims as the main residents. After the prefectural government was established in Longwu in 1953, it quickly became apparent that the district where the old market town is located was too small for the rapidly growing seat of the prefectural government. Under these circumstances, a new town was built and developed to the west of the old town from 1954 onwards. Over the past five decades, most state-run businesses in the old town were gradually either closed down or moved to the new town. This led a number of mainly Han residents who were working in the state system to move from the old town to the new one. Meeting the requirements of these people for the education of their children, for whom it was hard to continue attending the First Primary in the old town, the Third Primary was established in the early 1970s in the new town.[6] The percentage of Muslim students in the First Primary thus rose compared to the Han population, which largely vacated it. This change eventually turned the Third Primary into the most prestigious school of its kind in the area, despite a shorter history than the First Primary, and this was cultivated by the government officials whose children were studying in the Third Primary.

This demographic move also meant that better-off customers (state employees) were drawn away to the new town. Gradually, a growing number of Muslim families had to close down their small stores or restaurants in the old town and open businesses in the new town. After this 'upward' mobility of residents from the old town, particularly in the past one or two decades, the traditionally market area came to mainly function as a 'self-contained' residential area of the Muslim community, which was characterized by a declining economy and with daily life based around the Mosque.[7] When I revisited the town in 2006 and 2007, the old town almost stayed in the same situation whilst the areas of the new town and Longwu Monastery was seen to be restored and expanded on a daily basis.

This demographic change also impacted on local secondary education.

Originally there were two mainstream secondary schools in the Longwu area, Tongren County Secondary in the old town with Muslims as the largest group, and Prefecture Secondary in the new town. After moving their businesses to the new town, some Muslim families also transferred their children to Prefecture Secondary. According to some of my informants, this mobility was also propelled by the priority policy of the government towards Prefecture Secondary through, for instance, selecting students with higher achievement for Prefecture Secondary (with the result that less able students went to County Secondary). This was apparently at odds with the government policy of 'attending the neighbourhood school'. As with the Third Primary, Prefecture Secondary was located in the new town and children of public servants went there to study.

Meanwhile, over the past ten or fifteen years or so, students in Prefecture Secondary kept moving out to the schools in Xining, the capital of Qinghai province, and the vicinities, to pursue a higher level of education. In other words, while County Secondary declined substantially in the past decade, Prefecture Secondary was also experiencing a certain decrease in student numbers. As a result, County Secondary was annexed to Prefecture Secondary in 2002.

The educational level of Muslims

One Muslim community and three Tibetan villages

The Chinese education system is divided into a compulsory stage (from primary to junior secondary, that lasts nine years (*jiunian yiwu jiaoyu*)) and a post-compulsory stage. Longwu Township administered all three Muslim administrative communities in the Longwu area, and several Tibetan villages surrounding Longwu Township. Among these Tibetan villages, those closest to Longwu Township tended to have a higher educational level than those further away. The data in Table 5.1 show the educational level of one Muslim community and the three closest Tibetan villages,[8] from which some trends can be observed.

- Traditionally Muslims in the Longwu area had a much lower illiteracy rate compared to Tibetans. The rate of the Muslims born before the 1970s was 24.70 per cent.[9] By contrast, the Tibetans in three villages had an illiteracy rate of 44.58 per cent on average.
- The illiteracy rate of Muslims did not reduce by as much as that of Tibetans over the past two decades (see D1 and D2). Even in absolute terms, among the Muslim population who were born after the 1970s, there were still eleven people who were illiterate. Amongst the Tibetans, the corresponding number was thirty for three villages, that is, ten for each on average. Amongst those born after the 1980s, the corresponding number for the Muslim community was three (2.17 per cent out of the

Table 5.1 Illiteracy rate and college students rate of Muslims in comparison to those of Tibetans

		A: TP	B: BA70	C: BA80	D1 (%)	D2 (%)	D3 (%)
M	PU	458	292	138			
	IR	12.01	3.77	2.17	−8.24	−1.60	−9.84
	CR	0.66	0.68	0	0.02	−0.68	−0.66
T1	PU	321	194	116			
	IR	15.26	0.52	0	−14.74	−0.52	−15.26
	CR	4.67	6.70	2.59	1.84	−4.11	−2.08
	PU	418	253	153			
T2	IR	23.44	5.93	0.65	−17.51	−5.28	−22.74
	CR	0.96	0.79	0	−0.17	−0.79	−0.96
	PU	518	320	187			
T3	IR	18.73	4.36	0.53	−14.37	−3.83	−18.20
	CR	0.39	0.63	0	0.24	−0.63	−0.39

Key
A: TP = Total population
B: BA70 = Born after 1970
C: BA80 = Born after 1980
CR = College students rate
D1 = Discrepancy A–B
D2 = Discrepancy B–C
D3 = Discrepancy A–C
IR = Illiteracy rate
M = Muslim community
PU = Population
T1, T2, T3 = Tibetan village 1, 2, 3

Source: Fieldwork 2003

cohort) and for the three Tibetan villages was two in total (0.59 per cent out of the cohort).

• At the other end of the spectrum, the rate of Muslim population at college level was the second lowest as a whole. Nevertheless, this rate was not significantly higher than the lowest rate of a Tibetan group (T3), whereas it was significantly lower than the highest rate possessed by another Tibetan group (T1). In other words, the Muslim community did not appear to be in an advanced position in comparison with three Tibetan villages at college level.

We can thus see that, both from a developmental perspective and in absolute terms, Muslims as a whole in the Longwu area lagged behind in education over the past one or two decades. This was particularly striking when taking into consideration the fact that the Muslims were urban dwellers, whereas the Tibetans were rural residents.

Parents of students in the mainstream school and the Tibetan minority school

Table 5.2 gives the illiteracy rate and average years of schooling of the parents of my respondents in both the mainstream school (MS) and a Tibetan minority school (TMS). The information here echoed the educational trend of the Muslim community.

Table 5.2 Illiteracy rate and years in school of Muslim parents in comparison to rate and years in school of parents from other ethnic backgrounds

	Illiteracy rate		Average schooling years	
	Father	*Mother*	*Father*	*Mother*
Tibetans in MS	0	0	12.36	10.55
Han and others in MS	2.56	5.13	10.74	9.38
Muslims in MS	13.33	43.33	7.10	3.97
Tibetans in TMS	19.51	43.90	6.41	3.59

Key
MS = mainstream school
TMS = Tibetan minority school

Sources: Fieldwork 2003

In MS, the parents of Tibetans and of students from other ethnic backgrounds constituted one end of the spectrum, characterized by lower illiteracy rates (0 and 3.85 per cent respectively regardless of difference caused by gender, the same hereafter) and longer schooling years (11.46 and 10.06). At the other end were Muslim parents with higher illiteracy rates (28.33 per cent) and shorter schooling years (5.54). As urban dwellers, the educational level of Muslim parents of children in MS was just slightly higher than that of Tibetan parents of children in TMS, the vast majority of whom were rural. Therefore, in the mainstream school, where the students were from the urban areas, Muslim students possessed the poorest educational capital. This echoed a widely reported lower educational level of Muslims in the GQN borderlands (see, for example, Liu 1997 and M. Ma 1999).

The school performance of Muslim students

There were no local official statistics available that set out the academic achievement of students along the lines of ethnicity. As Prefecture Secondary became the only choice for the Muslims in Longwu, Muslim students made up the second largest part of the student body (31.63 per cent) after the Han (34.79 per cent). The following three sets of data in Table 5.3 were collected in the mainstream secondary. The first set (EJ) was the outcome of the end-of-year examinations of junior third year students in 2002. The second (ES) was that of the senior first year students in 2002. The junior third year was the final year of compulsory education, while the senior first year was the first year of

Table 5.3 Outcome of examinations in the mainstream school in 2002

Exam	Score	In total	Han	Muslim	Tibetan	Others*
EJ	NE	180	70	78	17	15
	AS	318.83	342.95	288.65	337.65	330.28
	BA		34.29%	60.26%	41.18%	50%
ES	NE	96	38	25	10	23
	AS	320.78	336.49	283.20	284.95	362.74
	BA		50%	68%	90%	43.48%
EE	NE		120	51	19	–
	AS	316.40	321.19	301.86	325.16	–
	BA		50%	62.75%	47.37%	–

Key
AS = Average score
BA = Below total average score
EE = Outcome of the senior secondary entrance examinations of the students in Tongren County in 2002
EJ = Outcome of end-of-year examinations of the junior third year students in Huangnan Prefecture School in 2002–2003
ES = Outcome of end-of-year examinations of the senior first year students in Huangnan Prefecture School in 2002–2003
NE = Number of examinees

* 'Others' include students from other ethnic backgrounds as well as from mixed ethnic background such as Han-Tibetan, Tu-Tibetan, etc. This group is thus highly heterogeneous in terms of both ethnic identification and academic achievement. This category does not include students from a mixed background of different Muslim minority groups such as Hui-Salar, Hui-Bonan. In other words, all the Muslims show a significant homogeneity in ethno-religious identification and academic achievement, and therefore make up a single group.

Source: Fieldwork 2003

post-compulsory education. The third set (EE) was the outcome of the senior secondary entrance examinations of students in the Tongren area in 2002.[10]

Table 5.4 gives the ethnic population in the mainstream school in 2002–3 and in Tongren County in 2002. Some conclusions can be drawn from the data in Tables 5.3 and 5.4:

- As a whole, Muslim students performed poorly when compared to students from other ethnic backgrounds. This can be seen in Table 5.3.
- Although the percentage of the Muslim students in the ordinary class (class two) was only 1.5 times that in the key class (class one), while this discrepancy among the Tibetan students was four times, this did not necessarily lead to a better outcome for the Muslim students for the year as a whole (see ES in Table 5.3 and SF in Table 5.4).[11]
- In the senior secondary entrance examinations in 2002, the number of Han examinees was nearly 2.5 times that of Muslim examinees (see EE in Table 5.3). On the other hand, the Han population in 2002 was less than twice the Muslim population (see EP Table 5.4). This demonstrated the lower proportion of Muslim students entered for the examinations.[12]

Table 5.4 Ethnic population in the mainstream school in 2002–2003 and in Tongren County in 2002

	Total	Han (%)	Muslim (%)	Tibetan (%)	Others (%)
JT	195	70 (35.90)	78 (40)	17 (8.72)	30 (15.38)
Class One	49	21 (42.86)	19 (38.78)	4 (8.16)	5 (10.20)
Class Two	49	13 (26.53)	22 (44.90)	6 (12.24)	8 (16.33)
Class Three	48	18 (37.5)	23 (47.92)	2 (4.17)	5 (10.42)
Class Four	49	18 (38.78)	14 (28.57)	5 (10.20)	12 (24.49)
SF	96	38 (39.58)	25 (26.04)	10 (9.60)	23 (23.96)
Class One	48	21 (43.75)	10 (20.83)	2 (4.17)	15 (31.25)
Class Two	48	17 (35.42)	15 (31.25)	8 (16.67)	8 (16.67)
EP	77165	7723 (10.01)	4285 (5.55)	55602 (72.06)	9518 (12.38)

Key
EP = Ethnic population in Tongren County in 2002
JT = Ethnic background of the junior secondary third year students of the prefecture school in 2002–2003
SF = Ethnic background of the senior secondary first year students of the prefecture school in 2002–2003

Source: Fieldwork 2003

• The percentage of Muslim students in post-compulsory education was significantly reduced. By contrast, the other three groups turned out to have a higher percentage at the post-compulsory stage (see JT and SF in Table 5.4).

Therefore, in terms of school performance, Muslim students tended to have a lower record in academic achievement and fewer would continue to study at the post-compulsory stage. In addition, in an interview with a Muslim community leader, I was also told that there were over ten Muslim students who dropped out in this academic year, a dropout rate of about 7 or 8 per cent. This was a high figure compared to what I was told in interviews with schoolteachers, administrators or parents – that drop-outs were rare in the school.[13]

Pessimistic views of Muslim parents: a key force

An overview of Muslims and school education

As expected, no Muslim parents told me that it was useless to send children to school. Meanwhile, according to three Muslim parents, there were two common ideas regarding school education among them. One was that, historically speaking, Muslims did not particularly invest in school education, and such a neglect of school education meant that they lagged behind Han, and more recently (over the past one or two decades) also lagged behind Tibetans because of this continuing neglect. Second, there existed a disparity between cadres (*ganbu*) and ordinary people (*qunzhong*)[14] in the degree of enthusiasm for sending their children to school. While cadres tended to encourage their children to study hard in order to eventually go to university, what ordinary Muslim parents expected their children to do with education was confined to achieving two primary goals (also see Chapter 3): to receive some basic education in relation to literacy and numeracy in order to be able to deal with (mostly family-run) business and daily life; and to obtain a graduation certificate (*biyezheng*), an essential qualification for the labour market. In addition, I was also told that the school was used as a 'nursery' by many ordinary Muslims to keep their children from hanging around with dubious characters whom they would otherwise encounter if they were not sent to school.[15]

Nevertheless, Muslim parents also admitted that their children could or were expected to stop studying when mature enough to help the family in business or with earnings, or to prepare for marriage. This usually occurred when the children were fifteen years old or so, at the age when they just finished their studies at the junior secondary phase, that is, completed the nine years' compulsory education required by the state. Therefore, this age was regarded by (in particular 'ordinary') parents as a turning point in their children's life in many respects.

On the whole, the historical 'tradition' of neglecting school education among the Muslims did not seem to have significantly reduced. This lack of enthusiasm for school study of their children was reflected in the poverty of their response to my question as to whether or not it was useful to send children to school. Instead, Muslim parents from both cadre and ordinary backgrounds spent much more time speaking about the barriers they encountered in the larger society that were directly or indirectly associated with the school education of their children, and the resulting hopelessness.

Barriers from the larger society

There were three main outlets (*chulu*) for Muslim children that were envisaged by their parents: to study in the Mosque or Arab countries, with the aim of becoming a Mullah; to be engaged in family business or any other business outside the state system, that is, irregular jobs such as temporary waiters, shop assistants, or drivers; or to become a cadre working in a state work unit. Among the three choices, there was very limited demand for more Mullahs in mosques, and to go to Arab countries to study is not a viable alternative when they could not afford to send their children to study abroad. Last, but not insignificantly, the change towards a knowledge economy also made the idea of ending up in a Mosque much less desirable. Muslim parents did not consider that their children could learn the kind of useful knowledge, such as sciences or English, which would prepare them for an increasingly standardized labour market, both nationally and globally, in mosques.

As for engagement in non-state business, given the hardship of this kind of job and the sluggishness of the local economy, this did not appear to be a more attractive choice to them. Moreover, the locally dominant Tibetans, over the past decade, started to take over quite a number of businesses from Muslims after realizing how much they 'lost' economically by not engaging in commerce, a field that was traditionally dominated or 'occupied' by Muslims. One reason I deduced from what I was told by several different Tibetans was an informal campaign of boycotting the Muslim enterprises among the Tibetans. That is, wherever possible, Tibetans would definitely consume in the businesses run by Tibetans rather than by Muslims. A Muslim community leader also offered an explanation that Muslims would rather move to a Muslim-dominated area in the GQN borderlands so long as they had plenty of economic capacity to allow them to do so, because they felt oppressed by the dominant Tibetans and were living a tiring life in Longwu. The enterprises these Muslims used to run were also abandoned as they left the area. In 2006 in the main commercial streets of the new town, half of the enterprises were run by Tibetans, while only a few Tibetan but more Muslim enterprises could be found some ten years ago. In 2007 when I returned to my field site, I found that many buildings on the main commercial street had already been rebuilt in the Tibetan style, and the rest were following suit too. This had been encouraged by the local government, to enhance the local tourist economy of this Tibetan town. Nonetheless, it had an important impact on Tibetans who had a sense of being the dominant group of the region, to whom the prefecture presumably belonged.

The last outlet for Muslim graduates was to become a cadre. This, compared to the other two outlets, was even more difficult, though it may have been more attractive to those Muslims who felt strongly in need of a better socio-economic status. This had several different causes. First of all, this was a Tibetan autonomous region, and therefore had a Tibetan-priority policy. Among local government officials, Muslims were under-represented, particularly at the highest rank of the prefectural level (see Table 4.3). Because Tibetans were in the majority, it was also difficult for Muslim candidates to be elected to government positions.

This disproportionateness of Muslims among top cadres meant that the Muslim community as a whole lacked social capital in relation to public institutions. This directly affected the number of Muslims who were recruited by state work units as a cadre. The perception that it was difficult for Muslims to enter the state system was also informed by the under-representation of Muslims in top leadership positions in both the central and provincial governments.[16] Top leaders of the prefecture or province seemed indifferent to this situation. Another practical obstacle preventing some Muslims from becoming a cadre was: the state in effect discouraged public servants from going on a pilgrimage to Mecca by making it difficult for them to get a passport until they are over 50 years old, when they are unlikely to take the opportunity to stay on abroad.

Muslims who worked in state units also had less opportunity for promotion. I was told that this was because they did not like to have social intercourse (*yingchou*) with their Han or Tibetan colleagues, because they would have to smoke, drink, play mahjong or go to Karaoke, as their colleagues normally do. Being able to do these things was regarded as very important for a public servant. More than this, some Muslim cadres who wore their caps or veils were disgusted by some of their superiors or colleagues, who 'wanted everyone to look like Han', and 'they would not feel comfortable until they could not distinguish on the basis of their appearance those who are Muslim from those who are Han', said a female Muslim cadre. Under such pressure, some Muslims gave way to these unofficial requirements made by officials, though they then faced pressure from their family or community, as I was told by one couple. Those who persisted in practising their cultural customs would be 'kindly' reminded by their leaders from time to time that they had better not do so, or simply had their names removed from the list of any promotion or award opportunity, which was directly linked to their salary and cadre welfare benefits.

Some respondents also talked about the possibility of working in Han-dominated China proper. But in their mind this was even more difficult, if not impossible, because of a lack of the necessary cultural level or social circles for competing with Han there, and a likely gap in daily life that was caused by their religious customs. In comparison, in Huangnan, in spite of the dominance of Tibetans, there was still some historically formed space in business for Muslims, though this was also seen under threat today.

In this light, while tuition fees steadily went up, to send children to school did not become a more persuasive option.[17] This was not to say that there was not a reasonable number of Muslims who would have liked to provide their children with a school education. On an individual level, cadre parents insisted on the necessity of education as mentioned earlier; on a community level, Muslim elites realized the importance of encouraging their younger generations to receive a reasonable level of education to enhance the public profile and status of the community, which would in turn create the opportunities to promote their economic performance. Nevertheless, due to significant barriers ahead of them, a Muslim government official admitted that some Muslim parents (elites), while expressing their definite willingness to give their offspring a school education, and also encouraging other Muslim parents to do so, presented their personal uncertainty and confusion about whether or not to keep their children in schools or to what extent they were able to manage this. These barriers became more serious when Muslim parents were ordinary people, who did not have any relations with the state system.

All in all, Muslim parents generally felt marginalized in society, and particularly in recruitment to and promotion in state work units. This caused the limited social capital they originally had to reduce. It cast a seriously pessimistic shadow on their motivation to send their children to school, or even to a public sector. In turn, their social and political status kept dropping as their political and social awareness of participation became weaker, as a Muslim cadre commented. This would eventually foster in Muslims an idea that they should stay in a peripheral position to the centre of power, and that normal participation in public life should be seen as a bonus honoured by the government.[18]

Barriers from the school

The enthusiasm of Muslim families for sending children to school was also affected by the school curriculum. This was reflected in their dissatisfaction with the school culture and what was being taught in school, and also in their desire for a Muslim minority school.

In schools, Muslim-related practice, such as praying, wearing caps or veils, and religious holidays, was discouraged.[19] Concern with this among Muslim parents was common. As most of them put it, even if Muslim children were required to stay in school during the holidays such as Muharram, they could not really concentrate on studying. By contrast, if they were allowed to go home for the holiday, parents and children would be grateful, and in return they would support the school more actively. Nonetheless, Muslims, including Muslim teachers, were subjected to this form of ethnic penalty. A Muslim teacher told me that he once decided to put on his white cap because he wanted to influence his Muslim students positively by publicly offering a model of disciplining himself in this way. As an unexpected result, one of the Han deputy head-teachers, who trusted and respected this teacher, stopped speaking to him for a week.

The more serious concern was that the curriculum excluded Islamic knowledge. One community leader traced this back to 1958, when the Religious Reform had terminated the course of Islamic knowledge that the school offered students.[20] He insisted that introducing a course of Islamic knowledge, even if only for one or two hours a week, would be politically significant, because it would embody the equality policy of the state in the sense that this would promote the status of the Muslim community and their religion. This was in particular important in this Tibetan-dominated area where the government encouraged and promoted Tibetan culture (also see the previous chapter). Given the low socio-political status of Muslims in the region, it was not surprising that many of my informants held a similar view.

In terms of knowledge itself, most parents also expressed the importance for their children and for themselves of having the opportunity to be educated in Islamic knowledge. They would otherwise become 'false Hui' (*jia Hui*). In other words, what concerned many parents was the potential sinicization of their children, which was informed by the fact that some Muslim children and parents resisted Islamic knowledge due to an atheistic education in school, which 'has already been branded [into their mindset]', a cadre commented.[21] This tendency was undermining the basis of their community in the sense that they were worried that the Muslim, as an ethno-religious community, would eventually be silenced or sinicized.

A call for Muslim minority school(s)

With these worries in mind, Muslim parents wished for a Muslim minority school that provided students with Islamic content rather than one which merely offered a Halal canteen, as can be found nationwide (Sun 1997).[22] In their mind, establishing a minority school with a relevant curriculum for Muslims would enhance enrolment rates of Muslim students.[23] Furthermore, Muslim parents mentioned that across the whole country, there were few institutions where people could learn Arabic, and, if this was introduced into the curriculum of Muslim minority schools, it would benefit both the community and country rather than do harm to the state. In other words, the country would benefit through cultivating personnel specializing in Islamic knowledge and the Arabic language, which was appropriate for an increasing development of the relationship between China and the Arab countries.

A desire for a Muslim minority school also revealed a concern about a safe space for the well-being of their children in schooling. Muslims were generally perceived not to be interested in or good at schooling. According to some parents, since teachers held such views about Muslims, they would be very likely to stereotype Muslim students: 'Do you want to learn?' 'Isn't it true that [Muslim] girls will get married and boys will run a restaurant when they are 18 years old?' Even Muslim parents themselves also encountered such prejudice. When some teachers rejected views or suggestions about school education from Muslim parents, they would say: 'Why do you have so much to say? You have just got such a [poor] child!' It was even difficult for Muslim students with high academic achievement to avoid such a label from teachers: 'Yes, you are capable [of study], this is not easy for you [as a Muslim].' Another reason for Muslims to call for a minority school was driven by the severe problem of bullying of Muslim children, both in and out of schools (in particular from Tibetan children, also see below), which was likely to end up with their dropping out of school due to a lack of intervention from relevant official parties.

A call for a state-run Muslim minority school was reflected in the Muslim community's lack of confidence in the Islamic knowledge imparted in their community-based education. In their words, religious education offered by their community was neither systematic nor deep enough. Some parents even said that they preferred not to send their children to the Mosque to study because of a concern with sectarianism. In the same vein, they would also not send their children to study in Arab countries. Interestingly enough, both sets of parents who either emphasized religious education or put school education in the first place shared the view that the state should support and organize religious education for Muslims, since this would make the education of Muslim students formal and systematic, and would also avoid the clashes that may be caused by Muslims who were running religious education themselves. This inevitably reminds us of the Hui's compromise choice of co-operating with Han in the Republican era in seeking legitimization in the wider environment dominated by the politico-cultural mainstream Han.

Nevertheless, their arguments usually ended up in pessimism. For Muslim parents, it would be extremely difficult if not entirely impossible to establish such a school in Longwu for two reasons: this was a Tibetan-dominated region and so Muslims did not have voice; the Muslim population was not large enough (less than 4,500 in Tongren) for a Muslim minority school.

To sum up, on the one hand, it was hard for Muslim parents to see the benefits that accrued to them by sending their children to school, and this reduced their enthusiasm for doing so. At the same time, encountering symbolic or physical hostility from the national mainstream cultural group, the Han, or locally dominant group, the Tibetan, in the process of schooling or the larger society, also negatively affected the school performance of their children. On the other hand, they were well aware that their public profile and socio-economic status would be even lower and finally result in less opportunity for them to prosper if their offspring did not receive school education as Tibetans and Han were doing. Nonetheless, they felt confused about and hence struggled over how (and how far) to reconcile the two contested sides.

Students' struggle between different 'cultures'

Where to study

As indicated earlier, Muslim students on the whole had lower achievement than average. The most salient phenomenon relating to their school performance was a reluctant attitude to schooling that permeated them. This could even be the case among high academic achiever Muslim students. Two of the high achievers, when asked if they would like to consider studying in the Mosque instead of the state school, clearly said they would. Their explanation was that to study the Koran would probably not be as difficult or tiring as studying the school subjects. That is, cultural discontinuity made their study unattractive. Nonetheless, most Muslim students wanted to study in a state-run Muslim minority school when compared to either a mainstream school or the Mosque. For them, to study in a Mosque was not realistic because they would not be able to access 'useful' knowledge, which would equip them for the labour market and a reasonably good life in the future. On the other hand, compared to mainstream schools, in a Muslim minority school they could study both 'ordinary' knowledge – as they were doing in the mainstream school – and their ethnic and religious culture. In addition, to study and stay with their Muslim peers would also make the study more effective and school life more relaxing. This would also comfort their parents in terms of the curriculum and tuition fees, as one student told me: 'My parents are always complaining about high tuition. If there was a Muslim minority school (though asking for the same tuition), they would definitely support me. Because this is good for both ourselves and our ethnic group.'

However, one sixth of the respondents expressed a preference for studying in mainstream schools, because there would be more opportunities to study something different or more time to study useful knowledge, and to benefit their social life rather than to only stay with the Muslims, a conservative and narrow-minded community, in their words. These students did not explicitly deny the need to study Islamic culture, but said that they were already taught it at a very young age or they could teach themselves in the future. For the moment, 'to study [school] knowledge is the most important thing'.

On the whole, for students who would either like to stay in the mainstream school or prefer a minority school, the fundamental obstacle they faced in their study and life in the mainstream school was caused by a feeling of discomfort. This discomfort was constituted by pressure from their community and family, and their school and the larger society, and was reflected in their confusion about and struggle for where to locate themselves in society with regard to their school study, cultural identity and socio-economic aspiration. In other words, they always found that any attempt to integrate these contested facets into a coherent whole resulted in a tiring failure. A prosperous socio-economic future required a relatively high educational level. In attempting to achieve a good school performance, they confronted severe barriers caused by the prejudice and hostility towards the Islamic cultural tradition of their community.

Barriers from outside the school

Although the abolition of assigning jobs to graduates in 1996 may have affected the motivation of Muslims to study hard in order to enter a university or college, the job ceiling Muslim students faced was nevertheless a significant obstacle to sustaining their motivation to aim for high school performance. Two respondents complained to me that political leaders, from the president of the country to provincial governors or mayors, were non-Muslim. In this region it was particularly the case that there was a very limited chance for Muslim graduates to find a job in the state system, yet this was relatively easy for both Han and Tibetans. They considered that this was caused by the ethnic difference between Han, Tibetans and Muslims, 'that is to say, people tend to look down upon Hui'. The most direct factors that reduced the motivation of Muslim students in the mainstream school were those from family and school. Although many student informants thought that their parents were concerned about their study, few of them considered that their parents would be effectively helpful, because they themselves had a very limited 'cultural level'. At the same time, they felt that their parents kept putting pressure on them by requiring them to work harder or complaining that they worked or consumed too much in schooling but without benefiting the family.

Low perceptions of Muslim students

The school, where students spent most of their time, played the key role in shaping its students' attitude towards and performance in schooling. Why did Muslim students on the whole perform poorly in school? While other people gave a number of explanations, I heard little from Muslim students themselves. However, this did not necessarily mean that among Muslims, nobody shared the views of Han or other ethnic groups to some extent about their school performance. In fact, comments from non-Muslims were actually a key element shaping both non-Muslim perceptions and treatment of Muslims and Muslims' self-perceptions, and therefore significantly influenced their school performance. A Muslim girl (M) explained when I (I) asked about Muslim academic achievement:

> M: I feel that usually Muslims, anyway in my class, according to my observation, apart from X [a boy's name], all Hui students do not perform well. Normally it is Han students who perform well.
> I: Then why is this so?
> M: Everyone has said this that Hui are people born for trading business, but culture, that is studied by Han. All have said so.
> [. . .]
> I: So what do you yourself think about this?
> M: I think, Han and Hui both are the same. Mainly because we Hui students, after hearing these [comments], do not seem to have confidence [in study, thus we do not perform well].

This particularly related to secondary school students who, compared to their primary counterparts, were much more aware of their image that was generated from other's perceptions and comments. As Du Boi articulates, this produces a double consciousness in minorities' self-understanding that arises from always looking at oneself through the eyes of others (1969[1930]: 45, cited in Young 1990: 60). Therefore, almost without exception, the Muslim low achievers I interviewed told me that they performed very well or not badly at primary level, and did not know why they could not continue to do so after entering the secondary school.[24] What in particular drew my attention was the association of Han but not Hui with schooling (culture-studying), as in the quote from the Muslim girl above. On the part of Muslims, this had two implications: (1) if a Muslim performed well it would be regarded as 'acting Han'; (2) if a Muslim could not perform well it would be natural and so would not be a problem because she or he was not supposed to have the obligation or merit to do well.

Thus, Muslim students were perceived not to be able to perform well, and, as a fact, they largely performed poorly. This in turn cultivated a negative attitude or treatment among non-Muslim teachers or students of Muslim students. Although most of my respondents did not reckon that teachers treated students differently because of their ethnicity, but because of their school performance, some stories obviously reflected prejudice towards Muslims from teachers. When asked whether or not his teachers' view of him was different from his own, a boy who was the only Muslim student with high achievement in a class told me of a conversation which happened between him and in his mind the most understanding and open-minded teacher:

> I think there is some difference [between my view and that of my teacher of me]. When I transferred [from County Secondary to Prefecture Secondary] in the second semester, I was registering with teacher X ... She asked me which nationality I belong to, I said 'Salar' [Muslim], then she sighed. I was feeling [at that moment], this might be generated from the ethnic difference, [this] seems [to generate from] some sort of barrier [between different ethnic groups]. Yes, it is.

In my observation inside classrooms, one of the common scenes was that Muslim students were mainly concentrated at the back of classrooms. Some Muslim students told me that '[t]he teacher arranges seats in the order of academic achievement. Higher achievers are arranged to sit in front of the classroom and lower achievers are behind.' 'We Hui usually sit behind ... Han and Tibetans sit at the front ... because we do not perform well.' The main reason teachers made such an arrangement was that 'teachers do not want to take care of poor performers any more, and only hope that they would allow other students to study by disciplining themselves.' 'The teacher said to the poor performers: "since you do not want to study hard, please just discipline yourselves, be a good person, so that you can receive a certificate [when graduating]".'

In this low view of poor Muslim students, I was told that, these students were much less likely to be asked to answer questions in classrooms, and less likely to be believed when they gave a correct answer. Meanwhile, teachers tended to criticize them more often and cruelly (scolding or beating), and were more likely to ask them to send messages to their parents for a meeting with teachers, at which the students were complained about to their parents. This treatment aroused complaints, reactions or rebellion among the students. They believed that it would help them with their confidence, motivation and performance if they sat at the front and were asked to answer questions more often; they also did not agree that all the students sitting behind were poor or bad. Some more radical actions were always taken by a few 'brave' girls and many boys, ranging from making trouble in classrooms, playing truant to dropping out. This was why most official punishments I could find on the public notice board of the school had something to do with Muslim students. Sometimes there were Muslim students who were trying to make progress by behaving themselves, but who were still likely to be driven back to the 'bad group' by teachers' careless punishment based on prejudice. A girl told me such a story about one of her fellow male students:

He is unlucky. He is recently trying to change himself, and making an effort to behave properly, but was asked again by the teacher to send his parents a message for a meeting with the teacher. He thus once again did not come to school recently. [Question: why did the teacher ask him to send the message to his parents if he was trying to change himself?] Before he started to try to behave properly, he was always playing, chatting, eating [in the classroom] with those [Muslim] boys, and was discovered by the teacher. But he was making an effort after these things, but he was still asked to go to see the teacher for what happened in the past, and was asked to send a message to his parents.

Cultural customs and the curriculum

According to my Muslim student respondents, religious practices of Muslims were also informally monitored by the school. Muslim boys were usually discouraged from wearing their religious caps (no Muslim girl was found in a headscarf. Also see below). Teachers would ask them not to bring their Islamic things (*zongjiao de dongxi*) to school, or would say that they did not look like a (serious) student in a Muslim cap, or would simply scold them for making trouble (*shiduo*). One boy described what he encountered on registration day when he came to the school in his Muslim cap:

> When I went to the school for registration, I was wearing a cap, and then it seemed that one of the teachers [after seeing me in the cap] said [to other teachers]: 'the [Muslim] students from the street district [the old town] usually do not study hard. Do not register him!' Then I took off the cap, and was registered . . . [Question: so why did you put on your cap when going to register?] At that time I did not know [that it was discouraged to put on Muslim caps in Prefecture Secondary School]. When I was studying in the First Primary, because the school is in the old town, I had been used to wearing [the cap]. All [Muslim] students wore [their caps there], so I also did the same. I did not know [about caps] when I came to the new town . . . However now nobody wears his cap, there are 23 Muslim students in my class [about half of the class], and none of us wears it.[25]

Another clash that occurred between Muslim students and the school was about Muslim holidays. Muslim students said it was unfair that, whilst the school had holidays for the Han and Tibetan new years,[26] it required them to go to school at Muharram. As Muslim parents also tended to support children asking for leave in Muharram, students then took a more open action against the school policy when told by teachers that they must stay in school. They collectively played truant that day. As expected, they were punished by their teachers when coming back to school. They were asked either to stand outside the classroom for several hours, or to write a self-criticism letter.[27]

Muslim students also felt uncomfortable about the curriculum. They complained that there was little content concerning their ethnic religion or culture. Many of them were also not satisfied with the content because it was too simple and boring for the students who were interested in their ethnic culture, and false and a waste of time for the students who were not keen on religious issues. Due to the irrelevance of the curriculum to their culture, some of them would show enthusiasm, motivation and confidence when coming across such content in textbooks, as a Muslim girl recounted to me:

> Last semester we touched upon the Koran in a history lesson . . . I usually do not understand history well, when talking about that [the Koran], because I myself knew it, and then it seemed that I suddenly became confident, that kind of feeling.'

At the same time, some other students would rather invest most of their time and energy in science subjects, as these subjects had much less to do with ideology of the politico-cultural mainstream.[28] One of the students, when explaining the reason why the school curriculum incorporated little Islamic culture, said:

> The School does not promote these [Muslim culture and customs]. Teachers, they do not have this habit . . . They consider that these things of ours, for instance, Buddhism of Tibetans or Islam of Muslims, all are superstitious. Although [they know] they are religious beliefs, [they think] they are still a bit superstitious.

The linguistic issue also precluded many Muslim children from full engagement in school study. They claimed that the local dialect they spoke was *gaidao hua* ('street language'), which was different from *putong hua* or Mandarin Chinese. In the school all the students were required to speak the standard language, especially in class and with teachers. Students described their embarrassment when they had to answer questions in Mandarin in class, because some of them (especially among boys) felt this was acting Han, while others felt unconfident and worried about the possibility of being teased by fellow students or criticized by teachers. This was particularly difficult for those who previously were students in County Secondary, where they were allowed to answer questions in class or communicate with teachers in the local dialect, because a large proportion of students as well as teachers in the school were Muslim.

The relationships between Muslim and other students

Another important reason why Muslim students felt uncomfortable in school was the relationships between themselves and the students from other ethnic backgrounds. Most of them told me that they tended to make friends with their Muslim fellows rather than Han or others. Some thought that some Han students were too self-confident about their assumed high quality. They therefore would not like to make contact with Muslim students, although some Muslims said that they were willing to make friends with Han if Han accepted them. However the reality seemed quite the reverse. One student told me: 'Sometimes Han students spend time with Han students, and do not do so with us. Sometimes they do not want to tell us when we are asking them questions ... When playing football, we are divided into two teams, one is Han and the other is Muslim ... [I think] sometimes they look down upon us.'

This lack of understanding of Muslim students among non-Muslims could also be seen in some verbal insults, or, more seriously, in bullying towards them, particularly that from Tibetans to Muslim boys. The bullying usually would develop into physical conflicts between Tibetan and Muslim boys, both within and outside school. A girl said this was because that

> [S]ome Muslims are very pious about their religion, and very honest. Some Tibetans or Han do not like these customs of Muslims ... They are only used to their own lifestyle, belief or religion, and thus do not like ours, just [because they] are not accustomed [to ours].

Conversely, Muslim students preferred to spend time with their Muslim fellow students. Some explained that they had stayed with their Muslim fellow students from a very young age, because their families lived in the same district, the old town, and also because they shared the same language and religious customs. All these factors would make it easier for them to understand each other and more congenial for them to spend time together. I pointed out that the 'language' they spoke was one of many Chinese dialects, which was also spoken by the local Han. They still emphasized that all the Han people, both teachers and students, tended to adopt standard Mandarin Chinese over the local dialect wherever this was possible. Given the high social status of Mandarin in China and the Han's overly high perception of themselves, Han's preference for Mandarin Chinese is not difficult to understand. Hence, Muslim children concluded that Mandarin was the language of Han and the local dialect was that of Muslims. They then told me that they usually spoke the local dialect because 'anyway we spend time with Muslims ... and usually do not speak Mandarin. If [we] speak to strangers or teachers, [we] will definitely use Mandarin.'[29]

The influence of modern cultural values

Muslim students were also inevitably influenced by modern cultural values. They were keen on music, painting, sports, fashion, Internet, studying abroad, individual development,[30] or even shouting, smoking, drinking or sex, though to a lesser extent. Correspondingly, they revealed less interest and knowledge in their religion-centred ethnic culture, while all parents, as I was told, were concerned that their children should study Islamic culture, although some of them did not feel it was so important or urgent to familiarize their children with the ethno-religious culture. These choices in modern cultural values, as students put it, were always discouraged or strongly criticized and opposed by either their parents or teachers. However, Muslim children usually did not share the same opinion as either their teachers or parents. They said that they were in the twenty-first century, they liked being pretty or fashionable. They rebuked their parents as feudalistic, their teachers as overly strict controllers.

This was particularly so in the case of Muslim girls. Beside the viewpoints mentioned above shared by both girls and boys, when talking about family or community life, some girls were unhappy with the lower level of attention their parents paid to them than that to their male siblings regarding schooling, because their parents considered that boys would have a more promising future. They also complained about stricter control over their freedom by their parents, who required that they stay at home, and help the family with housework. Girls also did not feel contented about the very limited opportunity for them to become a Mullah in mosques, which they considered to have reduced their career chances, although few of them showed interest in attending religious activities in the Mosque. 'Girls over thirteen years old are not allowed to appear in Mosques unless they are in a headscarf.' They all attributed their absence from the Mosque to Muslim customs.[31]

In school, in sharp contrast to Muslim boys' attitude towards caps, none of them showed willingness to wear a headscarf. While they laid the blame on school discouragement of ethno-religious practice, they also explicitly expressed their disgust at wearing headscarves. Two girls explained:

> [I]f you are a Muslim, you come to school in a headscarf . . . everyone will . . . tease you by saying 'disgusting, in a headscarf!' . . . So nobody [wears it], all of us care for face (*ai mianzi*) . . . Muslims themselves will also certainly say so: 'What? Wearing a headscarf in the school, in the classroom? Are you mad?'
>
> [It is] normal [for boys to wear] Muslim caps. [Fellow students] will not laugh at this . . . That is just a cap. If girls come along in headscarves, they will definitely laugh . . . When a girl is wearing a headscarf, what [we] will feel about it is: oh, a nanny is coming in!

Some girls admitted that this keenness on modern values particularly among girls distracted them from school study, which they did not know why, or just said that 'the study in the school is too much and too boring'. However, when speaking about the reason why they did not perform well in schools, a girl told me: 'Anyway people all are saying this, that after entering secondary school, boys perform well but all the girls have slowed down, fallen behind.'[32]

By and large, Muslim students felt uncomfortable in the school system.

This was because they were perceived to be poor academic performers and trouble-makers, who were believed to tend to flout the regulations and rules of the school. The school also restricted them in religious practice and in the use of dialect, and provided little Islamic knowledge in the curriculum. The discrimination or bullying from students of other ethnic groups made their stay in the school unsafe, which further exacerbated their negative situation in the school. In the meantime, a disagreement between Muslim children and their elders upon whether or not pursue modern cultural values distanced them from both their parents and teachers.[33]

Conclusion

Muslims living in this region lack social connections to access public institutions. This was the preferred choice in terms of career for its power to guarantee a high socio-economic status and financially secured life. Meanwhile, they also possessed limited cultural capital that would enable their children to compete meritocratically with their fellow students. Therefore, education became quite irrelevant to Muslims, and this led to their inertia in education. Community forces were an initial dynamic that did not make school education a priority while this was the absolute priority nationwide. The immediate experiences of Muslim students in the mainstream school exacerbated their negative attitude towards schooling. The fundamental cause of the marginalized status of Muslims was that Muslims were still regarded as 'difficult-to-transform' 'other' both institutionally and individually in many ways,[34] although they settled in China, particularly in the northwest, for several centuries. One of my cadre respondents evaluated the situation Chinese Muslims were in as follows:

> [For Chinese], Islam is an imported religion, [Muslims] are not a Chinese nation (*zhonghua minzu*) . . . [The state] speaks 'we descendants of Yan and Huang emperors (*Yan Huang zisun*) . . .'[35] which implies that you [Muslims] are not *Yan Huang zisun*. It reveals a tone of discrimination . . . [The state] has brought [some preferential] policies to you, provided your children with education, and let you have plenty to eat and drink, but still regards you as outsiders (*haishi ba ni dang wairen*).[36]

Muslims were barely identified by the larger society as Chinese people unless they sinicized themselves, involuntarily or voluntarily, like many of their compatriots in 'China proper', by substantially hiding or removing their ethno-religious markers.[37] This oppression was more apparent among those who strongly encouraged their children to study hard by emulating the Han model, and correspondingly did not regard it as appropriate to attend school with a recognizable Muslim appearance. A parent, when explaining why he did not encourage his child to attend school in his Muslim cap, said:

> This is a multi-ethnic area, Han and Tibetans do not consider this [Islam] is important, and meanwhile if they saw a Muslim wearing a white cap, they would have some discomfort in mind due to the symbolic difference emerging through capping between Muslims and non-Muslims; furthermore, after class, fellow students would be driven by their curiosity to ask about the meaning of capping, about holidays, customs of Islam, and then about Muslims themselves, many questions. So if Muslim students did not wear caps, other children would not have such ideas as who is Han, who is Tibetan or who is Muslim. There would not exist such a kind of clash.

The outsider status of GQN Muslims suggested in these two comments leads me to think about the different experiences Hui had from the ones Tibetans had in history. While Tibet tried to become independent throughout the first half of the twentieth century and therefore had serious tension with the Chinese government (see, for example, Goldstein 1998), Muslim Hui had experienced a co-operation with the Chinese after evaluating their situation in China. Nonetheless, this did not bring to them a welcoming societal culture. In my research region, Muslims faced oppression from both Han and Tibetans in spite of the fact that they had advantages as Chinese speakers and urban dwellers to (re-)establish a mutually constructive and beneficial relationship with the mainstream. Quite the reverse, they experienced ghettoization in the Chinese Han context of the larger society in general, and in this Tibetan-dominated region in particular. This placed them in a position of 'the minority of minorities', as a Muslim cadre articulated.

Formulated by external constraints that were especially associated with stigmatization, this ghettoization was also a result of the Muslim community's lack of strength within itself perhaps partially on account of its limited community size that collides with its supposedly internal sectarianism. Hence the ghettoization was seen to undermine the capability and enthusiasm of the Muslim community to organize and mobilize their social capital to benefit their community residents and assist social mobility, as a Muslim Bonan student commented to me as such: 'Hui are not of one mind.' This was in particular the case in some Muslims' fear of sectarianism among the community so that they would rather hand over their cultural rights to the state in their call for a Muslim school. This was also true when their elites tried to encourage their community to stress education, an effort which failed to prevent the continuing neglect of education among the Muslim masses as a result of the continuing exclusion of their culture from public institutions. It thus made up a different pattern of community forces in comparison with the Tibetan group who actively mobilized its members in political, economic and educational arenas as indicated in this chapter and Chapters 4 and 6. This distinction between the two communities forms two types of socio-ethnic capital that are elaborated by Zhou (2005): the enclave (constructive) pattern and the ghetto (destructive) pattern.

Similarly marginalized by the cultural mainstream, while Tibetans could be said to be excluded socio-culturally from within the local political system in Huangnan, Muslims were seen to be excluded entirely from public institutions (even though there were some Muslim cadres in the government) that deprived of their link to the centre of power. On the other hand, this Muslim status was also maintained by 'the damaging form' (Loury, Modood and Teles 2005: 13) of its community social capital. This is why Muslims in Huangnan were seen to increasingly become passive citizens and perfunctory students. Therefore, Muslims still had to struggle over whether or not it was worth engaging themselves more in state education by investing significant energy and finance in it if they could not see social systems delivering significant improvement with regard to the socio-cultural recognition, accommodation, and assistance of their community. Conversely, an improved policy would be able to bridge or narrow the gap between diverse cultural values that placed Muslim parents and children in the position of confusion about and disengagement from our societal culture.

6   Conclusion

Social systems

On the part of the government and public, as Kymlicka (2001: 20) articulates, standardized public education is seen as essential for citizens to have equal opportunity to access formal institutions, that is, to participate in a common societal culture. This is thought to enable citizens to have equal opportunity to work in the modern economy. On the other hand, to participate in a common societal culture is also regarded as essential for fostering a strong sense of common identity and membership amongst citizens, and at the same time to facilitate understanding between the people under the same government. Kymlicka thus concludes that 'promoting integration into a common societal culture has been seen as essential to social equality and political cohesion in modern states' (ibid.: 20–1). However, government policies and mainstream discourses are much more interested in *outcomes* than *processes* in which citizens are cultivated. This has masked hidden agendas disadvantaging ethnic minorities as culturally different peoples. I have uncovered these hidden agendas in the previous three chapters by scrutinizing processes of education and social mobility of ethnic minorities to emphasize the responsibilities that social systems should take in the process.

Government policies with regard to education largely exclude ethnic minority cultures from schools where the mainstream culture is institutionalized. This exclusion in the first place means there is little space for ethnic minority cultures appearing in the curriculum. Furthermore, the limited content involving minority cultures is likely to be politicized or tokenized as discussed in Chapters 3, 4 and 5. The politicization of minority cultures is in particular associated with the religious issue that is taken as a backward and extremist force (supposedly) hindering its disciples from modernization, and cultivating disloyal citizens for the state. The tokenization of minority cultures is evidenced in the way that minority cultures are superficially treated as colourful and so exotic, or historical, which serve as entertaining subjects, on the margins of public and private mainstream life. The absence of minority cultures from the curriculum, or the politicization and tokenization of them has resulted in precluding minority cultures of integrity from institutionalization.

This has sequentially prevented minority cultures from flourishing as living cultures, and in fact, has facilitated their decline.

Put simply, the policies towards minority cultures are driven by the pursuits of economic development or modernization of the state and ethnic unity and state stability. They are also embedded in age-old Chinese culturalism that has been strengthened by the more recently sinicized concept of social evolution, as discussed in Chapter 3. These discourses all tend to place the minority population in a position of anti-modernization, anti-unity or anti-progress in the larger society, which has presumably led to their 'low quality' in schooling or the workforce as illustrated in Chapters 3, 4 and 5. Therefore the aspect in need of fundamental change in the progress of the minority population is their modes of thinking, according to the government and public as illustrated in Chapter 3. The ideas of social equality, political cohesion and culturalism together have led Chinese public policy to appear to be similar to the idea of *laïcité* in French public policy (Favell 2001: 74–9) as briefly mentioned in Chapter 3.

Like the latter, Chinese policy allows religious freedom under the precondition that religious practice should recognize the principles of public political order. In other words, particularistic interests in and practices of one's own culture is structured or 'disciplined' through a state political engagement in the form of public associations in that the interests and practices would impair the liberty of others if an official sanction is not in place. As a result, the political structure imposes its priority over cultural interests when there is a conflict (Favell 2001: 74–9). Under this principle, the Chinese government has established national associations for several officially recognized religions (Buddhism, Islam, Daoism, Catholicism and Protestantism). All religious organizations need to register with the government to have lawful status (ZFS 2000). The explanation for this is that the government regards religion at one level as a personal affair, but also as a social phenomenon and entity, for the reason that religion draws the attention of society, and so gets involved with other entities and society as a whole. Religion therefore becomes a social or public affair that produces a variety of connections, actions and activities that are associated with social or public interests (ZFS 2000: 22–3). This policy has illustrated what Aihwa Ong called the 'pastoral' role the Chinese state plays in transforming backward (or disloyal) citizens into modern (and loyal) citizens, in spite of the different form this pastoralism has taken, due to the differential historical contexts (Murphy and Fong 2006).

This pastoral public policy towards minority cultures in general and their religions in particular has left a gap between the formal level of laws and constitutions and the informal level of public discourse and attitudes (Kymlicka 2001: 58) as discussed in Chapter 3. This is to say that public discourse, including the government discourse (such as the claim of descent from the Yan and Huang emperors; see Chapter 5), has not shown sufficient respect for diversity in spite of the fact that at the level of legal formalities it guarantees freedom of, for instance, religious belief. In other words, when the

Party-state guarantees citizens freedom of religion, the societal culture that the Chinese nation-state has offered to its citizens tends to exert control over a large number of other aspects except for a standard language, such as religion, recreation and economy. Among these, religion is a key factor that is under strict control throughout the history of the People's Republic of China (PRC), particularly after the Religious Reform in the late 1950s. Therefore, the societal culture is not a thin one that only centres on a shared language (Kymlicka 2001: 18), but rather, a thick one as can be seen from the exclusion of Muslim and Tibetan cultures illustrated in Chapters 3, 4 and 5. In a word, the gap between legal formalities and public discourse essentially lies in the ambivalence and ambiguity of Chinese political philosophy. This philosophy provides citizens with cultural rights in law on the one hand, and on the other hand keeps sanctioning citizens' exercise of these rights for the state agenda of nation-building and modernization, and so still holds 'the same old pastoral relationship' between the government and the masses as Murphy (2006: 17) points out. In this light, it is undesirable for the government to promote more societal cultures corresponding to different ethnic (or otherwise) cultures at the risk of undermining *the* societal culture based on the ethnic majority culture.[1]

Community forces and their consequences

State policy and public discourse, as discussed in Chapters 2, 3, 4 and 5, did not lead the CPC or the mainstream to full respect for minority customs or religious faiths. In the meantime, the idea of respect largely stays at the level of legal formalities, which conceals the real inequality between the Han and the minority population. This inequality is especially reflected in minorities lacking the cultural and social capital that enables them to meritocratically compete for schooling and to equally access resources, ideas and information from formal institutions so as to achieve upward social mobility. This inequality is revealed in three patterns of ethnic minorities' attainments in, interpretations of and responses to social systems as a result of their varied experiences of cultural exclusion, namely, *desperation, identity construction,* and *disengagement.* Firstly, some minorities *desperately* seek opportunities for social mobility and economic prosperity at any cost, including at the cost of their ethnic languages and cultures. This is evidenced in the case of a large number of rural Tibetans who are struggling at the bottom line of the living standard as shown in Chapter 4. In their opinions, as long as their children can study in better schools and find a state job or any other better job, it does not matter that the children would lose their community language or culture, as one old rural couple certainly confirmed.

By contrast, their elite counterparts who have a secure socio-economic status and life are keen to actively engage in the issue of *ethnic identity* that is backed by promotion of their culture – the latter is decreasing rapidly though, largely as a by-product of their achievement in social mobility. In this respect, elites and masses share little consensus on whether or not ethnic minority cultures are worth preserving and ought to be allowed to flourish whilst both are equally seeking empowerment. For the elites, without a valued and institutionalized culture, the value of its people can always be in danger in that its people have to pay a higher price in achieving prosperity in both schools and the wider society, and meanwhile risk (further) stigmatization of their symbolic image coupled by the rapid decline of their culture. For the masses, survival is the top priority so that their ethnic culture can be sacrificed for a presumably promising future – a future (hopefully) characterized with a material well-being. Nonetheless, this material attainment is likely to uproot them from their culture, as has occurred to their elite counterparts. Furthermore, this is also likely to make elites lack legitimacy when attempting to represent or speak for their ethnic community. As a consequence, socio-economic achievement has not led to an elimination of cultural identity claims as the Party-state expected, and in the meantime cultural diversity is under threat in the process of achieving social mobility.

In this light, minority communities have been caught in a dilemma through which they are demanded to absorb the behaviour, values and goals of the mainstream. This means that they accept and adopt an alien identity. In the meantime, although they make an effort to participate in the mainstream, they are actually also being reminded by both others and themselves of their identity, that is, of their negatively marked difference. This dilemma is irresolvable (Young 1990: 165).[2] Facing this dilemma, minorities can also opt for the third way in which they disengage from public institutions. This usually leads them to become perfunctory students in schools and passive citizens in society even though they are encouraged by the government to prosper or may be in fact better off economically, as the Muslim case I discussed in Chapter 5 demonstrates. Muslims supposedly benefit from their relatively close connections with the mainstream Han in geographical distribution and language use (Chinese), yet they are in reality more likely to be socio-culturally excluded from the larger society and, relatedly, be disadvantaged in schooling. On the other hand, the economic prosperity of Muslims owes little to their educational achievement, but rather to their 'habitus' of doing business in history. Nor does it lead them to being positive towards social systems. This is contrary to the government and academic assumptions that education plays the key role in socio-economic prosperity, and that poor minority educational performance is largely a result of poverty in economy or intelligence as can be seen in Chapters 3 and 5.

In the end, different community forces fostered two distinctive type of community social capital: the enclave (constructive) and the ghetto (destructive), as can be seen in Chapters 1, 4, 5, and the Postscript. The former type was largely seen among the Tibetan community that encouraged its members to act collectively in its attempt of gaining a larger stake whilst the latter type pervaded the Muslim community, where social capital was very limited and in fact was damaged from both within and without the community. The two types are closely associated with the different socio-political statuses the two communities had in both the larger and local society, which helped shape their internal attributes that in turn were intertwined with the former. It may be also related to their geographic and social distributions, which were discernible from each other, and their language. Whereas Tibetans were predominantly in the West and concentrated in rural areas, Muslims were dispersed in differential social strata and across the country, in spite of the fact that GQN borderlands were home to a large number of 'traditional' Muslims. In the meantime, Muslims are largely Chinese speakers while Tibetans are speakers of Tibetan. All of this might make it relatively easy to draw a line between the Han and the Tibetan communities and so to create an imagined community for the Tibetans. This probably did not occur to Muslims to the same extent. As a consequence, mobilization among Tibetans and Muslims appeared to be different in terms of its scale, constructiveness, and persistence. This is in particular manifest in recent development of education promoted by NGOs as shown in the Postscript.

Furthermore, the policy that disadvantages ethnic minorities has also complicated interethnic relations negatively. As argued in Chapters 4 and 5, Tibetans benefit from a larger number of state preferential policies and have a higher profile in the public domain compared to Muslims. However, politically, Tibetans still occupy second place compared to the Han due to their large absence from positions in the top CPC leadership, and culturally they are also marginalized as depicted in Chapters 3, 4 and 5. This has led them to oppress and ostracize Muslims below them in their autonomous region in attempts to gain more economic and political capital as part of their strategy to empower themselves against the Han domination. This political strategy is realized by them mobilizing their vertical social capital – which also means that they are mobilizing their bonding social capital as political elites. However, this strategy cannot lead them to gain mutual recognition from the cultural-politically dominant Han group in spite of their 'success' in oppressing Muslims.

Indeed, when Tibetans exercise their strategy against the Han domination, they also risk rousing clashes with the Han, which usually ends up with their 'defeat' whilst strengthening the Han consciousness of holding power against increasingly powerful Tibetans. That is to say, Tibetans always face the top-down monitoring from Han government officials at provincial or national levels. In this light, many Muslims, as Chinese speakers, attempt to justify their socio-economic and linguistic intimacy and so identify themselves with the Han in hope of some sort of coalition with the latter against the Tibetans.[3] Nonetheless, this goal is difficult to achieve. The Muslims possess limited vertical social capital on the one hand, and on the other hand are perceived by the Han as more alien as depicted in Chapters 3 and 5. And in fact, the ghettoized residential pattern of the Muslims (see Chapter 5) has forged (particularly) for Muslims at grassroots level, rejection, resentment towards or conflict with both the Han and Tibetans. Under these circumstances, interethnic relations are always a top political concern for government officials.

Economic development, political cohesion and cultural difference

In short, as a result of the lack of fully inclusive membership of minorities in terms of cultural rights in the larger society, minorities tend to appeal to identity and difference or even secession, or maintain a 'passive obedience to the law, and reluctant acceptance of the status quo' (Kymlicka and Norman 2000: 11). This is because for those who either emulate the Han model or opt for a minority environment in education or the wider society, to claim the importance of their ethnic culture is to attempt to construct strategies through drawing on 'many tacit assumptions from the existing culture' so as to shape a repertoire or 'tool kit' (Swidler 1986: 278). These strategies are expected to help reduce inequality or injustice between their 'unsettled' social position and the 'settled' position of the dominant group.[4] Moreover, the feeling of disempowerment can lead some minority groups to oppress those in more vulnerable positions where inequality is not only embodied in the relationships between the majority and minorities, but also between different minority communities. This tendency to minority disengagement from or resistance to the mainstream and ethnic disunity cannot be overcome even if minorities are encouraged to prosper or are better off economically. In other words, one cannot equate equality with economic well-being so as to ignore cultural rights or counter-pose these rights to survival or development rights (*shengcun quan, fazhan quan*), i.e. economic prosperity, in achieving the latter.

Indeed, equality has long been economically orientated as argued in Chapter 1. Nonetheless, it has been realized that different forms of inequality spring eternal. These forms of inequality are not only generated from class or economic difference, but the difference of ethnicity, race, gender, religious belief and language. Therefore, in seeking new equality, the idea should transform from equality as sameness to equality as difference (Modood 2001: 563). Equality as sameness is an embodiment of redistribution backed by rules of law while equality as difference is an appeal to recognition of cultural difference politically in the light of the importance of a culture for its people to be able to have a meaningful life (see also Kymlicka 1995 and Parekh 2000). This is to say that different groups should be treated positively but differently in accordance with their differences in ethnicity, religion, gender or sexual orientation. It would otherwise block 'the opportunity to exercise capacities in socially defined and recognized ways', which leaves minorities with 'uselessness, boredom, and lack of self-respect' (Young 1990: 54, 55). Hence, the idea of redistribution cannot displace or dissociate from that of recognition, and in fact redistribution always has 'an implicit or explicit cultural agenda' (Parekh 2000: 2).

Furthermore, an economically orientated agenda on the part of the Party-state is very likely – though this is partly – to attempt to distract public attention away from a hard-to-resolve tension between the Party-state ideology and minority ethnic cultures, which are run largely counter-ideologically or counter-scientifically, in the CPC's mind. However, as Kymlicka (2001: 84) rightly points out, based on his case studies in the West, 'the accommodation of ethnocultural diversity will remain a powerful source of conflict . . . even when all of these other goods are in place', namely, democratization, economic prosperity and personal tolerance. This is in the end about the way in which the state sensibly handles the package of (the majority based) nation building (national identity) and minority rights so as to move to the resolution of conflicts between the two.

Conversely, to recognize cultural difference in the public sphere does not *necessarily* conflict, but can be compatible with the state's agenda of turning supposedly 'disloyal' or 'troublesome' minorities into 'good citizens' or responsible citizens. In other words, minorities will be more likely to possess qualities encouraged by the state like public reasonableness, mutual respect, tolerance, active participation and responsibility (Kymlicka 2001).[5] This is to say; to become responsible citizens in the first place, people need to have a secure sense of belonging and then engagement. In order to achieve this goal, the first step is that social systems culturally free minorities from a position of being marginalized, oppressed or devalued by guaranteeing them minority cultural rights. This is because, as Levy suggests, 'symbolic recognition of the worth, status, or existence of various groups within the larger state community' is more important than others in the sense that this recognition will 'directly affect the well-being and self-respect of citizens of minority cultures, as well as their enthusiasm to participate in the political life of the larger state' (Levy 1997. Cited in Kymlicka and Norman 2000: 25, 29).

In this light, encouragement or promotion of the civic virtues of ethnic minority citizens is largely determined by a full recognition of their different cultures in state policy and by the public alike. This policy and public climate will then encourage ethnic minorities, as either individual or group members, to cultivate a sense of belonging both to their own ethnic community and the larger society or state. As a result, this will remove barriers preventing ethnic minority members from being fully engaged in public life and institutions with their own cultural heritage. In the educational arena, this policy will allow for a school culture for equality of educational opportunity, one that is responsive to ethnic minority cultures in both school life and curriculum, and 'is intended to assure that children will be rewarded, both in school and afterwards in the work place, according to their merit' (Feinberg 1996).[6] Without this responsive policy and attitude towards minority cultures, it is difficult to say that the government policy is built up on the principle of equality.

The new cultural landscape

Thus, culture matters, and cannot be displaced by or dissociated from either economic development or political cohesion. The findings offer a new direction that policy should take for the project of nation building and modernization of the state and minority rights in China. They first call for the redress of state policy that has excluded or politicized minority cultures while carrying out unequal treatments of different ethnic minority communities. This policy has been proved to be counter-productive for ethnic unity or cohesion and so for state stability. Furthermore, a call for a policy that promotes the cultural inclusion of ethnic minorities requires a re-examination of the assumption that it is inevitable that cultural rights will be ignored, or counter-posed to survival or development rights, in order to achieve the latter. Here the important balance that needs to be addressed is that between political, economic and cultural well-being.

Political citizenship and economic development are undoubtedly desirable to ethnic minorities.[7] However, even if ethnic minorities enjoy both economic well-being and political rights as formally equal members of the larger society, it will not foster in them an enthusiastic commitment to and a sense of moral and emotional identification with the nation-state where there is a limited place for their culture.[8] That is to say, without recognition, accommodation and cherishment of minority cultures, that is, without minority feeling of its cultural ethos and equal opportunity of self-expression, ethnic minorities will still feel that they are outsiders that do not quite belong to the larger society even if they are entitled to all the formal rights of citizenship. This is how my Muslim subjects feel about Chinese society, and why my Tibetan respondents struggle in between their own and the Han communities.

Nonetheless, the pursuit of an inclusive policy also necessitates a removal of the cultural superiority of the Han majority that is ingrained in the Han mindset both historically and at present, which can be seen throughout Chapters 2, 3, 4 and 5. This culturalism has underlain the hidden biases of rules and procedures in public institutions, which have caused inequality of treatment in significant areas of life such as employment, education and public services (Parekh 2000). This culturalism has in fact been a shifting discursive repertoire that has chronologically gone through the cultural contexts labelled as agrarianism, Confucian-based literariness and morality, science, democracy, and economic development in Chinese history. Concomitantly, minority cultures have been interpreted by this culturalism into nomadicism and militarism (so primitivism and barbarianism), feudalism and religiousness (so conservatism and self-enclosure), extremism, and sluggishness of economy.[9]

Under these circumstances, a new cultural landscape is needed that aims to ensure citizens equal opportunities to acquire the capacities and skills required to prosper in society; one that is inclusive of different ethnic cultures. To achieve this goal, it is necessary to create a common culture that emerges from a dialogue between equal citizens, what Parekh calls 'interculturally created and multiculturally constituted culture' (Parekh 2000: 221). Contents of this common culture should be broadly but not universally agreed by its citizens, and remain open to dispute. Furthermore, the dialogue should be carried out in both private and public realms (ibid.) in which citizens of different ethnic groups can equally be in dialogue with each other as well as with the state.[10]

Moreover, it is also the state's responsibility to protect its culturally diverse citizens from the side-effects of globalization that has been posing a threat to many, in particular, non-Western cultures, instead of pushing domestic minority cultures to a more peripheral position as a passive and so destructive response (largely one-way accommodation) to Western dominated globalization.[11] In this globalizing era, receiving countries of new industries and systems of management are required to create the cultural precondition, that is, to move towards a culture of 'international business civilization' (Hoogvelt 2001: 148. Also see Parekh 2000). This has been changing networks of social interaction, and creating new social norms globally, as well as reconfiguring domestic social structure with regard to, for example, employment, education and human rights. As a result, a new hierarchy of the world order has taken shape (Hoogvelt 2001). Playing in between domestic policies and those towards the international community, the state is being tested as to whether it can share its destiny with its citizens. This would mean it needs to transform both itself and its citizens to the resulting cultural hybridity, whilst reducing potential damages to its majority-based national culture in general and keeping damage to its diverse minority cultures in particular, to a minimum. Therefore, the central question that has emerged from my findings and should be addressed urgently by China in making up a united multiethnic country (*tongyi de duominzu guojia*) is: how does the sovereign reconstruct society with respect to such sensitive issues as the (re)definition of national identity, historical memory of culture, sense of citizenship, and the pursuit of a shared sense of economic well-being?

Postscript
Promoting education by NGOs?

This book has discussed the cultural exclusion of ethnic minorities in the state educational system, placing particular stress on the role that the state should play in the improvement of minority cultural participation in education. Nevertheless, with the coming to the fore of neo-liberalism as the state philosophy for development, so the devolution of (particularly) obligations down to the civil level was increased (though it is arguable whether there is such a thing as Chinese civil society). This neo-liberal governmentality thus left room for exploring more forms of education for ethnic minorities. As a result, schools or classes sponsored by domestic or international NGOs were established to promote community development in Tongren County and Qinghai Province. This mirrored a nationwide trend.

New educational programmes

In 2006 when I was conducting the follow-up fieldwork in Tongren County, my attention largely drawn to several education or education-related projects in Tongren and Xining (the capital of Qinghai) that were sponsored by NGOs. These projects had an important impact on local people, in particular Tibetans, in terms of alternative educational paradigms and opportunities. What follows is a sketch of these projects and an evaluation of the latest developments of education in the region, which is a reflection of and against the backdrop of globalization.

Two special classes in Tongren County Minority School were sponsored by the New York-based Trace Foundation between 2002 and 2005 to provide talented students from rural areas with special educational opportunities.[1] This initiative emphasized the study of language and the sciences, as well as intensive preparation for university entrance. It stressed in particular the teaching of sciences in Tibetan, so as to enhance students' performance in these 'cutting-edge' subjects. According to the foreign teacher in English of the two classes, the aim of setting up the two classes was to help Tibetan children to enter mainstream Chinese universities, rather than to attend minority institutes as they used to do. This supposedly would enhance their opportunities and competitiveness in the labour market. Nonetheless, according to an official of the Foundation, of 76 students, 58 went to minority institutes after sitting college entrance examinations in 2005. Moreover, most students were majoring in Tibetan-related subjects, as I was told by a teacher of these students.

Gedhun Choephel School in Tongren was founded by a French woman in 2001 and sponsored by a Monaco-based foundation. It consisted of primary and junior secondary parts of compulsory education. Students were mainly from the local rural area. The medium of instruction was Tibetan. English was emphasized due to the Western background of the school. Its graduates went to one of the secondary minority schools in Longwu Township to pursue senior secondary education. From 2005 onwards, students did not need to pay tuition fees, in accordance with a new law providing free education for pupils at the compulsory stage. Students boarded at school and their living expenses were covered by the Monaco foundation and the local government. Students had motivation for study, and in fact performed well in general, and in Tibetan and English in particular.

English Training Programme (ETP) was affiliated to Qinghai Normal University (*Qinghai Shifan Daxue*) in Xining and consisted of three levels: a preparation class (the equivalent of the senior secondary level), *dazhuan* (the equivalent of polytechnics), and the BA that commenced in September 2007. It was the first time that Tibetans of the five Tibetan regions, able to speak and write Tibetan, were brought together to major in English, and to learn practical skills in rural development and cultural preservation.[2] This programme produced some of the best students in English in Qinghai. This was due to the high motivation and the quality of these students, the quality of instruction their foreign teachers provided, and the amount of time that was dedicated to English learning. Students in the preparation classes had approximately 30 hours of instruction a week including 12–14 hours of English plus courses in the Tibetan language, the Chinese language, and other subjects.

In addition to learning English, students were also encouraged to become involved in small-scale grassroots sustainable development projects for their local communities. With assistance from foreign teachers, students successfully applied for and acquired funding. Once granted, students used funds to implement projects to build village schools, repair and provide village school equipment, provide solar cookers to rural households, construct water projects, and so on. In the process, these students learned how to write credible proposals, monitor and manage project finances, and write reports. These projects had very impressive effects on the local community, which in turn convinced students that learning English was more than an abstract mastery of odd sounds and grammar patterns, but something that could benefit their local communities.

Interested students were also encouraged to become involved with cultural preservation efforts with assistance from foreign experts. This included the collection of folklore in audio and video formats, transcription of the material in Tibetan using the International Phonetic Alphabet, and translation into English.

After graduation, most ETP students taught English in the countryside. A few also worked for some international NGOs. In addition, in recognition of the need for further English training, the United Board provided funds for sending some graduates abroad for further study. When these young Tibetans returned, they would become local Tibetan teachers of English that would replace the need for foreign English teachers, making the English training project truly sustainable. As a matter of fact, there has already been the first wave of ETP students who returned from abroad in the autumn 2007, and became teachers of English in local colleges.

Rebgong Cultural Centre was established in June 2004 in Tongren by a few local Tibetan monks with financial support from their US-based relatives and kin. It operated around two major projects: a library of mainly Tibetan collections that primarily served school people and monks, and a foundation that sponsored Tibetan children, especially girls and orphans, to receive education. In addition, it also ran summer and winter schools of English training, a monthly seminar series on Tibetan studies in 2006,[3] workshops and so forth.

As with the Trace Foundation, the Foundation of the Cultural Centre started to entrust Tongren County Minority Secondary School to teach two classes of 80 Tibetan children each year from 2005 onwards when the students of the two classes sponsored by Trace graduated. Students were selected with its entrance examinations from around 200 candidates. 'The criteria are exclusively merit-based', as I was told by the manager. According to the manager, the medium of instruction was Tibetan for Tibetan literature and language, Chinese for Chinese literature and language, with other subjects being taught in either Chinese or Tibetan, dependent upon the teacher's language. All the sponsored students were rural. However, I was told, they had quite a good command of Chinese that allowed them to study in colleges or universities without serious barriers when the medium of instruction was mainly Chinese. Among college students the Centre sponsored, the majority studied in minority institutes in Xining, Chengdu (the capital city of Sichuan Province), Lanzhou (the capital city of Gansu Province) and some prefectures in Qinghai. According to the manager, the most popular subjects with students were English, computer science and Tibetan.

In the meantime, emulating the model in TAR where Tibetan students were sent by the local government to inland China to pursue an education of better quality, the Huangnan Prefecture Government embarked upon a similar programme from 2002 onwards.[4] Nevertheless, I was told by a government official that this provision did not turn out to be as effective as expected. This was for several reasons. First, the selection of students was not by merit, nor was it confined to students from impoverished families which the programme initially targeted. Second, many Tibetan children were not well prepared with a good command of Chinese, which prevented them from fully understanding of lectures. Furthermore, the lack of discipline from parents and their 'own' teachers of Huangnan led students to indulge in material comfort rather than study. The same informant admitted that he was not in the position of telling parents the truth when parents blindly trusted in the quality of education in inland schools, nor could he do so at the risk of undermining his official career. This was in particular embarrassing when the Tibetan community was seen to actively and effectively work on diverse educational projects to promote its community development with resources obtained from abroad.

All of these projects targeted Tibetans, and so Muslims in the region still lacked support. This was true even though the wealthiest Muslim millionaire (*shoufu*) in the area (who was also a member of the local People's Congress) sponsored classes in Islamic culture and the Arabic language organized by the Mosque, and also sponsored Muslim children to study in schools. Put differently, although his action influenced individuals, it was unlikely to lead to significant impact either on the Muslim community or on the wider society. This was perhaps because even if there was a Muslim community organization that would like to sponsor their children to study, there was no Muslim minority school in the region to host their children. Furthermore, no (international) NGOs showed interest in engaging in the education of Muslims in Tongren that merely had a small population. As a consequence, this individual action had little effect upon helping establish constructive social capital both within the community and in relation to the larger society, especially to state agencies of the centre of power.

Discussion

The majority of Tibetan students in these programmes supported by NGOs had impressive motivation for study and in fact achieved highly. Nonetheless, their excellent performance did not improve their participation in mainstream society or mainstream universities as documented above. For instance, few of these Tibetan college (ETP) graduates found a job in a public sector, and at the same time, only a small number of these Tibetan school students managed to enter a mainstream university. One reason was the relatively narrow range of subjects that Tibetan graduates studied: English, Tibetan and management of projects, though few projects attempted to help students in scientific subjects such as the one sponsored by the Trace Foundation (yet, without effective outcomes as stated earlier).[5] This could neither bring them into socio-politically significant public institutions,[6] nor find them a sustainable job that required skills and knowledge in science or technology. Their stress on English over Chinese was partially informed by their negative assessment of possible opportunities to find a state job because of their somehow less fluent Chinese – Tibetan was usually not included in civil service examinations. Meanwhile, this was also caused by their lack of social connections with the socio-cultural mainstream (most of these Tibetan students were from rural areas). On the other hand, there were a limited number of graduates in Qinghai who were fluent in English and so these Tibetan children could in theory stand ahead of the vast majority of graduates to capture some scarce opportunities with their English skills. As a consequence, for example, most graduates of ETP became teachers in English in rural areas. A few worked for international NGOs or went abroad to pursue further education mainly in social sciences. This latter opportunity was predominantly dependent upon their foreign teachers who had contact with NGOs or information about development projects carried out in foreign countries.

Another source inhibiting Tibetans from engaging in public institutions stemmed from their high interest in 'advanced' foreign countries. Being educated in English and western management culture were the cultural preconditions of participating in international business (see Chapter 6 and Hoogvelt 2001: 148). In this light, a Western scholar expressed her optimism to me about these Tibetans who were said to be trained to manage and consume Tibetan culture rather than to follow their traditional way to preserve their culture that was without explicit direction and skills. Nevertheless, this learning experience created among Tibetans an illusion that took what they were studying as advanced human knowledge. This illusion led them to an idea that they could leap into the most advanced stage of human development without experiencing the less advanced 'Chinese stage'. According to an ETP student, her fellow students would usually rather work as an occasional translator or tourist guide than become a cadre in a public institution, in spite of the fact that the latter job would enable them to have a financially secure life and a stable socio-economic status. They thought they would deal with foreigners in their future career anyway, and so to master Chinese or find a job in a public institution was not particularly in their interest.[7] In fact, many of them hoped very much to be able eventually to go abroad to study, though this rarely occurred (only about 5 per cent were sent abroad, according to some ETP students and teachers).

This interest in 'advanced' foreign cultures was associated with the idea that Tibetans had a closer affinity with foreign countries than with China, as argued in Chapter 4. This idea even led some to think that the Tibetan language is pronounced in a similar way to the English language, which was said to enable Tibetans to achieve highly in learning English.[8] In the same vein, these Tibetan children believed that they were equipped with the kind of first-world cultural capital – which not only referred to their English skills, but was also associated with the international management culture that they acquired, or with their ability to teach English using the Western pedagogy and ideas. As an ETP student said to me, for an (ordinary or minority) school in China that needed to recruit teachers, these graduates were overqualified. In comparison, they were not very keen to learn Chinese, partly because of the poor teaching methods their Chinese teachers used, partly due to less encouragement from their projects. For example, ETP did not include Chinese but Tibetan, English and mathematics in its *dazhuan* entrance examinations, as I learnt from ETP teachers.

As a result, most of these Tibetan children were seen to remain in a peculiar situation in which they, with their excellent English language skills, gained some kind of privilege and perhaps more potential opportunities in comparison with the vast majority alongside them, of whom many were privileged Han. On the other hand, they were detached from the centre of power within the Chinese context where public institutions (using Chinese as the working language) were located, and so remain at the margins of society. Therefore, when these would-be Tibetan elites became quite localized through effectively helping with their community development (in the case of ETP, for instance), they at the same time also faced being uprooted from their Han dominated larger local context of China. Hence, the crucial issue that concerned me was whether all of this would lead to a further segregation of the Tibetan community from the Han and other communities (Muslims, for example) as a result of new cleavages created between these potentially elite Tibetans and other ethnic communities or the state when a growing number of NGOs became involved with the education of Tibetans in the area.

In the meantime, the lack of support for the education of Muslims from the government and NGOs in the region exacerbated Muslims' enthusiasm towards social systems and so widened the gap between Muslims and other ethnic groups. In fact, many Muslim families moved to Xining as a response to the ways in which they were treated in Tongren. In their mind, Xining at least could provide their children with a better education and also had a far larger Muslim community in which they hoped to enjoy cultural well-being and to pursue a meaningful life.

Therefore, whilst Muslims were still staying in a similar disadvantaged (if not worse) situation, Tibetans were dragged away by a more 'advanced' and yet 'alien' force which distanced these largely grassroots-based but potentially elite Tibetans. In the meantime, it is also apparent that the local government's initiative of sending Tibetan children to inland mainstream schools proved counterproductively suffocating, rather than realizing their potential. The primary reason why these 'preferential' initiatives did not work along the lines of what the Party-state very much expected still lies in its (intentionally or otherwise) exclusion of minority cultures in maintaining its own legitimacy, which did not foster a sense of belonging to mainstream society among either Tibetans or Muslims. Equally important, minority communities in general, and the Tibetan community in particular, have shaped their new framework of development particularly in the light of neo-liberalism, which dichotomizes advanced countries, such as the USA and UK, from the backwardness of China, a discourse exactly and ironically promoted by the politico-cultural mainstream of China in relation to its peripheral groups (also see Chapter 3).

Reflecting upon these recent developments regarding minority education in Tongren and Qinghai, which were seen to be cultivating a high-flying grassroots generation of the Tibetan community whereas breeding new disjunctures between different ethnic communities, and between minority communities and mainstream society, it became even more urgent for the central and local governments to consider an inclusive policy as discussed in Chapter 6. Such a policy would build up an inclusive cultural environment in which minority communities would fit as a sense of belonging to the larger society among them was forged. This would in consequence allow for creating a trustworthy and constructive relationship between the state and grassroots minority communities as well as between different ethnic groups. Otherwise, even with excellent English and other skills (so that they were not regarded as intellectually inferior by themselves or many others), or economic prosperity, it is still likely that minority students and communities would be deprived of the opportunity to exercise their capacities.

Appendices

Appendix 1

History timeline

Dates	Dynasty
ca. 2000–1500 BC	Xia
1700–1027 BC	Shang
770–221 BC	Eastern Zhou
	770–476 BC Spring and Autumn period
	475–221 BC Warring States period
221–207 BC	Qin
206 BC–AD 9	Western Han
AD 9–24	Xin (Wang Mang interregnum)
AD 25–220	Eastern Han
AD 220–280	Three Kingdoms
	220–265 Wei
	221–263 Shu
	229–280 Wu
AD 265–316	Western Jin
AD 317–420	Eastern Jin
AD 420–588	Southern and Northern Dynasties
	Southern Dynasties (420–588)
	420–478 Song
	479–501 Qi
	502–556 Liang
	557–588 Chen
	Northern Dynasties (386–588)
	386–533 Northern Wei
	534–549 Eastern Wei
	535–557 Western Wei
	550–577 Northern Qi
	557–588 Northern Zhou
AD 581–617	Sui
AD 618–907	Tang
AD 907–960	Five Dynasties
	907–923 Later Liang
	923–936 Later Tang
	936–946 Later Jin
	947–950 Later Han
	951–960 Later Zhou
AD 907–979	Ten Kingdoms
AD 960–1276	Song
	960–1127 Northern Song
	1127–1276 Southern Song
AD 916–1125	Liao
AD 1038–1227	Western Xia
AD 1115–1234	Jin
AD 1279–1368	Yuan

(Continued overleaf)

Dates	Dynasty
AD 1368–1644	Ming
AD 1644–1911	Qing
AD 1911–1949	Republic China (in mainland China)
AD 1949–	People's Republic of China

Appendix 2
Fieldwork

My fieldwork in 2003 lasted four months, from February to June, in Longwu Township (Longwu *Zhen*), the seat of Huangnan Tibetan Autonomous Prefecture, Qinghai Province. It consisted of classroom observation, questionnaires and interviews, as well as informal conversations. The follow-up fieldwork in 2006 and 2007 lasted one month respectively in August, and comprised interviews and informal conversations.

In 2003, I observed the final year of compulsory education (the third year in junior secondary) and the first year of the post-compulsory education (the first year in senior secondary) in the mainstream school. This is a transitional point through which one can tell if a student (and/or her/his family) expects to finally move on to tertiary education, which reflects different aspirations among parents and/or students towards their children's future. I observed one class in each grade for four days. In addition, I also attended a physics lesson in the Tibetan minority school.

I distributed ninety-four questionnaires in total to students from Han and ethnic minority groups in the two classes, and received back eighty-one. Of these respondents, thirty-six were Han, thirty-one were Muslim, twelve were Tibetan, and two were from other minorities. The questionnaires aimed to collect personal information to help in selecting samples for interviews at a later stage. I distributed a further forty-eight questionnaires in the Tibetan minority school where forty-four questionnaires were returned. These questionnaires contained an extra set of questions excluded from the questionnaires for the ordinary school respondents. This was primarily to compensate for the lack of time to interview these students (and their parents). The majority of these families were scattered widely in difficult-to-reach rural areas. The extra questions were simplified ones that I used in interviews with the Tibetan students in the mainstream school.

The essential goal that I aimed to achieve through interviewing was to listen to different ethnic voices on such issues as state education, school performance and perceptions of both others and self while at the same time verifying some figures or facts against government or public accounts. I conducted fifty-one semi-structured interviews in person with students from the mainstream school. This included nineteen Han students (ten girls), nineteen

Muslim students (twelve girls), eleven Tibetan students (five girls) and two students from other ethnic groups. All interviews were conducted in the flat of a retired teacher in the mainstream school where I had lived throughout my fieldwork. Most interviews lasted around thirty to forty minutes and were recorded with a Sony Walkman with permission from the interviewees. With their consent, most interviews were carried out with two students at a time, and usually they were from the same ethnic group.

I further conducted fifteen semi-structured or in-depth interviews with Tibetan and Muslim parents from different socio-economic backgrounds, including government officials, public servants, manual workers, self-employed people, farmers and community leaders. This type of interview aimed to explore what Ogbu calls community forces, and the ways community forces are formed and the potential impact they have on minority students. Interviews were conducted in schools, offices, urban dwellings or farmhouses. Most interviews lasted one to two hours and were recorded with the Walkman or pencil and paper, according to the informants' individual preferences. In interviewing some rural Tibetan parents who had difficulties in understanding Chinese, I invited the retired teacher I was living with to be my interpreter, who speaks the Tu language (his mother tongue), Chinese and Tibetan fluently.

I then conducted ten semi-structured interviews with schoolteachers or school administrators mainly from the mainstream school and a few from the minority school. All interviews were recorded with the Walkman or pencil and paper, as with the parents. This part of the work aimed to examine the ways social systems works at a micro level by probing school policy – the hidden curriculum or the mainstream group's perceptions and treatments of minority communities and students. This part of the data was analysed in conjunction with the data collected from Han Chinese students from the mainstream school.

In 2006 and 2007, in Tongren, Xining, Chengdu, and via email, I interviewed more than ten ETP students and had an informal conversation with some other ETP students. I visited the Rebgong Cultural Centre and interviewed the manager. I also visited Gedhun Choephel School and interviewed two teachers. In addition, I interviewed two government officials. One worked in the local bureau of education, and the other worked in the office of family planning. I also had opportunities to meet some foreign teachers teaching English in local schools and a couple of western scholars conducting field research in Tongren. In Xining, I obtained information from its foreign and Tibetan officials about the two classes in Tongren County Minority School sponsored by the Trace Foundation. I was also invited by an ETP foreign teacher to observe an English lesson in his class and then interviewed him. In addition, I had a long conversation with a Tibetan teacher of ETP over a meal. Through the ETP people I met in Qinghai, I visited a few more ETP graduates and their employer in Chengdu, where interviews with them were conducted. Interviews conducted in these two periods of fieldwork were all semi-structured or in-depth, and recorded with pen and paper or a follow-up note.

Appendix 3
The questionnaire for the mainstream school[1]

My name is Lin Yi, a PhD student in the Department of Sociology at the University of Bristol, England. I need to collect some data and information on ethnicity and education in Northwest China for my thesis, and hope to have your assistance in this case. Below is a questionnaire of your personal information, could you please complete it? Your information may only be used in my research, hence I will not let any third party in any form know about it, and your real name will not appear in my research wherever you are cited. Thanks for your cooperation! (If there is no enough space, could you write your answer(s) on reverse side with the number of question(s)?)

1. Your name:
2. Your gender:
3. The date you were born:
4. The place you were born (family village, county and province):
5. The place your family is from (if different from 4.):
6. The grade you are in:
7. Do you take any responsibilities for your classmates (subject representative, group head, classmonitor or a member of the Class Committee):
8. Are you a member of the Communist Youth League of China:
9. Are you transferred from another school? If so, where and when:
10. Have you ever been rewarded (*jiangli*) or punished (*chufen*) in the school:
11. The nationality group you belong to:
12. The group your father belongs to:
13. The group your mother belongs to:
14. Your first language(s)/dialect(s) or the language(s)/dialect(s) you use at home:
15. Any other language(s)/dialect(s) you can speak (quite) fluently:
16. How many years did your father attend school (from primary school onward)?

1 This is to be conducted in order to select student samples, and will not be formally conducted again in individual interviews.

17. How many years did your mother attend school (from primary school onward)?[2]
18. Your father's occupation:
19. Is he retired or laid-off (*xiagang*)?
20. Your mother's occupation:
21. Is she retired or laid-off?
22. Do you have any brothers or sisters?
23. Have they been to school?
24. If so, how long?
25. What are your brothers/sisters doing if they are not in schools?
26. And where?
27. Generally speaking, your academic achievement (grade) in your class is: high, upper intermediate, average, lower intermediate, low:
28. Your attendance rate:[3]
29. Are you boarding in the school? Who pays for your boarding fees?
30. If you are not boarding, how do you get to the school (walking, cycling, etc.)?
31. How much is the tuition fee per semester and who pays?
32. Are there any other fees (books and exercise books, computing or miscellaneous fees):
33. Do you sometimes assist in your family's work or business or do some work somewhere else to supplement your family's income?
34. I will interview some of you individually at your spare time, in March or April. The interview will be lasting 30 to 40 minutes, on ethnicity and education. Our conversation will be recorded by me. This interview is confidential and anonymous, i.e., I will not let any third party in any form know about our conversation, and your real name will not appear in my research wherever you are cited. If you would like to accept an interview and your parents also approve it, could you leave your contact information below? You do not need to do it otherwise.[4]
35. Have your parents approved:
36. Your telephone no.:
37. Your email address:
38. Your family address:
39. Time you prefer to have an interview:
40. Place you prefer to have an interview (must be quiet enough and with least interruption):
    1) school 2) your place 3) my place 4) any other places (please specify).

2 Students are to be asked to obtain the information for questions 16 and 17 in consultation with their parents.
3 The data in questions 27 and 28 will also be collected through teachers.
4 Questionnaires were given to students on a Friday and collected on the next Monday so that students could consult their parents as to whether the latter would be happy if their children had an interview later on.

41. If you have any further inquiries or requests (for instance if you prefer to be interviewed with some of your fellow students together), please do not hesitate to let me know.
42. Below is my current contact information:

Appendix 4
The questionnaire for the minority school

1. Your name:
2. Your gender:
3. The date you were born:
4. The place you were born (family village, county and province):
5. The place your family is from (if different from 4):
6. The grade you are in:
7. Do you take any responsibilities for your classmates (subject representative, group head, classmonitor or a member of the Class Committee):
8. Are you transferred from another school? If so, when:
9. And where:
10. Why:
11. Which primary school were you studying:
12. What were the subjects:
13. What was the medium of instruction:
14. Which junior secondary school were you studying:
15. What were the subjects:
16. What was the medium of instruction:
17. The nationality group you belong to:
18. The group your father belongs to:
19. The group your mother belongs to:
20. Your first language(s)/dialect(s) or the language(s)/dialect(s) you use at home:
21. Any other language(s)/dialect(s) you can speak (quite) fluently:
22. How many years did your father attend school (from primary school onward)?
23. How many years did your mother attend school (from primary school onward)?
24. What does your father do:
25. What does your mother do:
26. Do you have any brothers or sisters?
27. Have they been to school?
28. If so, how long?
29. What are your brothers/sisters doing if they are not in schools?
30. And where?

31. Generally speaking, your academic achievement (grade) in your class is: high, upper intermediate, average, lower intermediate, low:
32. Your attendance rate:
33. Are you boarding in the school? Who pays for your boarding fees?
34. How often do you go back home, how, and how long does it take:
35. If you are not boarding, how do you get to the school (walking, cycling, etc.) and how long does it take?
36. How much is the tuition fee per semester and who pays?
37. Are there any other fees (books and exercise books, computing or miscellaneous fees):
38. Do you sometimes assist in your family's work or business or do some work somewhere else to supplement your family's income?
39. Are your parents concerned about your study (keep supervising and accelerating (*ducu jiancha*) or tutoring your study, or keep in touch with your teacher(s))? Do you like the way they are concerned about your study and why?
40. Are they also concerned about your study of your own nationality's culture, religion, and language and script? Do you like their concern?
41. The reasons you come to this school rather than an ordinary school (for example the Prefecture School) (you may choose more than one answer according to your actual situation):

    - You can sit in the college entrance examinations in the Tibetan language
    - You have opportunity to learn the language, culture, etc. of your own nationality in the subject(s) of . . .
    - You can relatively easily keep up in the study because . . .
    - You can more easily set your mind to study in an environment in which the compatriots of your own nationality are surrounding
    - You need to board in the school
    - The fees you need to pay is less (than that in the ordinary school)
    - A decision made by your parents
    - Any other reasons (please specify):

42. If possible, would you like to study in an ordinary school (for example the Prefecture School), and why?
43. Your contact information:
44. There are any other things or comments you want to say or make:
45. If you have any questions or suggestions with regard to the questionnaire, please get in touch with me via:

    Tel: xxxxxxxx
    Address: xxxxxxxx

Please put the completed questionnaire back into the envelope provided and give it to me.[1] Thanks!

---

1 Questionnaires were given to students on a Thursday and collected a week later.

Appendix 5

Interview questions for Han, Muslim and Tibetan students

Study life

1. Do you usually like the study life in your school? If so, is this because the study is interesting or to stay with your fellow students is interesting, or for any other reasons? Or sometimes not? Why?

2. Are your parents concerned about your study (keep supervising and accelerating or tutoring your study, or keep in touch with your teacher(s))? If not, why? If so, do you like it, why? (*For minority*) Are they also concerned about your study of your own nationality's culture, religion and language?

3. Students from different ethnic groups may sometimes confront different problems in the study life in the school. Could you tell me some specific causes that would affect the minority/Muslim/Tibetan student's achievement in study:

   - Personal: gender, personality, age and previous achievement, etc.
   - Familial: ethnic and religious background, parents' educational level, parents' occupation and family's economic condition, etc.
   - Social: the relationship between study and development in the future, attractions as well as unhealthy atmosphere in society, etc.

4. (*For minority*) Can you learn (about) the culture, religion, history or language and moral values of your own nationality and other minority nationalities in some subjects, activities or from teachers in the school? If so, did you find them useful and interesting? Is it necessary and interesting to you to learn more (about) them? If you have not learnt (about) them, do you feel necessary or interested to learn? Why?

   (*For Han*) Can you learn (about) the culture, religion, history or language and moral values of minority nationalities in some subjects, activities or from teachers in the school? If so, did you find them useful and interesting? Is it necessary and interesting to you to learn more (about) them? If you have not learnt about them, do you feel necessary or interested to learn? Why?

5. May this happen that the way in which the teachers treat the students is

different according to the student's gender, achievement, personality, appearance, seat in the classroom and the socio-economic status of the family, ethnic background etc.? (For instance, are the teachers equally patient in responding to different students' requests/questions in the classroom, what kind of students they prefer to ask for answering questions in the class, whether they discipline and punish students differently, etc.)

6. Is there this situation that the school disciplines students not to practice (some of) their own cultural customs in the school (or maybe on certain occasions) (for example, dress, food, holiday/festival, language/dialect, religion and so on)? Or they would be punished otherwise? If so, would it be verbal or physical punishment, or administrative one?

Association and identity

7. (*For minority*) Generally speaking, among your fellow students, with whom do you feel easier to have social intercourse (*jiaowang*) or close contact (*shenjiao*), those from your own ethnic/religious group or from other groups? If the latter, from the Han group or other minority groups and why? What about with teachers from different ethnic groups?

   (*For Han*) Generally speaking, among your fellow students, with whom do you feel easier to have social intercourse or close contact, those from your own ethnic group or from other groups? If the latter, from the Muslim, Tibetan or other minority groups and why? What about with teachers from different ethnic groups?

8. (*For minority*) Can you describe any customs listed below that affect your everyday life?

   - Banning certain food and drink
   - Participating in your own nationality's cultural entertainments (music performing, dancing or singing), or other cultural activities
   - Taking classes in your own nationality's culture, language, religion, etc.
   - Practising your religion
   - Speaking your ethnic language or dialect
   - Celebrating certain holidays/festivals in a given way

9. Bullying and giving some fellow students nicknames (*waihao*) are quite common in school life. Do you think that some students would be more likely to be bullied or given a nickname because of their differences in gender, achievement, personality, appearance, ethnic or faith background, or socio-economic status?

   (*For Han*) What would you think about them if you got to know some of your fellow students who have a religious belief? Would you mind if you had a religious belief and the others also knew this? If not, would you possibly believe in a religion? If so, what, and why?

10. (For Tibetan) Last I would like to ask you, how and by whom the decision was made that you came to this ordinary rather than a minority school to study? If possible, are you willing to study in a minority school? Are you interested in studying in the Monastery (*siyuan*)?

(For Muslim) Last I would like to ask you, if there was a minority school that exclusively or mainly recruited Muslim students, and in which you could study common knowledge of science and culture, as well as Islamic culture and knowledge, would you prefer to study in that school? Would you like to have the Islamic education (*jingtang jiaoyu*) in the Mosque (*qingzhensi*)?

(For Han) If you were a Tibetan or Muslim student, is it possible for you to go to the minority school for Tibetans or Muslims to study? Why?

Is there anything else you would like to say that has not been covered?

Appendix 6
Interview questions for teachers

1. Are you concerned with the attendance of your students? What do you think are the main reasons that some students play truant? Are minority students more likely to play truant? If so, why?
2. Is dropout a severe problem? What do you think are the main reasons that some students drop out? Are minority students more likely to drop out? If so, why?
3. Roughly speaking, how do you perceive the academic achievement of minority students: are they more likely to have higher or lower achievement than their Han peers or have similar one? Are there differences between the Tibetan and Muslim students?
4. Minority students may sometimes confront special problems in the study life of the school that other students do not face. Could you tell me some specific causes that would affect their study (personal, familial, social, economic, cultural, linguistic, religious, etc.)? Are there differences between the Tibetan and Muslim students?

   - Personal: gender, personality, age or previous achievement, etc.
   - Familial: ethnic and religious background, parents' educational level, parents' occupation and family's economic condition, etc.
   - Social: the relationship between study and development in the future, attractions as well as unhealthy atmosphere in society, etc.

5. Can the students learn (about) the culture, religion, history, language or moral values of ethnic minorities? If so, how are they offered and how did you find the content? If not, what would be your viewpoint about it?
6. Among your students, who do you feel you can more easily communicate with, female, male, the Tibetan, Muslim, Han, or those from certain place, family of certain socio-economic status, or with other backgrounds or characteristics? Why?
7. If you knew some of your students hold pious religious belief, would you think this has an effect on their study? If so, positive or negative, and why?
8. Is there such a situation that the school disciplines students not to practice (some of) their own cultural customs in the school (or maybe on

certain occasions) (for example, dress, food, holiday/festival, language/
dialect, religion and so on)? Or they would be punished otherwise? If
so, would it be verbal or physical punishment, or administrative one?

9. May this happen that the way in which some of the teachers treat the
students is different due to the students' gender, achievement, personality, appearance, seat in the classroom, the socio-economic status of the
family, and ethnicity, etc.? (For instance, are the teachers equally patient
in responding to different students' requests/questions in the classroom,
what kind of students they prefer to ask for answering questions in the
class, whether they discipline and punish students differently, etc.)

10. Last I would like to ask you that from your point of view, what are the
severest problems in the education of minority areas?

Is there anything else you would like to say that has not been covered here?

Notes

1 Introduction

1 Even within the same ethnic group the educational gap is also observable. See Kao and Thompson (2003).

2 There is overwhelming literature on this issue. What follows is merely a simplified review of a wide range of factors explored in British and American literature that cause the failure of ethnic minorities in either schools or the larger society. Of which some are only applicable to certain minority groups while other may be to different ones. This review aims to present, not exhaust, some main academic findings so as to inform my study in the remaining chapters.

3 All the page numbers for Bourdieu (1986) refer to Halsey et al. (1997).

4 The notion of social capital that Bourdieu suggests is approached in a significantly different way from that of American positivists. Here the conflation of the views of different theorists from distinctive traditions is based on the idea that as a theory that is loosely defined as social relationships, differential approaches to social capital can be temporarily ignored when introducing it in a more general and broader sense of 'relationships'. For an examination of the problem and properties of social capital and its intellectual history, see Woolcock (1998).

5 The terms of 'bonding' and 'bridging' are not originally coined by Putnam; 'linking' is by Woolcock despite the fact that the idea is in part inspired by others' work. See Putnam (2000) and Woolcock (2001) for details.

6 Social capital may be regarded as negative if it discourages, restricts or stifles personal initiative and innovation within the group. Interested readers can also consult the pair of notions in relation to different patterns of social capital for different minority groups put forward by Zhou (2005): ghetto (destructive) and enclave (constructive), as discussed earlier.

7 A distinction between multicultural society and multiculturalist society must be made here. The former is a term describing diversity of society whereas the latter refers to recognition of diversity. In other words, a multicultural society could be a monoculturalist society where other cultures than the dominant one are marginalized. In fact it is rarely the case that a society is not multicultural whilst recognition of cultural diversity by the public, academics or in policies, is not always the case in many multicultural societies. Also see Parekh (2000: 6).

8 For the explanation of this term see the closing section of this chapter.

9 See Map 1.1 and Map 4.1.

10 The eminent sociologist Fei Xiaotong puts forward the idea of *liang nan xing zang* ('prosper Tibet under the impact of two "nans" ', the names of two prefectures, which are located in the borderland areas between Qinghai and Gansu). This is the idea of integrating Tibet into the rest of China economically, and also culturally

and politically by moving the Tibetan centre from Lasa to the *Liangnan* area. However, whilst *Gannan* prefecture in Gansu is agreed on by all researchers as one of the two 'nans', the other prefecture appears differently in different accounts or quotations: *Sunan* in Gansu (Fei 1998), *Huangnan* in Qinghai (R. Ma 1996: 503), or *Hainan* in Qinghai (XKT). Nevertheless, all three prefectures are located in the borderland areas. Also see Chapter 2 for a further discussion of state agenda of integration.

11 My research subjects do not include Dongxiang Muslims on the borderlands simply because I conducted fieldwork on the Qinghai side of the borderland areas whereas Dongxiang are primarily concentrated on the Gansu side. Chapter 5 provides more information of Muslim communities in China.

12 Both Gladney and Mackerras consider that ethnicity plays more important role than religion in the Hui identity whereas Israeli holds the view in favour of religion (Mackerras 2005). This is, as Mackerras suggests, an issue that is not clear-cut. However, what is in need of distinguishing first here is the difference of identification between the government and the Hui. Second, it is also very important to break the Hui community down as context-specific sub-groups (which Mackerras also agrees on), for example, those in China proper and those on Qinghai-Gansu borderlands.

13 This is a simplified categorization. Actually amongst the four Muslim groups in the region, the first language of the three non-Hui groups is not Chinese. I have defined all of them as Chinese speakers because these three Muslim groups are very small in numbers (see Chapter 5 and Table 3.1), and have largely mastered Chinese. Also see Gladney (2003).

14 Ogbu does not distinguish mainstream schools from minority schools. In my systematically reading of Chinese academic literature (1994–2004) on the education of ethnic minorities, I have only found one short article dealing with minority students in mainstream schools (Huang 1997). An exception is that Tibetan students studying in inland mainstream schools have drawn academic attention. However these students are separately educated and so have limited opportunities to have contact with their Han schoolfellows. Hence both in terms of culture preservation and socialization, their situation is more similar to that of their counterparts studying in Tibetan minority schools in minority regions. For further information see Chapter 4 and Postiglione, Zhu and Ben (2004).

15 For a description and information of the three periods of fieldwork, see appendices. Separate minority school is a controversial issue in many countries, for example, in Britain and France. This is particularly true in the case of separate religious schools, which is usually regarded as promotion of segregation, denomination, patriarchy or inequality over cohesion, secularity, democracy or equality. More information of the debate around separate (faith) schools in the UK can be consulted in such works as Chadwick (2001), Connolly (1992), Dobson (2002), Dwyer (2000), Halstead (1994), Haw (1995), McLaughlin (1992), Modood and May (2001), Osler and Hussain (1995), Rex (1986), Watson (2000), Yuval-Davis (1992).

16 More information on the official 'Ethnic (Minorities) Identification Project' (*minzu shibie gongzuo*), such as its rationale, criteria and arbitrariness, can be found in Fei (1980) and other scholars (for example, Gladney 2004, Tapp 2002 and Xie Jian 2004).

17 In fact, a new Chinese word for 'ethnicity' that was adopted in Hong Kong and Taiwan before being accepted by mainland China is used within academic circles, *zuqun* (lit. 'ethnic group'). In spite of this, *minzu* is still the only name for 'ethnicity' or 'nationality' that is bewared and used by other entities or people.

18 For an examination of heterogeneity of the Han, readers can consult works by researchers like Blum (2001), Ebrey (1996) and Gladney (2004).

2 The trajectories of Chinese culturalism and its educational legacy

1 Chinese culturalism is not agreed upon by all scholars. Duara (1993) observes that the threat towards Chinese cultural values arose on several occasions and produced various reactions in history. He thus suggests that culturalism that assumes the cultural superiority of the Chinese is difficult to be identified as a distinct form in history. In fact, the supposed cultural superiority of Chinese, even under threat at times, has never faded away. Quite the reverse, since China has successfully accepted and sinicized alien cultures such as Buddhism in history, this has in turn reinforced its belief in the power of its (literally and morally grounded) culture. Thus, Chinese hold a general view towards the power of '(soft) culture', while other 'hard' forces (for example, technology or military) are not considered to be as advanced as 'culture'. In addition, the imagined cultural superiority of the Chinese should also be understood from a context-specific view – this culturalism is not exercised as aggressively or tangibly as, for example, racial superiority in the West (so this difference itself appears to be cultural). This is perhaps, though partly, why it is regarded as not being constant or continuous from a Western perspective.

2 Despite its broad historical perspective, this chapter does not attempt to specifically historicize 'events' with primary historical materials, as many historians would expect – and nor does it always display the 'history' chronologically. Rather, it takes history on the stage but as a background simultaneously to spell out an ingrained discourse of culturalism as a thematic strand in Chinese history. Correspondingly, the terms used referring to ethnic communities are essentially concerned with the Han and non-Han division than a reflection of their precise weight of popularity in certain historical periods.

3 Strictly speaking, this is not a suitable or 'scientific' way of categorization of group membership and I argue below that the boundaries between the Han and non-Han groups are fluid. The more accountable terms may be 'the group at the centre and periphery of culturalism', the essential idea of difference between 'Han' and 'non-Han'. However, for the reason that the term 'Han' is much more familiar to readers, I have decided to use 'Han' as the main term to reduce the complexity of the concept. For much the same reason, 'Fan', a term for non-Han, is 'ahistorically' used prior to 'Yi'. Also see note 4.

4 However, the term *Yi* (as in Yi/Xia or Hua/Yi) was much more common in premodern discourse as a general appellation for 'barbarians'. See below.

5 There are somewhat different opinions, and one suggests, on the basis of different archaeological evidence, that East Asian culture was shaped through the path in which southern culture diffused to the north. See Qiaoben (1985: 186).

6 However, some other scholars believe that Chinese dialects in the northwest have been influenced by the Tibetan language. A very recent argument further infers that the Sino-Tibetan language family was derived from the same family as the Altaic family. Given the linguistic assumption that Chinese and Tibetan are developed from the same language family, it is too difficult to convincingly map out the relationships between Han, Tibetan and languages from the Altaic family in the region when both historical development and territory based communication between different languages need to be taken into account. Interested readers can find out more information in Alede'ertu (2004), Jin (1995), Dai and Fu (2001).

7 The classics cited in this and the following paragraphs are not listed here because they are widely available in numerous versions or sources.

8 For example, owing to a different historical development, the Chinese Han culture in the south is distinctive compared to its northern counterpart.

9 However, this case is interestingly different from Bourdieu's (1986, 1990) observation of the process in which the culture of a certain group is capitalized through

institutionalization by the same cultural group. To what extent this process has influenced the shaping of the relationship between Chinese intellectuals and the regime, and the attitude of scholars towards their rulers is worthy of further exploration.

10 However, this democracy was not applicable to women. In this sense, gender disparity can also be considered another legacy of the imperial examinations system although it is not the phenomenon only in China. Moreover, gender disparity was not only the legacy of the examination system, but fundamentally was the legacy of Confucianism that located women in a subordinated position in both families and society before the establishment of the examinations system. In this light, whereby an ideal man was said to be the combination of both moral and literary matters (see below), a woman could not be regarded as possessing morality unless she had no literary/literacy knowledge (*nüzi wu cai bian shi de*).

11 When agreeing that the civil service examinations that actualized and reinforced culturalism are largely an intellectual enterprise, I am not naively assuming that, what we call 'Chinese culture' is solely an intellectual legacy too. Without the masses being a significant part of this enterprise, it is doubtful if there would be such a thing called Chinese culture. However, when Watson was wondering if the standardization of rituals that held Chinese society together across social strata 'is a consequence of state-sponsored social engineering' or 'the result of voluntary adoption by the general populace' (1988: 18), and Rawski contends that ritual was 'the preserve of the privileged' (1988: 29), both authors have delivered a similar message that, this 'Chinese culture of rituals' was essentially a vertical expansion of 'high/elite culture' – though this was never a one way game. Indeed, it is otherwise difficult to understand, as Watson has similarly doubted, as to how this massive country with regionally or ethnically diverse languages and traditions would find it possible to reach this uniformity.

12 For more details about this culture fever, see Chen (1995), Gu (1999), Wang (1996), Zhang (1996).

13 For a concise discussion of the concept of China and Chinese from a Han-minority relationships perspective, see Mackerras (2004).

14 The notion of 'legal formalities' is borrowed from Kymlicka (2001). Xie's expression here is 'a furious political equality'. More information can be found in Chapter 6.

15 This shift is not agreed by all scholars, for example Duara (1993). (Also see note 1.) However the paradigm that holds this perspective was termed by Townsend (1992) as the 'culturalism to nationalism thesis'. In his article, Townsend distinguishes between culturalism and nationalism, and at the same time points out the connections between both. In the meantime, he also criticizes the weaknesses of the concept of culturalism that leads him to stress the value of the notion as a 'heuristic device'. For more details, and in particular for more technical analysis of culturalism as identity and as movement, see Townsend.

16 However, 'culture' is also shifting from a traditionally 'soft' notion to being linked with or incorporating some hard dimensions – scientific, technological or military.

17 Recently *dujing* (reading the Confucian classics) is flourishing among Chinese children, which emerged in Taiwan in the mid-1990s and spread to Mainland China, Hong Kong and the Chinese communities in the North America and Southeast Asia. In spite of its potential philosophy of blind loyalty to the regime and neglect of the role law plays in modern society, it is nevertheless believed to be able to bring out the potential of children, to help to improve language skills, enhance morality and develop their intelligence (Wanwei Wang 2004).

18 Also see the concept of plurality and unity (*duoyuan yiti*) of the Chinese nation in the next chapter.

19 So the view as to whether one culture is better than others can in fact shift dependent

upon economic development, which contradicts the contention that when it comes to propelling economic and political progress of human beings, some cultures are clearly more effective than others. How does culture matter then?

20 This idea is more associated with economic development rather than with trans-formation of Chinese culture or civilization that *Heshang* advocated.

21 The inequality between rural and urban residents that is represented in the system of residence registration has drawn growing public attention recently, which has led to a call among academics for the termination of different policies for rural and urban areas. See Lu (2004) for further information about this system.

22 This is a highly contested notion and is often used rhetorically by governments to justify a range of disparate policies/interventions. To counter-pose cultural rights to economic development is one example. For a discussion of this, see the concluding chapter.

23 In 2005, a new law providing free education for pupils at the compulsory stage was introduced by the government.

3 Ethnicization through schooling

1 The number of minority groups that are recognized by the state is much fewer than the number of groups (more than 400) who claimed their minority identity when China embarked on its 'Ethnic (Minority) Identification Project' in the early 1950s. In the 2000 census there are still 728,113 individuals 'unidentified' and awaiting recognition (RhSKTS and JF 2003; RPB and RhSKTS 2002).

2 Both the Nationalist Party and the CPC used to propose the conception of minority self-determination that they eventually gave up. In the CPC case, the conception of self-autonomy displaced that of self-determination. For a detailed examination of this shift, see Dreyer (1976: 141–6), Songben (2003).

3 In my research, western regions are referred to the traditional category.

4 For political purposes peculiar to itself, the Chinese government classifies people as 'believers' by very superficial criteria that have little to do with whether and what people 'believe'.

5 'Level of received education', a more neutral term, replaced 'cultural level', a term underpinned by China's 'civilizing mission' (Gladney 1999: 58) in the fifth census in 2000 (PBRSKT 2002). For a concise and persuasive discussion of the constella-tion of culture-related terms in the educational context, see Gladney (1999: 58–62). Also see the section of 'the *wenhua* discourse of China' in the previous chapter.

6 Different levels are labelled as: no schooling, literacy class, primary school, junior secondary school, senior secondary school, secondary vocational school, junior college, university and postgraduate.

7 In different censuses information provided with reference to (il)literacy is not identical. The information that the third census of 1982 provided is illiteracy and semi-illiteracy figures and rates of the 12-year-old-plus population, and illiteracy figures of the 6-year-old-plus population; the census in 1990 produced illiteracy and semi-illiteracy figures and rates of the 15-year-old-plus population; the census in 2000 provided figures of the 6-year-old-plus population who have non-schooling and attended wiping-out illiteracy classes (*saomang ban*). Meanwhile in the *Tabulation on Nationalities of 2000 Population Census of China*, the illiterate population aged 15-year-old-plus is available.

8 Whilst it is difficult to tell the general reliability of government data on which my analysis is based owing to limited resources, some unreliability with respect to this data was observable during my qualitative fieldwork. For example, according to a government official who was involved in the fifth census, her superior required that they should exaggerate of the level of education that people received by one level when reporting to the higher government in official documents. Doing so, it is said

will have the effect of boosting the superior's achievement in his or her official career (*zhengji*, lit. political achievement). The same informant also said that this is a phenomenon spreading to different government levels and in various official statistics. In fact, general figures relating to the ethnic population in national censuses can be problematic as the example of the Han population in Tibetan Autonomous Region in the 1990 and 2000 censuses given by Mackerras (2004: 225) shows.

 9 Compared to the six groups, all other ethnic groups have a significantly lower illiteracy rate than 50 per cent, that is, from about 30 per cent to 2 per cent.

10 According to Yuan Shaofen (1991. Cited in Songben 2003: 30), the largest minority group, *Zhuang* people, did not have the consciousness of belonging to the Zhuang ethnic group but were being sinicized when the CPC came to power and embarked upon its 'Ethnic Identification Project' over 50 years ago. Dreyer (1976: 269) further points out that Zhuang ('Chuang' in her spelling) had also had indigenous communist movement of some strength. This may partially be able to explain Zhuang's educational performance. Also see Goodman (2002) and Mackerras (2004). However, this is not the only case among the minority population, particularly in non-western regions, where minorities have long lived and communicated with Han that led to their sinicization, for example the She in Fujian and the Tujia in Hunan (whose illiteracy rates are 11.81 and 11.71 that are very close to that of the Han). Given the status as the first minority autonomous region, a relatively high educational level among the Mongolians in the Inner Mongolian Autonomous Region is also understandable.

11 Some Chinese scholars distinguish between three types of group by the illiteracy criterion, namely, elimination (*xiaochu xing*), transition (*zhuanhuan xing*) and expansion (*kuozhan xing*). However, the Tibetan, Dongxiang and Salar still fall in the expansion category. For more details see Zhang (1995); Zhang and Chen (1995).

12 On the trajectories of state policies of bilingual education and the religious issue in education, see Teng and Wang (2002: 292–319). *Guojia Jiaowei* (The National Education Commission) is the former name of *Jiaoyu Bu* (The Ministry of Education).

13 In his discussion of state policies of ethnic minorities in Eastern Europe, Kymlicka (2001) also illustrates the intersection between the ethnic issue and the religious issue, and how this affects state policies.

14 Dreyer argues that the ethnic issue or 'the minorities problem' is essentially a problem of integration that constitutes four concerns in Chinese policymaking: defence, economic and social well-being, and national pride (1976: 3–4). This concise insight into the whole national policy system towards ethnic minorities can serve as a general background of my analysis of government policies in educational and cultural dimensions, through which issues of security, socio-economic well-being and national ideology of propaganda come to light. For detailed information of Chinese policies towards ethnic minorities from imperial to communist times, see Dreyer.

15 While the CPC believes that religion is an historical phenomenon that follows an emergence $\rightarrow$ development $\rightarrow$ disappearance law, the Party also holds the same viewpoint towards ethnicity (*minzu*), that is to say, *minzu* will eventually disappear. See for example Z. Jiang (1992), D. Li (2000) and R. Li (2002). Kymlicka (2001) has also observed that Western political theorists, in a similar fashion, had long viewed ethnicity in much the same way in that it would gradually disappear in the course of modernization.

16 The idea of *laïcité* in French public policy is comparable to the policy of religion in China, both place emphasis on state sanction over particularistic interests in and practices of one's own culture (Favell 2001: 74–9). A further discussion on this

issue of relationships between the state and minority cultures can be found in Chapters 1 and 6.

17 A similar evolutionary order is also allegedly found in the educational system of different ethnic groups that corresponds four types of socio-economic patterns, although this is not part of the history curriculum. Education in primitive society is not an independent and special activity that has particular education institutions or full-time teachers. Education in slavery society is characterized by school education that gradually replaces social and family education. Meanwhile education becomes the privilege of the ruling class. Education in feudal society is largely associated with religious education particularly among religious ethnic groups, which is characterized by independent education institutes and full-time teachers. Education in modern society is found among ethnic minority groups that are at the similar social development stage to the Han. This type of education includes education not only in the traditional culture, but also in such subjects as foreign languages, sciences and mathematics (Teng and Wang 2001: 88–92).

18 For more information about the discourse of 'culture' in general sense, and in the notion of 'minority cultures', see the previous chapter.

19 According to the fifth national census, the rural population in western China amounts to 72.1 per cent while the percentage of the coastal provinces and municipalities is 42.18 per cent (Beijing, Tianjin, Shanghai, Shandong, Jiangsu, Zhejiang, Fujian and Guangdong) (Zhongguo Guojia Tongjiju 2000).

20 Harrell (1995) compares three types of civilizing projects carried out respectively by Confucian, Christian and Communist, and shows similarities, differences between them, as well as succession between Confucian theory and Communist theory.

21 On the issues concerning relationships between physical environment, cultural differences and mental ability, interested readers can consult, among innumerous others, Glacken (1967); Rushton and Jensen (2005); Herrnstein and Murphy (1994); Fischer et al. (1996).

22 For a recent discussion of the integral relationships between minority cultures and socio-economic patterns, see Liu (2005).

23 There is another problem, which is how to render concepts from science, philosophy, etc. into the vocabularies of minority languages. This is something that was faced by the Chinese, beginning in the late nineteenth century, but is of course largely resolved by now. Even so, due to the dominance of integrative programs with regard to minority education, minority languages are still faced by the question of how to survive more effectively as a living language, as one of my Tibetan cadre respondents pointed out.

24 The kind of schools discussed here are minority schools. This reflects a consensus amongst the government, academic and public that minority education equates the education in minority schools. In fact, minority education, or more precisely, the education of ethnic minorities, should also include the education of minority children in ordinary or mainstream schools given the fact that many ordinary or mainstream schools in minority areas have a large number of minority students as evidenced in my qualitative research case. Relevant information is also presented in Chapter 1.

25 Separate minority school is also a controversial issue in many other countries. For more information, see note 15 Chapter 1.

26 Relatedly, a negative by-product of preferential policies is said to be that these policies have seduced numerous Han to change their ethnicity to minority, which has brought about chaos in implementing state policy and exercising social justice (see, for example, Min 1996).

27 To name a few, Fei (1989: 34–5); Lin, Jin and Chen (1990: 531); Teng (2002).

28 For more critiques of the concept of *suzhi* and its place in current Chinese

developmental discourse, also see Anagnost (2004); Kipnis (2001, 2006); Murphy (2004).

29 Empirical evidence of the issue can be found in Chapters 4 and 5.

30 This is also a consensus among Muslim parents and students as my interviews with them showed. They complained about the 'unfairness' in finding a job in the state system. They thought that due to a lack of connections with state work units, when Muslim students are equally good school performers compared to their Han or Tibetan peers, they are very unlikely to be offered a job in the state system in competition with the latter. For further information with regard to the social status/background of Tibetans and Muslims, and how this affects their competitiveness in the labour market in general, and in recruitment by the state system in particular, see Chapters 4 and 5.

31 Head-teachers in the minority schools in the Longwu area complained that more financial aids went to minority schools in more impoverished and remote areas, which produced less effectiveness.

32 The view of Muslims in this section is by no means merely held by my respondents who inhabit this Tibetan dominated area, but in fact by those in Han dominated regions elsewhere, and even in Muslim dominated regions nearby. This was revealed in many informal conversations I had with Han across the country and at various times. Academic accounts mentioned earlier expressed a similar opinion.

33 For more information of this Muslim 'compact village', also see Chapter 5.

34 Indebted to the era of the global knowledge economy, Chinese society no longer belittles commerce. Yet, mainly self-employed Muslims are evaluated within the traditional frame. However, there are contradictions here, too. All over Southeast Asia, the Chinese (Han) are thought of as 'innate merchants', whose mode of organization is described by Gates as petty capitalist (1996). A comparable phenomenon is that the so-called Chinese Han from south-eastern China, who constitute the majority of the overseas Chinese in Southeast Asia, are widely viewed by the rest of China as innate merchants. It is also worth noting the striking disparity of educational performance between Han and Muslims in this region despite the fact that these days, both similarly value commercial attainments. See Chapter 5.

35 This is exactly what many other minorities say about the Han. See, for example, Chapter 4.

36 Apple (2006: 231–3) discussed two types of school, one focuses on national test and so is teacher-directed. This type of school usually promotes the kind of 'qualities' Han Chinese praise, which Apple criticizes. The other type of school emphasizes project-based instruction and so is child-centred.

37 In theory, this could be the case with Han students who studied in a minority school in the minority language, as some of my minority respondents pointed out.

38 The people working in state work units are traditionally called *ganbu* (cadre), who are in opposition with *laobaixing* or *qunzhong* (ordinary people, the masses), the rural people (for example, numerous Tibetans, Mongolians and Tu) and self-employed urban dwellers (mainly Muslims). This is to say that *ganbu* have *tiefanwan* (iron rice bowl, that is, a secure job), which entitles them to full state welfare services ranging from an urban residence permit to health care and education. In this sense, *ganbu* can also be used to refer to working class people in state work units, despite the fact that their socio-economic status is far lower than those non-working class *ganbu*. Recently there is a tendency that in many ways the line between *ganbu* and *laobaixing* is coming to be blurred under privatization and marketization, but the titles are still popular for the reasons of tradition and the fact that privatization and marketization have also resulted in a great number of used-to-be 'cadres', particularly working-class 'cadres', losing their job and becoming laid-off worker (also see Chapter 2). As a fact, it becomes more difficult

to get a job in the state system owing to the significant decline in the numbers of the state work units while state welfare package for public servants keep improving recently (also see Chapter 2). This is particularly desirable in remote areas of West China due to a sluggish economy that precludes private enterprises from being prosperous on a massive scale. In a word, the disparity between cadres and the masses in China is still conspicuous, though in some different ways. Therefore 'cadre' in this book refers to anyone working in the public sector regardless of his/her status, and so includes governmental officials or manual worker.

39 When asked about bilingual education, a Tibetan informant assessed that it is not because the Tibetan language is unable to express certain concepts in sciences or technology; rather, because these kinds of expressions have not been translated into Tibetan or not timely. This is largely the reason why the Tibetan language is perceived handicapped compared to the 'expressive' Chinese. By the same token, he evaluated that Chinese may be seen as inferior to English.

40 We also see an astonishingly similar situation in the USA and England where a new alliance made up by neo-liberalism, neo-conservativism, authoritarian populism, and managerialism is educating the 'right' way. That includes, among others, the drastic reduction of government responsibility for social needs, the 'disciplining' of culture and the body, and the popularization of a form of Social Darwinist thinking (Apple 2006: 9, 55).

4 Choosing between 'ordinary' and minorities

1 The Mongolians were concentrated in the Henan Mongolian Autonomous County (99.34 per cent) while the vast majority of Muslim (Hui, Salar and Bonan) resided in Jianzha (70.53 per cent) and Tongren (25.08 per cent).

2 The minority population in Huangnan in 2005 accounted for 91.35 per cent with the breakdown being as follows: Tibetan 71.44 per cent, Mongolian 14.83 per cent, Muslim 8.77 per cent, and Tu 4.92 per cent (HZT 2006). The ethnic population in Tongren was 72.06 per cent Tibetan, 5.56 per cent Muslim, 10 per cent Han and 12.16 per cent Tu (HZT 2006).

3 The figures are from the fifth census (see HZT 2002: 93–112).

4 Xunhua is the only Salar Autonomous County in Qinghai as well as in China.

5 The detail of this demographic transition, which was mainly caused by the move of the Muslim population from the county part to the prefecture part, can be found in Chapter 5.

6 This did not necessarily mean that they were also appointed as the top leaders of the Party committees, which were the factual top positions in the government system.

7 Zhonghua Renmin Gongheguo Minzu Quyu Zizhi Fa (Self-Autonomous Law of Ethnic Minority Regions in People's Republic of China) (see Wang and Chen 2001: 285–314); Huangnan Zangzu Zizhizhou Zizhi Tiaoli (Self-Autonomous Rules in Huangnan Tibetan Autonomous Prefecture) (see HZZBW 1999: 1605–15).

8 Rebgong is the Tibetan name for Tongren, renowned for its Tibetan painting, sculpture and the similar art works. Rebgong Art Gallery is a collection place of these art works.

9 About this resurgence among the Tibetans in general, see Goldstein (1998) and Mackerras (1999).

10 Actually most urban Tibetans had an extended family based in rural areas, where they were originally from.

11 Because the local cadre team was approaching saturation point, it was getting more and more difficult to become a cadre, particularly a non-working class one, without a degree, although there was the policy that privileged Tibetans in recruitment into state work units.

12 Traditionally for financial and some other practical reasons, they tended to let their children have a job earlier, for instance when children finished their junior secondary school study, their parents preferred to send them to *zhongzhuan* (secondary vocational school), where they could learn some practical skills (*shiyong jishu*). There were basically two benefits they could get by doing so: the period of time they needed to sponsor their children became shorter, and their children could start to earn money earlier to supplement family income.

13 The Muslim students were made up of the Hui, Salar, Bonan or their mixture.

14 The number of Tibetan students offered by the school official was quite different from my investigation. My estimation, which was based on over 90 questionnaires and 50 interviews as well as observation, informal conversations with the people in this school, was that the number of the Tibetan students in terms of naming, language, heredity and psychology was around 10 per cent. This is the figure used in the following analysis. The higher proportion provided by the school official was mainly a result of the change of nationality or ethnicity (*minzu chengfen*) among some Han and Tu, including those mixed ethnic children of Han, Tibetan or Tu who used to opt for Han for an 'advanced' status. For these Han, the good thing with a Tibetan identity *de jure* and a Han cultural background (capital) *de facto* is that they can benefit from preferential policies (in particular their children can benefit in school or college enrolment) on the one hand, and on the other, enjoy the benefit of higher cultural or symbolic status in society that is brought by their Han ethnic origin; the Tu who changed their nationality were either not satisfied with the categorization of them by the state or because compared to the Tibetan, they were less visible or heard culturally or politically. An official working in the local bureau of education also said many figures that local schools reported to them were not accurate.

15 From 2005 onwards, students did not need to pay tuition fees in accordance with a new law providing free education for pupils at the compulsory stage. Also see Chapter 5 and the Postscript.

16 These were again different from my investigation: the proportion of the Han, Muslim and Tibetan teachers was respectively 75 per cent, 9.21 per cent and 2.63 per cent.

17 In a letter from a schoolteacher in January 2005, I was told that in the first semester of 2004–5, under a new prefectural policy, more than 10 teachers in the school requested for retirement, of which 10 were approved. The ages of the 10 teachers ranged from 38 to early 50s. Given the high proportion (13.16 per cent) and the young ages of the retired teachers, it was said that this was largely a resistance to the strict and ridiculous punitive regulations of the school.

18 This is the policy called *minkaomin*, an idea that allows minority students to sit college entrance examinations in minority languages. Also see Sautman (1999) and Chapter 3.

19 According to some teachers in this school, most students in the past got less than 20 per cent of the exam questions correct in college entrance examinations.

20 Correspondingly, they also pointed out that a Han student would not be able to perform as well as Tibetan students if she or he were studying in a minority school.

21 To adopt Chinese as the medium of instruction in secondary minority schools did not seem to be compulsory though this was encouraged by the local government policy, particularly in senior secondary schools. For instance, my investigation showed that in Huangnan Prefecture Minority Senior Secondary School, Chinese was thoroughly used as the medium of instruction, while in the Tongren County Minority School, the Tibetan head-teacher required that the school adopted Tibetan as the teaching language. The consequence was that Huangnan School was made a model by the government for bilingual education whilst it was not necessarily affirmed by some Tibetan elites. By contrast, Tongren School

encountered pressure from its largely rural Tibetan parents, who saw its usage of Tibetan was inappropriate for their children's future career.

22 I was told that the only opportunity when Tibetan was employed as the main means of communication is during the period of the Two Conferences (*Lianghui Qijian*), i.e. of the Prefectural People's Congress Conference and the Prefectural Committee of the People's Political Consultative Conference.

23 On how hegemonies of race, civilization and economy are entangled with one another, Ong (1996) provides some interesting and insightful observations.

24 According to Harrell, Crossley also observes a similar view of difference between pastoral and farming populations (Harrell 1995: 19).

25 An interesting point of comparison is the language ability of the Tibetan students in inland boarding schools where they study all subjects in Chinese, with the obvious exception of Tibetan language. This has made their language ability in Tibetan inferior to that of their counterparts who remain in Tibet while their Chinese ability is not necessarily strong though surely better than those remaining in Tibet. For more information see Postiglione, Zhu and Ben (2004).

26 See note 18.

27 This segregation becomes more serious with the Tibetan students studying in inland boarding schools. Details can be found in Postiglione, Zhu and Ben (2004).

28 I used to be a pupil in this primary school more than 20 years ago. I still remember that among my some 50 fellow pupils, there were less than five who were Tibetan.

29 The pair of term 'in/voluntarily' is partially inspired by Ogbu's (1987, 1998) distinction between voluntary and involuntary minorities though the pair of concept is quite misleading itself and is not adopted in this book. For further details, see Chapter 1.

30 Some research has also discussed the significant role in education with regard to ethnic minority cultures that the school itself cannot play alone. See for example Nieto (1999) and Tomlinson (1996).

5 The social disengagement of 'familiar strangers'

1 Also see Chapter 1.

2 More information on the sects of these Islamic groups, their conflicts with the Qing dynasty, and their history in China, see, for example, Bai (2000), Gladney (1996), Lipman (1997), Dillon (1999), T. Ma (2000).

3 Most figures or numbers in this section are extracted from HZZBW (1999) and TXBW (2001).

4 The Second Primary was closed down some ten years ago.

5 This is also a reflection of a province-wide informal consensus that minority education prioritizes Tibetans or Tibetan speakers over Muslims. Also see M. Ma (1999).

6 New cadres from outside the town were also an important source of the growing number of Han households in the new town.

7 A similar residential segregation of Muslims from other ethnic groups is also observed elsewhere in the GQN region by Liu (1997).

8 In the Muslim community, there were also 89 Han residents, accounting for about one sixth of the community population.

9 I chose the two age groups, those who were born in 1970 and in 1980, in comparison with the whole community and the older group for two reasons. First, those born in 1970 should have gone to school in around 1977 when China embarked on its reform and opening-up policy and re-instituted its system of college entrance examinations. This triggered a wave of schooling after a ten years' gap during the Cultural Revolution. Second, from 1986 or 1987 onwards, the desire to take advantage of new economic opportunities at the cost of education emerged when those born in 1980 should have started schooling. This wave drew

a great number of both teachers and students to abandon education to jump into the 'commercial sea' of the larger society (also see Chapter 3).

10 In order to enter the post-compulsory level, students were required to sit senior secondary entrance examinations (*zhongkao*) and must meet a certain standard. However, due to a decline in student numbers, in the past few years the school tended to take in all examinees, as I was told by one of the school officials.

11 The distinction between the two classes was determined by students' senior secondary entrance examinations grades. The top half of the students were allocated to the key class and the poorer half to the ordinary one. This streaming of students by academic achievement was abolished officially on the principle of non-discrimination. This was also the reason why the school officials denied that they were still streaming students in this way when asked. Nonetheless, both the students and teachers in the senior first year told me that the students in this year were streamed though this was not a school-wide policy.

12 It is inappropriate to include Tibetan students in this comparison because the majority of Tibetans were rural. According to my observation, almost all the Tibetan students from the Longwu urban area continued into senior secondary study. This can also be seen from the percentages of Tibetan students in junior third and senior first year, 8.72 and 9.60.

13 Poor school performance is a widespread phenomenon in GQN borderlands. See, for instance, Liu (1997) and M. Ma (1999).

14 More information on the concept of *ganbu* can be obtained in note 38 Chapter 3.

15 This 'nursery' view of the state school among Muslims particularly annoyed and insulted some mainstream teachers, who defined this as 'typical' Muslim thought.

16 On the situation in Qinghai, see M. Ma (1999).

17 From 2005 onwards, students did not need to pay tuition fees in accordance with a new law providing free education for pupils at the compulsory stage. Also see the previous chapter and the Postscript.

18 A telling example is that, when religious and community leaders were invited by government and school officials to sit on the rostrum in a conference to promote an incentive for them to help recruit students, Muslim community leaders were deeply touched (Teng 2002: 269–70).

19 Contrary to my expectations, few Muslim parents addressed the issue of a mixed gender school, which seems to be a major concern of the Muslims Gladney (1999) observes. This is probably associated with the distinction between rural and urban areas.

20 The relevant information can be obtained from HZZBW (1999: 1430); Teng (2002: 297); Teng and Wang (2001: 197–8).

21 Based on John Bowen's model generated from a Muslim Malay community, Gladney (1999: 85) proposes a similar suggestion of two disparate streams in the transmission of Islamic knowledge – the Muslim community and the state education. These two streams are respectively characterized by those educated in Islamic knowledge and those in the Marxist-Leninist view of Islam and religion. 'This two track system has led to increasingly distinct public and private spheres among Muslims in China.'

22 Gladney (1999) observes that Arabic language study is much more advanced in Xinjiang Uygur Autonomous Region due to the influence of the Arabic script in Uygur and the proximity to Pakistan from the Region.

23 Unfortunately, a higher enrolment rate did not necessarily lead to a better school performance according to some of my respondents who were from those Muslim autonomous regions in the GQN borderlands. The main reason to appear in their descriptions was that (most) Muslims in these regions were rural. Relatedly, these Muslims appeared to be more religious. For similar findings of poor performance of Muslims, see Gladney (1999), Liu (1997) and M. Ma (1999).

24 Some teachers claimed that Muslim students tend to perform poorly from the very beginning when they start to go to primary school due to the poor educational capital they could get from their family. In my informal observations, this was not the case, or at least not a phenomenon particularly associated with Muslims at primary level. This no doubt needs to be explored further.

25 I noticed that there were some Muslim boys wearing caps when I arrived in the school on my first day. Interestingly enough, most Muslim boys I interviewed in the junior third year or senior first year were unaware of this phenomenon when I pointed it out to them. After close observation in the following several months, I found that the boys in caps were largely from the first two years, that is, the junior first or second year. One explanation from my respondents was that the older Muslim boys preferred fashion to 'conservative' customs of their community; another was that students in the more senior stage were disciplined more strictly, which it was believed could help them better concentrate on study, i.e. preparation for college entrance examinations.

26 The Tibetan New Year takes place coincidentally sometime around the time of the Chinese New Year.

27 After this 'accident', the school official introduced a policy that Muslim students would be allowed to leave for half a day for Muharram in the future.

28 Some Muslim parents discouraged their children from studying sciences which they reckoned were 'wrapped' in Chinese. See M. Ma (1999).

29 Nonetheless, differences between the Chinese language spoken by Hui and by Han in vocabulary and pronunciation are found, which are significantly associated with their different cultural norm and values. See Yang (1996).

30 When explaining why Muslim parents were not keen to keep their children in school after compulsory education, a boy offered this analysis: to go to school for some basic knowledge will benefit the family in business. More knowledge is not necessary for family business, and merely good for the individual development of students. So parents will not encourage them to study further even if they themselves might like to.

31 One Bonan student respondent told me that in his hometown in Gansu province, quite a number of female Muslims went to study in some mosques in Linxia Hui Autonomous Prefecture, the traditionally cultural centre of Muslims in the GQN borderlands, or Lanzhou, the capital of Gansu. A few of them, usually those who started to study earlier, became Mullahs; most of them went back home to play the same role of mother, wife or daughter in their family. The only difference before and after their study in mosques was that they may start to instruct their children or husband in the Islamic knowledge they acquired.

32 As a whole, female Muslim students did not have a lower, but rather, a similar level of achievement compared to their male counterparts in my survey. One of the possible reasons might be that a number of Muslim girls never attended school or dropped out at a very early stage while their brothers stayed much longer in schools. This was particularly the case in the ordinary Muslim families I interviewed. That the family needed someone to do housework when both parents had to stay away from home to earn money was one of the explanations.

33 Gladney (1999) attributes the reluctance of Muslims in schooling primarily to the exclusive and negative curriculum of Islamic knowledge and the mixed sex school environment. This seems to be a more complicated issue to me, as can be seen from the arguments presented in this chapter.

34 On the mainstream perception of Muslims, also see Chapter 3.

35 Legendary rulers of China in remote antiquity. This is taken to refer to the ancestors of the Chinese people.

36 Buddhism, also an 'imported' religion, was well accepted by Chinese society. On the difference in the accommodation of Islam and Buddhism, see M. Ma 1999.

37 In a prestigious school in Xining I was told that Hui students of high achievers did not wear their caps, and nor did their parents. Most of these parents worked in the state system. Those who tended to wear their caps, parents as well as students, were usually from self-employed families.

6 Conclusion

1 The Party's ambivalence towards the relationship between cultural and political loyalty and cultural tolerance when trying to integrate the ideas of political control, cultural diversity, citizenship cultivation, and economic development into a coherent whole has also been primarily portrayed by Potter (2003) as can be seen from his comprehensive arguments over the Party's contested attempt to maintain a balance between political loyalty and popular autonomy with particular regard to the religious issue. Also see Chapter 3.

2 Nonetheless, this dilemma was seen to be gradually resolved after some international and local NGOs engaged in development of education for Tibetans in the region, and a mobilization of both elite and grassroots forces among Tibetans was in particular effective. For more information see Postscript.

3 For instance, some of my Muslim informants told me that they were very happy when the top CPC leadership in the region was back in hands of 'our Han' from the Tibetans. In fact many Muslims explained to me that the Muslims actually have little difference from the Han but the Tibetans are really different.

4 The pair of terms 'settled' and 'unsettled' is borrowed from Swidler (1986).

5 Responsible citizens, Galston suggests, possess civic virtues that include qualities such as courage, law-abidingness, loyalty, independence, open-mindedness, work ethic, capacity to delay self-gratification, adaptability to economic and technological change, and capacity to discern and respect the rights of others, willingness to demand only what can be paid for, ability to evaluate the performance of those in office, willingness to engage in public discourse (Galston 1991. Cited in Kymlicka and Norman 2000: 7).

6 This raises the further question of what recognition would mean in practice. However, this is quite beyond the scope of this book that centres on the explanatory direction of the cultural exclusion rather than the prescriptive dimension.

7 However, the concept of 'political citizenship' cannot be generalized, that is to say, it is always associated with a sense of identification with the nation-state. Modood (1997) argues that there are different conceptions of state or citizenship, and each has a different state-individual, or public-private idealization, and therefore each has a different response to cultural diversity. Also see the discussion on multiculturalism in Chapter 1, Passerin d'Entreves and Vogel (2000), and Weintraub and Kumar (1997). Given the difference between the West and China in the concept of private-public, interested readers can also consult McDougall and Hansson (2002), although it is based more on literary criticism.

8 The arguments made here are mainly based on Parekh (2000: 236–7).

9 When criticizing his community of being uncultured, a Muslim respondent said that it was the Han who invented technology, medicine and other sciences.

10 Harrell (1996) argues there was and is some room for local minorities to negotiate ethnicities with the Party-state. Nevertheless this is still very far from freedom of expression and debate on a large scale but more associated with passive or individual reaction.

11 A Tibetan college student judged that the more money Tibetans have, the higher their living standard is, and the more they forgot their own culture. And with or without the Chinese, that would be happening (Sautman and Eng 2001. Cited in Mackerras 2004: 225). This is a good example demonstrating the vulnerability

of minorities when confronting the global modernization, and implying the responsibility that the state should take.

Postscript

1 On further information and other projects sponsored by the Trace Foundation, see its website.
2 I simply put here the original text in which Stuart and Wang (2003) illustrated the programme. The text has been shortened with some minor changes I have made to fit in with my context.
3 In 2004 and 2005 the frequency for seminars was every three or four months.
4 For more information on the programme in TAR, see Postiglione, Zhu and Ben (2004).
5 Nevertheless, some students were sent abroad to pursue further education in some social-economically important subjects, such as education leadership, international studies or development management. This would hopefully improve their participation in major public institutions when they return to China. In the meantime, the University of Hong Kong helped to establish a project promoting Chinese language teaching in Qinghai. It is still too early to predict how (far) these initiatives will go and how much they will help Tibetan children participate in mainstream society in due course (for further information of the Chinese teaching programme, see Huazheng Zhongxin et al.).
6 However, many of them I interviewed also said that they were not interested in working as a public servant: they felt that to work in a government sector would involve coping with 'dirty' politics or politicians. Also see below.
7 Also see note 6.
8 Their high achievement is not difficult to understand if we think about the amount of time they dedicated to English study: apart from classroom study, every ETP student I interviewed said they usually did not go to sleep before midnight and got up about five or six o'clock in the morning to study English. Also see above.

Bibliography

Ai, Y., Meng, H., and Postiglione, G. A. (1995) 'An Investigation of Dropout in Some Frontier Minority Areas', *Jiaoyu Yanjiu* (Educational Research), 1: 60–6. (In Chinese)

Alede'ertu (2004) ' "The Theory of Dog/Deer" Constructs the New Configuration about the Same Origin and Unity of the Chinese Nation', *Zhongguo Minzubao* (China Ethnic Newspaper), 12 November. Online available HTTP: <http://www.cass.cn/minzusuo/jianbao/F001540.doc> (accessed 1 February 2005). (In Chinese)

Anagnost, A. (2004) 'The Corporeal Politics of Quality (Suzhi)', *Public Culture*, 16(2): 189–208.

Apple, M. W. (2001; 2nd edn 2006) *Educating the 'Right' Way: Markets, Standards, God, and Inequality*, New York and London: Routledge.

Bai, J. (Postiglione, G.) (1994) 'Chinese Ethnic Minorities – Modernization and Education', trans. Feng Xinzeng, *Minzu Jiaoyu Yanjiu* (Research of Minority Education), 3: 28–36. (In Chinese)

Bai, S. (2000) *A Brief History of Islam in China*, Yinchuan: Ningxia People Press. (In Chinese)

Blair, M. (2001) 'The Education of Black Children: Why Do Some Schools Do Better Than Others?' in Richard Majors (ed.) *Educating Our Black Children: New Directions and Radical Approaches*, London and New York, RoutledgeFalmer: 28–44.

Blum, S. D. (2001) *Portraits of 'Primitives': Ordering Human Kinds in the Chinese Nation*, London: Rowman and Littlefield.

Bourdieu, P. (1977) *Outline of a Theory of Practice*, Cambridge: Cambridge University Press.

—— (1986) The Forms of Capital, in J. E. Richardson (ed.) *Handbook of Theory of Research for the Sociology of Education*, New York: Greenword Press: 241–58; reprinted in A. H. Halsey, Hugh Lauder, Philip Brown and Amy S. Wells (eds) *Education, Culture, Economy, Society* (1997), Oxford: Oxford University Press: 46–58.

—— and Passeron, Jean-Claude (1977) *Reproduction in Education, Society and Culture*, trans Lois Wacquant; reprinted in 1990 with a preface to the new edition by Pierre Bourdieu, London, Newbury Park, New Delhi: Sage Publications.

Cairangcuo, Chen A. and Liu H. (1997) 'A Study of Correlation Between Tibetan Family Education Methods and Children's Intelligence Level', *Qinghai Shifan Daxue Xuebao* (Journal of Qinghai Normal University), 1: 111–15. (In Chinese)

Chadwick, P. (2001) 'The Anglican Perspective on Church Schools', *Oxford Review of Education*, 27(4): 475–87.

Chen, L. (1988) 'Zhongguo, Huayi, Fanhan, Zhonghua, Zhonghua Minzu – A Process of Realization of An Inherent Link and Development', in Fei X., Chen L., Jia J. and Gu B. (eds) *Zhongghua Minzu Duoyuan Yiti Geju* (1989), Beijing: Central Institute for Ethnic Minorities Press, 72–113. (In Chinese)

Chen, X. (1995) *Occidentalism: A Theory of Counter-Discourse in Post-Mao China*, New York: Oxford University Press.

Chen, X. (1998) 'Develop the Education of the Miao, Promote Ethnic Equality', *Bijie Shifan Gaodeng Zhuanke Xuexiao Xuebao* (Journal of Bijie Teachers Training College), 3: 36–44. (In Chinese)

Coleman, J. S. (1988) 'Social Capital in the Creation of Human Capital', *American Journal of Sociology*, 94: S95–S120.

Connolly, C. (1992) 'Religious Schools: Refuge or Redoubt', in M. Leicester and M. Taylor (eds) *Ethics, Ethnicity and Education*, London: Kogan Page: 137–45.

Crossley, P. K. (2000) *A Translucent Mirror: History and Identity in Qing Imperial Ideology*, Berkeley: University of California Press.

——, Siu, H. F., and Sutton, D. S. (2006) 'Introduction', in their (eds) *Empire at the Margins: Culture, Ethnicity, and Frontier in Early Modern China*, Berkeley, Los Angeles, London: University of California Press: 1–24.

Cui, Y. (1995) 'A Study of Enculturation and Minority Education', *Xinjiang Shifan Daxue Xuebao* (Journal of Xinjiang Normal University), 4: 78–84. (In Chinese)

Cui,Y., Zhang D., and Du C. (eds) (1999) *General History of Qinghai*, Xining: Qinghai People Press. (In Chinese)

Dai, Q. and Fu, A. (2001) 'V-O Pattern in the Tibetan-Burmese Language and A Comparison with the Han Language', *Fangyan* (Dialects), 4 (November): 289–300. (In Chinese)

Deng, S. (1997) 'To Deeply Study the Personality of Minority Students Is the Important Prerequisite for Practising Quality Education of Minorities', *Zhongguo Minzu Jiaoyu* (China Minority Education), 1: 33–5. (In Chinese)

Dikötter, F. (1992) *The Discourse of Race in Modern China*, London: Hurst and Company.

Ding, H. (1991) 'A Brief View of the Education of the Hui', *Gansu Minzu Yanjiu* (Research of Gansu Ethnic Minorities), 3. Online available HTTP: <http://www.edu.cn/20011115/3010085.shtml> (accessed 9 August 2003). (In Chinese)

Ding, Y. (1997) 'A Synthesis of Studies of Psychological Characteristics and Education of Minority Children in China', *Minzu Jiaoyu Yanjiu* (Research of Minority Education), 2: 50–63. (In Chinese)

Dobson, F. (2002) 'Open Up Faith Schools', *The Guardian*, 8, February.

Dongfang Minzu Wang (Oriental Ethnic Net): http://www.e56.com.cn. (In Chinese)

Dreyer, J. T. (1976) *China's Forty Millions*. Cambridge (US) and London: Harvard University Press.

Duara, P. (1993) 'De-Constructing the Chinese Nation', *The Australian Journal of Chinese Affairs*, 30 (July): 1–26.

Dwyer, C. (2000) 'Negotiating Diasporic Identities: Young British South Asian Muslim Women', *Women's Studies International Forum*, 23(4): 475–86.

Ebrey, P. (1996) 'Surnames and Han Chinese Identity', in Melissa J. Brown (ed.) *Negotiating Ethnicities in China and Taiwan*, Berkeley: University of California Institute for East Asian Studies: 19–36.

Elliot, M. C. (2006) 'Ethnicity in the Qing Eight Banners', in P. K. Crossley, H. F. Siu, and D. S. Sutton (eds) *Empire at the Margins: Culture, Ethnicity, and Frontier in Early Modern China*, Berkeley, Los Angeles, London: University of California Press: 27–57.

Elman, B. A. (2000) *A Cultural History of Civil Examinations in Late Imperial China*, Berkeley, Los Angeles, London: University of California Press.

Favell, A. (2001) *Philosophies of Integration: Immigration and the Idea of Citizenship in France and Britain*, Basingstoke and New York: Palgrave.

Fei, X. (1980) 'Ethnic Identification in China', *Zhongguo Shehui Kexue* (Social Sciences in China), 1: 94–107. (In Chinese)

—— (1989) 'Configuration of Plurality and Unity of the Chinese Nation', in Fei X., Chen L., Jia J. and Gu B. (eds) *Zhonghua Minzu Duoyuan Yiti Geju* (*Configuration of Plurality and Unity of Chinese Nation*). Beijing: Central Institute for Ethnic Minorities Press: 1–36. (In Chinese)

—— (1998) 'The Youth Acts As Companion Returns Home: Writing for 'The Marriage of The Tu People in Gansu'. Online available HTTP: <http://tiger.berkeley.edu/wdluo/reading/vol-220> (accessed 17 January 2005). (In Chinese)

Feinberg, W. (1996) 'The Goals of Multicultural Education: A Critical Re-Evaluation', *Philosophy of Education*. Online available HTTP: <www.ed.uiuc.edu/EPS/PES-yearbook/96_docs/feinberg.html> (accessed 28 August 2003).

Ferguson, R. F. (2005) 'Why America's Black-White School Achievement Gap Persists', in G. C. Loury, T. Modood and S. Teles (eds) *Race, Ethnicity and Social Mobility in the US and UK*, Cambridge: Cambridge University Press: 309–41.

Fischer, C. S. et al. (1996) *Inequality by Design: Cracking the Bell Curve Myth*, New Jersey: Princeton University Press.

Fong, V. and Murphy, R. (2006) 'Introduction', in their (eds) *Chinese Citizenship: Views from the Margins*, London and New York: Routledge: 1–8.

Foucault, M. (1980) *Power/Knowledge: Selected Interviews and Other Writings 1971–1977*. New York: Pantheon Books.

Gates, H. (1996) *China's Motor: A Thousand Years of Petty Capitalism*, Ithaca, NY: Cornell University Press.

Gibson, M. A. (1988) *Accommodation without Assimilation: Sikh Immigrants in an American High School*, Ithaca, NY: Cornell University Press.

Gibson, M. A. et al. (1997) 'Ethnicity and School Performance: Complicating the Immigrant/Involuntary Minority Typology', *Anthropology and Education Quarterly*, 28(3): 315–462.

Gillborn, D. (1997) 'Ethnicity and Educational Performance in the United Kingdom: Racism, Ethnicity, and Variability in Achievement', *Anthropology and Education Quarterly*, 28(3): 375–93.

—— (2005) 'Education policy as an act of white supremacy: whiteness, critical race theory and education reform', *Journal of Education Policy*, 20(4): 485–501.

Glacken, C. J. (1967) *Traces on the Rhodian Shore: Nature and Culture in Western Thought from Ancient Times to the End of the Eighteenth Century*, Berkeley and Los Angeles: University of California Press.

Gladney, D. C. (1996) *Muslim Chinese: Ethnic Nationalism in the People's Republic*, Cambridge and London: Harvard University Press.

—— (1999) 'Making Muslims in China: Education, Islamicization and Representation', in G. A. Postiglione (ed.) *China's National Minority Education: Culture, Schooling, and Development*, New York and London: Falmer Press: 55–94.

—— (2003) 'Islam in China: Accommodation or Separatism?' *The China Quarterly*, 74: 451–67.

—— (2004) *Dislocating China: Reflections on Muslims, Minorities and Other Subaltern Subjects*, Chicago: University of Chicago Press.

Goldstein, M. C. (1998) 'Introduction', in Melvyn C. Goldstein and Matthew T. Kapstein (eds) *Buddhism in Contemporary Tibet: Religious Revival and Cultural Identity*, Berkeley, Los Angeles and London: University of California Press: 1–14.

Goodman, D. (2002) 'The Politics of the West: Equality, Nation-Building and Colonization', *Provincial China*, 7(2) (October): 127–50.

Gramsci, A. (1971) *Selections from the Prison Notebooks*, New York: International Publishers.

Gu, E. X. (1999) 'Cultural Intellectuals and the Politics of Cultural Public Space in Communist China (1979–1989): A Case Study of the Three Intellectual Groups', *Journal of Asian Studies*, 58(2): 389–431.

Guo, Y. (2003) 'A Brief Diagnose of Symptoms in Minority Education Being Divorced from Reality and Society', *Xinan Minzu Xueyuan Xuebao* (*Journal of Southwest Minority Institute*, 24(1): 15–17. (In Chinese)

Guojia Jiaowei and Guojia Minwei (The State Education Commission, the State Ethnic Affairs Commission) (1992) 'Some Suggestions on Several Questions in Strengthening Minority Education Work'. Online available HTTP: <http://www.edu.cn/ 20010823/ 207458.shtml> (accessed 8 September 2003). (In Chinese)

Guojia Minwei and Guojia Tongjiju (The State Ethnic Affairs Commission, The National Bureau of Statistics) (2000) *2000 Nian Zhongguo Minzu Tongji Nianjian* (China's Ethnic Statistical Yearbook 2000). Online available HTTP: <http://www.e56.com.cn/publish/dianzi/2000/main2000.htm> (accessed 17 October 2004). (In Chinese)

Guojia Minzu Shiwu Weiyuanhui (i.e. Guojia Minwei) (2002) *The Chinese Communist Party's Basic Viewpoint and Policy of the Ethnic Issue*, Beijing: Ethnic Publishing House. (In Chinese)

Guowuyuan (The State Council) (2002) 'Resolution of Deepening Reform and Speeding up Development of Minority Education'. Online available HTTP: <http://www.moe.edu.cn/wreports/20020009/13.htm or http://www.moe.edu.cn/edoas/website18/level3.jsp?tablename=146andinfoid=1089> (accessed 22 September 2004). (In Chinese)

Halike Niyazi and Muhabaiti Hasimu (1997) 'Mastery of Chinese Should Be One of the Necessary Qualities of Minority College Students', *Xinjiang Daxue Xuebao* (Journal of Xinjiang University), 25(1): 90–2. (In Chinese)

Halstead, M. J. (1994) *Parental Choice and Education*, London: Kogan Page.

Harrell, S. (1995) 'Introduction: Civilizing Projects and the Reaction to Them', in his (ed.) *Cultural Encounters on China's Ethnic Frontiers*, Seattle and London: University of Washington Press: 3–36.

—— (1996) 'Introduction', in M. J. Brown (ed.) *Negotiating Ethnicities in China and Taiwan*, Berkeley: University of California Institute for East Asian Studies: 1–18.

Harrison, L. E. and Huntington, S. P. (eds) (2000) *Culture Matters: How Values Shape Human Progress*, New York: Basic Books.

Haw, K. (1995) 'Why Muslim Girls Are More Feminist in Muslim Schools', in M. Griffiths and B. Troyna (eds) *Antiracism, Culture and Social Justice in Education*, Stoke-on-Trent Trentham Books: 43–60.

Heberer, T. (1990) *China and Its National Minorities*, Armonk, NY: M. E. Sharpe.

Herrnstein, R. J. and Murphy, C. (1994) *The Bell Curve*, New York: Free Press.

Hoogvelt, A. (2001) *Globalization and the Postcolonial World: The New Political Economy of Development*, Hampshire: London: Palgrave.

Hu, A. and Wen, J. (2002) 'Social Development as the Priority: The New Catch-Up Strategy in Western Minority Regions', in Tie Mu'er and Liu W. (eds) *Minzu Zhengce Yanjiu Wencong (1) (Collection of Studies of Minority Policies (1))*, Beijing: Ethnic Publishing House: 181–203. (In Chinese)

Huang, B. (1997) 'The Education of Ethnic Minorities in Non-Minority Schools', *Minzu Gongzuo (Ethnic Work)*, 8: 42–3. (In Chinese)

Huazheng Zhongxin (Wah Ching Centre of Research on Education in China) et al. 'A Proposal in Support of Bilingual Education and Cultural Exchange in Tibetan Areas of West China'. Online available HTTP: <http://www.cte.edu.cn/localuser/ajcr/qh/index.html> (accessed 16 September 2006). (In Chinese)

HZT (Huangnan Zhou Tongjiju (Huangnan Prefectural Bureau of Statistics)) (1999) *Huangnan Tibetan Autonomous Prefecture Statistical Yearbook 1978–1998*, Huangnan (Qinghai): Huangnan Zangzu Zizhizhou Tongjiju. (In Chinese)

—— (2002) *Huangnan Statistical Yearbook 1999–2001*, Huangnan: Huangnan Zangzu Zizhizhou Tongjiju. (In Chinese)

—— (2003a) '2002 Statistical Communique of National Economy and Social Development in the Huangnan Prefecture', *Huangnan Bao (Huangnan Newspaper)*, 15, March. (In Chinese)

—— (2003b) *Major Statistical Indexes of National Economy in the Huangnan Tibetan Autonomous Prefecture 2002*, Huangnan (Qinghai): Huangnan Zhou Tongjiju. (In Chinese)

—— (2006) *Major Statistical Indexes of National Economy in the Huangnan Tibetan Autonomous Prefecture 2005*, Huangnan (Qinghai): Huangnan Zhou Tongjiju. (In Chinese)

HZZBW (The Huangnan Zangzu Zizhizhouzhi Bianzuan Weiyuanhui (The Compiling Committee of Huangnan Tibetan Autonomous Prefecture Annals)) (1999) *Huangnan Prefecture Annals*, Lanzhou: Gansu People Press. (In Chinese)

Jia, J. (1989a) 'A Research of 'Han People', in Fei X., Chen L., Jia J. and Gu B. (eds) *Zhongghua Minzu Duoyuan Yiti Geju* (1989), Beijing: Central Institute for Ethnic Minorities: 137–52. (In Chinese)

—— (1989b) 'Han Elements in Ethnic Minorities in History', in Fei X. et al. (eds) *Zhongghua Minzu Duoyuan Yiti Geju* (1989), Beijing: Central Institute for Ethnic Minorities Press: 159–77. (In Chinese)

Jiang, H. (2004) 'Over Competitiveness in Basic Education and Socialization of The Youth'. Online available HTTP: <http://www.sociology.cass.net.cn/shxw/qsnyj/P020041228285355310853.pdf.> (accessed 31 December 2004). (In Chinese)

Jiang, Z. (1992) 'Enhance Ethnic Unity, Go Forward Hand in Hand to Build the Socialism with Chinese Characteristics', in Guojia Minzu Shiwu Weiyuanhui (ed.) *The CCP's Basic Viewpoint and Policy on the Ethnic Issue* (2002), Beijing: Ethnic Publishing House: 277–94. (In Chinese)

Jiaoyu Bu (Ministry of Education) (1986) 'Compulsory Education Law of People's Republic of China', in *Education Law and Relevant Regulations* (2001), Beijing: China Legislation Publishing House: 14–17. (In Chinese)

—— (1995) 'Education Law of People's Republic of China', in *Education Law and Relevant Regulations* (2001), Beijing: China Legislation Publishing House: 1–13. (In Chinese)

—— (1998) 'Higher Education Law of People's Republic of China', in *Education Law and Relevant Regulations* (2001), Beijing: China Legislation Publishing House: 25–37. (In Chinese)

Jin, D. (1998) 'Enhance The Education of Ethnicity, Set Up A New Minority Image – A Discussion of the System of the Textbook 'General Knowledge of Ethnicity', *Zhongguo Minzu Jiaoyu* (China Minority Education): 1, 38–9. (In Chinese)

Jin, Y. (1995) 'A Brief Analysis of Several Special Usages of the "Ba" Sentence in the Qinghai Dialect', *Qinghai Minzu Xueyuan Xuebao* (*Journal of Qinghai Ethnic Institute*), 3: 64–6. (In Chinese)

Kalmijn, M. and Kraaykamp, G. (1996) 'Race, Cultural Capital, and Schooling: An Analysis of Trends in the United States', *Sociology of Education*, 69 (January): 22–34.

Kao, G. and Thompson, J. S. (2003) 'Racial and Ethnic Stratification in Educational Achievement and Attainment', *Annual Review of Sociology*: 29, 417–42.

Kipnis, A. (2001) 'The Disturbing Educational Discipline of "Peasants" ', *China Journal*, 46: 1–24.

—— (2006) '*Suzhi*: A Key Approach', *China Quarterly*, 186: 295–313.

Kymlicka, W. (1995) *Multicultural Citizenship: A Liberal Theory of Minority Rights*, Oxford and New York: Oxford University Press.

—— (2001) 'Western Political Theory and Ethnic Relations in Eastern Europe', in W. Kymlick and M. Opalski (eds) *Can Liberal Pluralism be Exported? Western Political Theory and Ethnic Relations in Eastern Europe*, Oxford and New York: Oxford University Press: 13–105.

Kymlicka, W. and Norman, W. (2000) 'Citizenship in Cultural Diverse Societies: Issue, Contexts, Concepts', in their (eds) *Citizenship in Diverse Society*, Oxford and New York: Oxford University Press: 1–41.

Lamont, M. (2001) 'Symbolic Boundaries', in N. J. Smelser and P. B. Baltes (eds), *International Encyclopedia of the Social and Behavioral Sciences*, London: Pergamon Press: 15341–7.

Lamontagne, J. (1999) 'National Minority Education in China: A Nationwide Survey Across Counties', in G. A. Postiglione (ed.) *China's National Minority Education: Culture, Schooling, and Development*, New York and London: Falmer Press: 133–71.

Lareau, A. and Horvat, E. M. (1999) 'Moments of Social Inclusion and Exclusion: Race, Class, and Cultural Capital in Family-School Relationships', *Sociology of Education*, 72 (January): 37–53.

Li, D. (2000) 'Essential Characteristics and Developmental Trend of the Ethnic Issue of the Contemporary World', *Minzu Tuanjie* (*Ethnic Unity*), 9 and 10. Online available HTTP: <http://www.56-china.com.cn/mztj/9/yi9M2.htm> (accessed 18 February 2003). (In Chinese)

—— (2002) 'A Summary Speech in the Fifth National Minority Education Working Conference'. Online available HTTP: <http://www.moe.edu.cn/minority/ jianghua/ 1.htm> (accessed 22 February 2003); <http://www.moe.edu.cn/edoas/website18/ info12112.htm> (re-accessed 21 May 2006). (In Chinese)

Li, D., Cai, B., Li, J., Wang J. (1995) 'Development Strategies for Minority Basic Education in Northwest', *Sheke Zongheng* (Society Branch Vertically and Horizontally), 6: 17–28. (In Chinese)

Li, R. (2002) 'Must Attach Importance to The Ethnic and Religious Issue', in Guojia

Minzu Shiwu Weiyuanhui (ed.) *The CCP's Basic Viewpoint and Policy of the Ethnic Issue*, Beijing: Ethnic Publishing House: 1–7. (In Chinese)

Li, X., Li, Y., Zheng, Y., and Yang, H. (1994) 'The Development of Minority Education in Impoverished Areas – An Investigation into and Thoughts of Minority Education in Linxia Hui Autonomous Prefecture and Jishishan County', *Minzu Yanjiu* (Research of Ethnic Minorities), 3, 14–24. (In Chinese)

Lipman, J. N. (1997) *Familiar Strangers: A History of Muslims in Northwest China*, Seattle and London: University of Washington Press.

Lishi (Qi Nianji Shangce) *(History* for Grade Seven vol. 1) (Textbook) (2001), Beijing: Beijing Normal University Press. (In Chinese)

Liu, X. (1994) 'Research of Basic Education Development in Qinghai Minority Areas', *Minzu Jiaoyu Yanjiu* (Research of Minority Education), 1, 7–15. (In Chinese)

Liu, Y. (2005) 'To protect the subjectivity of ethnic (minority) cultures', *Zhongguo Minzu Bao (China Nationalities Newspaper)*, 9 December. (In Chinese)

Loury, G. C., Modood, T. and Teles, S. M. (2005) 'Introduction', in their (eds) *Ethnicity, Social Mobility and Public Policy: Comparing the US and UK*, Cambridge: Cambridge University Press: 1–17.

Lu, X. (2004) 'Walk Out from the Predicament of 'Separate Government of Urban and Rural, One Country with Two Policies'. Online available HTTP: <http://www.sociology.cass.net.cn/shxw/xcyj/t20040727_2304.htm> (accessed 2 January 2005). (In Chinese)

Lu, X. and Yang, B. (eds) (2000) *Formulation and Development of the Cohesion of the Chinese Nation*, Beijing: Ethnic Publishing House. (In Chinese)

Ma, C., Siqin, Ma, W., Su, Z. and Ma, H. (1996) 'Heavy Wings – An Investigation into the Education of Xunhua Salar Girls', *Qinghai Minzu Yanjiu (Qinghai Minority Research)*, 1: 16–25, 2: 18–26. (In Chinese)

Ma, M. (1999) 'On Several Problems in the Education of the Hui in Qinghai', *Huizu Yanjiu (Hui Studies)*, 2: 44–62. (In Chinese)

Ma, Q., Xiao, L. (2002) 'Cultural Discontinuity and Minority Education – A Sensible Attitude Towards Minority Education', *Shaanxi Shifan Daxue Xuebao (Journal of Shaanxi Normal University)*, 31(1): 119–24. (In Chinese)

Ma, R. (1996) 'Sociology of ethnicity', in *Shehui Wenhua Renleixue Jiangyanji (Lectures on Socio-Cultural Anthropology)*, Tianjin: Tianjin People Press: 498–532. (In Chinese)

—— (2001) *Ethnicity and Social Development*, Beijing: Ethnic Publishing House. (In Chinese)

—— (2003) 'On Ethnic Consciousness', *Xibei Minzu Yanjiu (Northwest Ethno-National Studies)*, 3: 5–17. (In Chinese)

Ma, R. and Wang, T. (2002) 'An Investigation Report of Economic and Social Development of Ethnic Minorities with a Small Population in China', in Tie Mu'er and Liu W. (eds) *Collection of Studies of Minority Policies (1)*, Beijing: Ethnic Publishing House: 289–315. (In Chinese)

Ma, T. (2000) *Islamic Sects and the Menhuan System in China*, Yinchuan: Ningxia People Press. (In Chinese)

McDougall, B. S. and Hansson, A. (2002) *Chinese Concepts of Privacy*, Brill, Leiden.

Mackerras, C. (1999) 'Religion and the Education of China's Minorities', in G. A. Postiglione (ed.) *China's National Minority Education: Culture, Schooling, and Development*, New York and London: Falmer Press: 23–54.

—— (2004) 'What is China? Who is Chinese? Han-minority relations, legitimacy, and the state', in P. H. Gries and S. Rosen (eds) *State and Society in 21ˢᵗ-Century China*, New York and London: RoutledgeCurzon: 216–34.

—— (2005) 'Some Issues of Ethnic and Religious Identity among China's Islamic Peoples', *Asian Ethnicity*, 6(1): 3–18.

McLaughlin, T. (1992) 'The Ethics of Separate Schools', in M. Leicester and M. Taylor (eds) *Ethics, Ethnicity and Education*, London: Kogan Page: 114–36.

Meng, L. (2002) 'A Cross-Culturally Comparative Study on Intelligence and Achievement of Mongolian and Han Students', *Nei Menggu Shifan Daxue Xuebao (Journal of Inner Mongolia Normal University)*, 15(2): 30–3. (In Chinese)

Meng, X., Qi, S., Kan, B. (1998) 'Educational Needs of the Tibetans in Qinghai – A Survey of Two Tibetan Communities', *Zhongguo Shehui Kexue (Social Sciences of China)*, 3: 122–36. (In Chinese)

Min, D. (1996) 'Cannot Sell "False Ethnicity" ', *Minzu Tuanjie (Ethnic Unity)*, 1: 31. (In Chinese)

Minzu Jiaoyu Si (Minority Education Section, State Education Commission) (1992) 'Outline of Guidelines for National Minority Education Development and Reform (trial edition)'. Online available HTTP: <http://www.edu.cn/20010823/207457.shtml> (accessed 8 September 2003). (In Chinese)

—— (2002) 'Present Situation and Future of Education Development in Minority Areas in Our Country', in Tie Mu'er and Liu, W. (eds) *Minzu Zhengce Yanjiu (1) (Studies of Minority Policies*, Beijing: Ethnic Publishing House: 204–12. (In Chinese)

Mitter, R. (2004) *A Bitter Revolution: China's Struggle with the Modern World*, Oxford and New York: Oxford University Press.

Miyazaki, I. (1981) *China's Examination Hell: The Civil Service Examinations of Imperial China*, trans. C. Schirokauer, New Haven and London: Yale University Press.

Modood, T. (1997) 'Introduction: The Politics of Multiculturalism in the New Europe', in T. Modood and P. Werbner (eds) *The Politics of Multiculturalism in the New Europe: Racism, Identity and Community*, London and New York: Zed Books Ltd: 1–25.

—— (1993; 2nd edn, 2001) 'Multiculturalism', in *The Oxford Companion to Politics of the World*, Oxford: Oxford University Press: 562–4.

Modood, T. and May, S. (2001) 'Multiculturalism and Education in Britain: An Internally Contested Debate', *International Journal of Educational Research*: 35: 305–17.

Murphy, R. (2004) 'Turning Peasants into Modern Chinese Citizens: "Population Quality" Discourse, Demographic Transition and Primary Education', *China Quarterly*, 177: 1–20.

—— (2006) 'Citizenship education in rural China: The dispositional and technical training of cadres and farmers', in V. Fong and R. Murphy (eds) *Chinese Citizenship: views from the margins*, London and New York: Routledge: 9–26.

Navarro, R. A. (1997) 'Commentary', *Anthropology and Education Quarterly*, 28(3): 455–62.

NESF (The National Economic and Social Forum) (2003) 'The Policy Implications of Social Capital', 28 (May), Dublin. Online available HTTP: <http://www.nesf.ie/documents/No28SocialCapital.pdf> (accessed 28 March 2004).

Nieto, S. (1999) 'Critical Multicultural Education and Students' Perspectives', in

S. May (ed.) *Critical Multiculturalism: Rethinking Multicultural and Antiracist Education*, London and Philadelphia: Falmer Press: 191–215.

Ningxia Jiaowei (Jijiaochu) (Ningxia Education Commission, Section of Basic Education) (1998) 'Basic Situation of Minority Education Development in Ningxia Hui Autonomous Region', *Zhongguo Minzu Jiaoyu (Minority Education of China)*, 5: 5–7. (In Chinese)

Noguera, P. A. (2004) 'Social Capital and the Education of Immigrants Students: Categories and Generalizations', *Sociology of Education*, 77: 180–3.

Nye, J. S. Jr. (2005) 'The Rise of China's Soft Power', *The Wall Street Journal Asia*, 29 December.

Ogbu, J. (1987) 'Variability in Minority School Performance: A Problem in Search of an Explanation', *Anthropology and Education Quarterly*, 18: 313–34.

Ogbu, J. and Simons, H. D. (1998) 'Voluntary and Involuntary Minorities: A Cultural-Ecological Theory of School Performance with Some Implications for Education', *Anthropology and Education Quarterly*, 29(2): 155–88.

Olneck, M. R. (2000) 'Can Multicultural Education Change What Counts as Cultural Capital?' *American Educational Research Journal*, 37: 317–48.

Ong, A. (1996) 'Cultural Citizenship as Subject-Making: Immigrants Negotiate Racial and Cultural Boundaries in the United States', *Current Anthropology*, 37(5): 737–62.

O'Reilly, K. (2005) *Ethnographic Methods*, London and New York: Routledge.

Osborne, J. W. (2001) 'Academic Disidentification: Unravelling under Achievement among Black Boys', in R. Majors (ed.) *Educating our Black Children: New directions and radical approaches*, London and New York: RoutledgeFalmer: 45–58.

Osler, A. and Hussain, Z. (1995) 'Parental Choice and Schooling: Some Factors Influencing Muslim Mothers' Decisions About the Education of Their Daughters', *Cambridge Journal of Education*, 25(3): 327–47.

Palden Nyima (1998) 'An Exploration of Ways of the Education of Tibetans', *Jiaoyu Yanjiu (Educational Research)*, 10: 50–4. (In Chinese)

Parekh, B. (2000) *Rethinking Multiculturalism: Cultural Diversity and Political Theory*, Basingstoke and New York: Palgrave.

Passerin d'Entreves, M. and Vogel, U. (2000) (eds) *Public and Private: Legal, political and philosophical perspectives*, London and New York: Routledge.

Postiglione, G. A. (1999) 'Introduction: State Schooling and Ethnicity in China', in his (ed.) *China's National Minority Education: Culture, Schooling, and Development*, New York and London: Falmer: 3–19.

Postiglione, G. A., Zhu, Z. and Ben, J. (2004) 'From Ethnic Segregation to Impact Integration: State Schooling and Identity Construction for Rural Tibetans', in *Asian Ethnicity*, 5(2): 195–217.

Potter, J. and Wetherell, M. (1987) *Discourse and social psychology: Beyond attitudes and behaviour*, London: Sage.

Potter, P. B. (2003) 'Belief in Control: Regulation of Religion in China', *China Quarterly*, 174: 317–37.

Putnam, D. R. (2000) *Bowling Alone: The Collapse and Revival of American Community*, New York: Simon and Schuster.

Qiaoben, W. (Mantaro, H.) (1985) *Yuyan Dili Leixing Xue (Linguistic Typology)*, trans. Yu Zhihong, Beijing: Peking University Press. (In Chinese)

Quanguo Renmin Daibiao Dahui (The National People's Congress) (2004)

'Constitution of People's Republic of China'. Online available HTTP: <http:law.people.com.cn/bike/reg/loggin.btml> (accessed 30 September 2004). (In Chinese)

Rawski, E. S. (1988) 'A Historian's Approach to Chinese Death Ritual', in J. L. Watson and E. S. Rawski (eds) *Death Ritual in Late Imperial and Modern China*, Berkeley, Los Angeles, London: University of California Press: 20–34.

Renmin Ribao Shelun (People's Daily Editorial): 'Closely Unite Religious People, Jointly Devote to the Great Cause of Building Up Socialism with Chinese Characteristics', *Renmin Ribao* (People's Daily), 13 December 2001. (In Chinese)

Rex, J. (1986) 'The Concept of a Multicultural Society', in his (1996) *Ethnic Minorities in Modern Nation State*, London: Palgrave Macmillan: 11–29.

RhSKTS and JF (Guojia Tongji Ju Renkou he Shehui Keji Tongjisi, Guoji Minzu Shiwu Weiyuanhui Jingji Fazhansi) (Department of Population, Social, Science and Technology Statistics, National Bureau of Statistics; Department of Economic Development, State Ethnic Affairs Commission) (2003) *Tabulation on Nationalities of 2000 Population Census of China*. Beijing: The Ethnic Publishing House. (In Chinese)

RPB and RhSKTS (Guowuyuan Renkou Pucha Bangongshi, Guojia Tongjiju Renkou he Shehui Keji Tongjisi (Population Census Office under the State Council and Department of Population, Social, Science and Technology Statistics, National Bureau of Statistics of China) (2002) *Tabulation on The 2000 Population Census of the People's Republic of China*, Beijing: China Statistics Press. (In Chinese)

Rushton, J. P. and Jensen, A. R. (2005) 'Thirty Years Research on Race Differences in Cognitive Ability', *Psychology, Public Policy and Law*, 11(2): 235–94

Sautman, B. (1997) 'Racial Nationalism and China's External Behavior', *World Affairs*, fall.

—— (1999) 'Expanding Access to Higher Education for China's National Minorities: Policies of Preferential Admissions', in G. A. Postiglione (ed.) *China's National Minority Education: Culture, Schooling and Development*, New York and London: Falmer Press: 173–210.

Schirokauer, C. (1981) 'Introduction', in I. Miyazaki *China's Examination Hell: The Civil Service Examinations of Imperial China*, trans. C. Schirokauer, New Haven and London: Yale University Press: 7–10.

Shen, H. (1995) 'Marginalization of the Minority Population in Chinese History – An Historical Perspective of the Poverty of the Minority Population', *Xibei Minzu Xueyuan Xuebao*) (Journal of Northwest Minorities Institute): 53–60. (In Chinese)

Songben, Z. (Matsumoto, M.) (2003) *A Study of Ethnic Policies of China: Nationalism from the End of Qing Dynasty to 1945*, trans. Zhan Zhonghui, Beijing: The Ethnic Publishing House. (In Chinese)

Strategy Unit (2003) 'Ethnic Minorities and the Labour Market: Final report'. Online available HTTP: <http://www.number10.gov.uk/su/ethnic%20minorities/report/ex_summary.htm#fn002> (accessed 21 May 2004).

Stuart, K. and Wang, S. (2003) 'Ethnicity, language and school success', *China Education Forum*, Hong Kong: Wah Ching Centre of Research on Education in China, 4(1), 1–3. Online available HTTP: http://www.hku.hk/chinaed (accessed 23 June 2004).

Sun, Y. (1997) 'My View of Point of the Education of the Hui', *Gongzuo Tongxun* (*Working Bulletin*), 8. Online available HTTP: <http://www.edu.cn/20011115/3010098.shtml> (accessed 9 August 2003). (In Chinese)

Swidler, A. (1986) 'Culture in Action: Symbols as Strategies'. *American Sociological Review*, 51: 273–86.

Tang, D. (2002) 'On Preferential Policies for Minority Education in Our Country', *Minzu Jiaoyu Yanjiu (Research of Minority Education)*, 13(50): 42–7. (In Chinese)

Tang, M. (2003) 'An Analysis of Economic Causes of Ethnic Conflicts in the Present Stage in China', in Yu Zhen and Dawa Cairen (eds) *Ethnic Relationships and Ethnic Development of China*, Beijing: Ethnic Publishing House: 1–38. (In Chinese)

Tapp, N. (2002) 'In Defence of the Archaic: A Reconsideration of the 1950s Ethnic Classification Project in China', *Asian Ethnicity*, 3(1): 63–84.

Teles, S. M., Mickey, R. and Ahmed, F. S. (2005) 'Regime effects: ethnicity, social mobility, and public policy in the USA and Britain', in G. C. Loury, T. Modood and S. M. Teles (eds) *Ethnicity, Social Mobility and Public Policy: Comparing the US and UK*, Cambridge: Cambridge University Press: 522–70.

Teng, X. (2002) *Ethnicity, Culture and Education*, Beijing: Ethnic Publishing House. (In Chinese)

Teng, X. and Wang, J. (eds) (2001) *Chinese Ethnic Minorities and Education in the 20th Century: Theory, Policy and Practice*, Beijing: Ethnic Publishing House. (In Chinese)

Teng, X. et al. (1997) 'Middle-Aged and Young Scholars in Bejing Talking about Minority Education', *Minzu Jiaoyu Yanjiu (Research of Minority Education)*, 1. Online available HTTP: <http://www.cbe21.com/zhuanti/minzujy/minzujydd/0010.htm> (accessed 17 October 2004). (In Chinese)

Tomlinson, S. (1996) 'Ethnic Minorities, Citizenship and Education', in J. Demaine and H. Entwistle (eds) *Beyond Communitarianism: Citizenship, Politics and Education*, London: Palgrave Macmillan: 114–30.

Townsend, J. (1992) 'Chinese Nationalism', *The Australian Journal of Chinese Affairs*, 27: 97–130.

Trace Foundation: http://www.trace.org.

TXBW (Tongren Xianzhi Bianzuan Weiyuanhui (The Compiling Committee of Tongren County Annals)) (2001) *Tongren County Annals*, Xi'an: Sanqin Press. (In Chinese)

van Zanten, A. (1997) 'Schooling Immigrants in France in the 1990s: Success or Failure of the Republican Model of Integration?' *Anthropology and Education Quarterly* 28(3): 351–74.

Wang, G. and Chen, J. (2001) *The Development of the Minority Regional Autonomy System)*, Beijing: Ethnic Publishing House. (In Chinese)

Wang, J. (1996) *High Culture Fever: Politics, Aesthetics, and Ideology in Deng's China*. Berkeley: University of California Press.

Wang, K. and Liu, J. (2002) 'Chinese Minority Education Practice and State Education Principles', *Gansu Gaoshi Xuebao (Journal of Gansu Higher Teachers Training College)*, 7(3): 99–101. (In Chinese)

Wang, L. (2006) 'The Urban Chinese educational systems and the marginality of migrant children', in V. Fong and R. Murphy (eds) *Chinese Citizenship: views from the margins*, London and New York: Routledge: 27–40.

Wang, M. (1997) *The Peripheries of Huaxia – Historical Memory and Ethnic Identity*, Taibei: Yunchen Wenhua Shiye Gufen Youxian Gongsi. (In Chinese)

Wanwei Wang (Chinese News Net) (2004a) 'Reading the Confucian Classics Becomes Popular with Children in China', 7 November. Online available HTTP: <http://

news.creaders.net/headline/newsPooL/7A220928.html> (accessed 8 November 2004). (In Chinese)

Watson, C. W. (2000) *Multiculturalism*, Buckingham: Open University Press.

Watson, J. L. (1988) 'The Structure of Chinese Funerary Rites: Elementary Forms, Ritual Sequence, and the Primacy of Performance', in J. L. Watson and E. S. Rawski (eds) *Death Ritual in Late Imperial and Modern China*, Berkeley, Los Angeles, London: University of California Press: 3–19.

Weintraub, J. and Kumar, K. (1997) *Public and Private in Thought and Practice*, Chicago and London: University of Chicago Press.

Wetherell, M. (2001) 'Introduction', in M. Wetherell, S. Taylor and S. J. Yates (eds) *Discourse Theory and Practice: A Reader*, London, Thousand Oaks and New Delhi: Sage Publications: 1–8.

Wetherell, M. and Potter, J. (1992) *Mapping the Language of Racism: Discourse and the Legitimation of Exploitation*, New York: Columbia University Press.

White, R. (1991) *The middle ground: Indians, empires, and republics in the Great Lakes region*. Cambridge and New York: Cambridge University Press.

Woo, D. (2002) 'Ethnicity and Class as Competing Interpretations: The Socio-economic Mobility of Asian Americans', in S. Fenton and H. Bradley (eds) *Ethnicity and Economy: 'Race and Class' Revisited*, London: Palgrave Macmillan: 98–118.

Woolcock, M. (1998) 'Social Capital and Economic Development: Toward a Theoretical Synthesis and Policy Framework', *Theory and Society*, 27: 151–208.

—— (2001) 'The Place of Social Capital in Understanding Social and Economic Outcomes', ISUMA *Canadian Journal of Policy Research*, 2(1): 11–17. Online available HTTP: <http://www.isuma.net/v02n01/woolcock/woolcock_e.pdf> or <http://www.isuma.net/v02n01/woolcock/woolcock_e.shtml> (accessed 28 March 2004).

Xiao, J. (1995) 'An Historical Investigation of the Course of Chinese Ethnic Minorities Identifying with Confucianism', *Kongzi Yanjiu* (*Studies of Confucius*), 2: 96–102. (In Chinese)

Xie, J. (2004) *Minzuxue Lunwen Ji* (*Collection of Ethnological Essays*): Yilan (Taiwan): Fo Guang College of Humanities and Social Sciences. (In Chinese)

Xie, X. (2004/2005) 'Chinese Civilization Integrates the Globe'. Online available HTTP: <http://www.chinesenewsnet.com> (accessed 30 October 2004). (In Chinese)

(Guowuyuan) Xinwen Bangongshi (The Information Office of the State Council) (2005) 'White Paper on Regional Autonomy for Ethnic Minorities'. Online available HTTP: <http://www.china.org.cn/ch-book/20050228/index.htm> (accessed 3 March 2005). (In Chinese)

Yan, H. (2003) 'Neo-Liberal Governmentality and Neo-Humanism: Organizing Value Flow Through Labor Recruitment Agencies', *Cultural Anthropology*, 18(4): 493–523.

Yan, Y. (2002) 'Managed Globalization', in P. Berger and S. P. Huntington (eds) *Many Globalizations: Cultural Dynamics in the Contemporary World*, New York: Oxford University Press: 19–47.

Yang, Z. (1996) *Hui Language and Culture*, Yinchuan: Ningxia People Press. (In Chinese)

Young, I. M. (1990) *Justice and the Politics of Difference*, New Jersey: Princeton University Press.

Yuan, X., Yang, J. and Li, J. (eds) (2003) *An Investigation and Analysis of Present*

Situation of the Basic Education in Sichuan Minority Areas and Research of Solutions to It, Chengdu: Sichuan Ethnic Press. (In Chinese)

Yuval-Davis, N. (1992) 'Fundamentalism, Multiculturalism and Women in Britain', in J. Donald and A. Rattansi (eds) *'Race', Culture and Difference*, London: Sage: 278–91.

ZFS (Guojia Zongjiaoju Zhengce Fagui Si) (2000) *A Reader of Chinese Laws, Regulations and Policies of Religion*, Beijing: Religion and Culture Press. (In Chinese)

Zhang, C. and Huang, L. (1996) 'Research of Present Situation and Causes of Illiteracy and Solution to Wiping Out Illiteracy in Southwest', *Minzu Jiaoyu Yanjiu* (*Research of Minority Education*), 4: 36–41. (In Chinese)

Zhang, T. (1995) 'The Threat Brought About by Population – China Minority Population and Poverty', *Minzu Tuanjie* (*Ethnic Unity*), 9: 35–6. (In Chinese)

Zhang, T. and Chen, X. (1995) 'An Analysis of Cultural Quality of Minority Women in China', *Renkou Yanjiu* (*Population Studies*), 19(4): 40–4. (In Chinese)

Zhang, X. (1996) *Chinese Modernism in the Era of Reforms: Cultural Fever, Avant-Garde Fiction, and the New Chinese Cinema.* Durham, NC: Duke University Press.

Zhang, Y. (1994) 'An Analysis of Minority Physical and Cultural Quality in China', *Renkou Xuekan* (*Journal of Population*), 5: 38–42. (In Chinese)

Zhongguo Guojia Tongjiju (National Bureau of Statistics of China) (2000) 'The Fifth Census: Urban and Rural Population Distribution'. Online available HTTP: <http://www.stats.gov.cn/detail?record=2andchannelid=52984> (accessed 20 September 2003). (In Chinese)

Zhongguo Lishi (4) (*History of China 4*) (Textbook) (1995), Beijing: People Education Press. (In Chinese)

Zhou, E. (1957) 'Several Questions in Minority Policies in Our Country', in Guojia Minzu Shiwu Weiyuanhui (ed.) (2002) *The CCP's Basic Viewpoint and Policy on the Ethnic Issue*, Beijing: Ethnic Publishing House: 233–60. (In Chinese)

Zhou, M. (2005) 'Ethnicity as Social Capital: Community-Based Institutions and Embedded Networks of Social Relations', in G. C. Loury, T. Modood and S. Teles (eds) *Race, Ethnicity and Social Mobility: Comparing the US and UK*, Cambridge: Cambridge University Press: 131–59.

Index

academic discourse: concern with community forces 50–1; concern with social systems 51–3; evaluation 53–5; of minority education 50–5; on minorities' intelligence 51; on minority modes of thinking 50; on religious tradition 51
Apple, Michael 38, 151n36

biological racism 32
Bourdieu, Pierre 4, 6, 38, 144n4, 146n9; *see also* cultural capital

child-centred school 151n36
China: assimilationist model of ethnic minorities 32–3; culture discourse 15, 19, 27–33, 38; current ethos in education 36–9; disparity between cadres and the masses 152n38; education of ethnic minorities in 40–7, 145n14, 150n24; ethnic minorities of 40–2; fluidity of ethnic boundaries 20–1; history of acculturation 24
Chinese culturalism 11, 15, 35, 38, 40, 112, 146n1; and Confucianism 23, 26, 27, 34, 35, 147n10; and its educational legacy 19–39; historical development of 20–7; institutionalization of 25–7; under nationalistic sentiment 30–3, 147n15
Chinese education system 1, 90; blindness to difference in 37–8; college entrance examinations (*gaokao*) 26, 36, 52; examinations-driven schooling 37; new programmes 120–3; streaming of students by academic achievement 155n11
Chinese Muslim *see* Muslims

civil service examinations system 19, 22, 52, 123, 147n11; and Chinese characters (*hanzi*) 27–8; and cultural elites 27; embedding careerist attitude 26; gender disparity in 147n10; history of 25–6
civilizing projects 33, 35, 57, 150n20
community forces 2, 3, 4, 5, 50–1, 108, 132; and consequences 16, 113–15; and social systems or 3, 53–5
cultural capital 1, 7, 8, 16, 64, 108, 124; and class disparity 4–5; in educational achievement 3–5; three forms of 4
cultural citizenship 48, 49, 61
cultural difference 4, 150n21; economic development, political cohesion and 116–17; inequality and 9; and social mobility 10; and symbolic boundaries 21, 22; *see also* culture
cultural discontinuity 3, 4, 10, 100
cultural orientations 2, 4; *see also* cultural difference; culture
culture: new landscape 117–19; and power relations 6–8; as the primary criterion in distinguishing ethnic groups 21–5

discourses: 'cultivation' 54, 61; 'cultural level' 28, 42, 81, 101, 148n5; 'culture fever' 31, 34, 147n12; 'culture war' 55; 'minority of minorities' 109; 'useful' knowledge 84, 95, 100, 101
discursive repertoire 11, 19, 35, 40, 62, 118
dominant culture: acquisition of 8; 'meritocracy' of 5; *see also* mainstream culture
dominant group 2, 6, 7, 8, 17, 23, 61, 96, 100, 116

For Product Safety Concerns and Information please contact our EU
representative GPSR@taylorandfrancis.com
Taylor & Francis Verlag GmbH, Kaufingerstraße 24, 80331 München, Germany

www.ingramcontent.com/pod-product-compliance
Lightning Source LLC
Chambersburg PA
CBHW050712280326
41926CB00088B/2988